CRIMINAL REMINISCENCES

AND

DETECTIVE SKETCHES.

CRIMINAL REMINISCENCES

AND

DETECTIVE SKETCHES.

BY

ALLAN PINKERTON

BOOKS FOR LIBRARIES PRESS
FREEPORT, NEW YORK

First Published 1878
Reprinted 1970

STANDARD BOOK NUMBER:
8369-5241-3

LIBRARY OF CONGRESS CATALOG CARD NUMBER:
70-109632

PRINTED IN THE UNITED STATES OF AMERICA

CONTENTS

CONTENTS

CHAPTER X.

PREFACE.

IN presenting this volume to the public, I have but
few words of preface to offer.

Those sketches pertaining to my own caree as a detective have been taken at random from the thousands
of incidents which have occurred during my detective
experience, and are simply a sample of the numberless
circumstances daily occurring, that, like swift shuttles,
have woven back and forth, over and under, through and
through, my large business the golden threads of humor
and the sable threads of pathos and sorrow.

Of the criminal reminiscences gathered together, 1
claim no particular merit of originality for, or of them.
They are merely memories of the past, in a criminal
sense—of occurrences ripe with thrilling interest in their
time, and still full of fascination and attractiveness , and
of men, brilliant, talented men, who have lived their
unworthy lives of magnificent crime, occupying great
stations and high eminences, as these are measured,

among the strange and mysterious class to vhom we give the generic term of criminals.

In my estimation, although my thousands of readers may differ with me, all these interesting sketches and reminiscences speak their own lesson of caution and warning; and, doing so, have their honest place in the world by the side of all those aids tending to make better men and women of us all.

ALLAN PINKERTON.

CHICAGO, 1878.

DETECTIVE SKETCHES

CHAPTER I.

HOW I BECAME A DETECTIVE.

ON the romantic Fox River--called the **Pish-ta-ka** in the original Potawatamie language—and about thirty-eight miles northwest of the city of Chicago, is located the beautiful village of Dundee. It has probably at this writing a population of three thousand inhabitants, and is one of the brightest and most prosperous towns of Illinois.

The town was originally settled by a few sturdy people, the hardy Scotch, as its name would indicate, as also that of the splendid little city of Elgin, but five miles distant, and who occupied to some extent the outlying farms; so that the place and community, while never accomplishing anything remarkable in a business way, has had a steady, quiet growth, has lived its life uninterruptedly and peacefully, and possesses the pleasantest evidences of steady prosperity and constant, quiet happiness.

1*

If this would be easily observed by the visitor, its **beau-**
tiful location would attract still greater attention.

Before you, looking up-stream, you would see at your
feet the rapid river which has just leaped the great dam
from which the mills and manufactories are fed, and, above
this, stretching and winding away into the distance like a
ribbon of burnished silver, it would still be seen, gliding
along peacefully with a fair, smooth bosom, wimpling
fretfully over stony shallows, or playing at hide-and-seek
among the verdure-covered islands, until the last thread-
like trail of it is lost in the gorges beyond.   To the right,
just beyond the little basin which holds its part of the village, rise huge hills from which here and there issue forth
beautiful springs, while now and then a fine roadway,
hewn out between, leads to the Indian Mounds and the
splendid farms beyond.   To the left, over the opposite
portion of the village, the eye ranges over a succession
of elevations dotted with handsome residences and em-
bowered by gardens, with the hills and the uplands
beyond, as well as the highway, or " river road," thread-
ing along in and out of sight among the tree-covered
bluffs ; while, facing about, you will see the river moving
peacefully along, until lost in the valleys and their forests
below.

The town rests there on the banks of this beautiful
stream, and between the guardian hills upon either side,
like twin nests where there is always song and gladness.

In the time of which I write, however, all this was
different ; that is, the town was different.   The river ran

down like a silvery ribbon from among the islands just the same ; the splendid hills were all there crowned with fine forests as they are now ; but the town itself did not contain probably over three hundred inhabitants all told, the business portion only consisting of a few country stores, a post office, a blacksmith-shop or two, a mill, and two small taverns able to accommodate a few travelers at a time, but chiefly depending for their support upon the custom of the farmers who straggled into the village on rainy days, "election time," or any other of the hundred and one occasions which mark out events in the lives of back-country people.

There was then one rough bridge across the river, built of oaken beams and rude planks in a cheap, common fashion ; and at either end of this were clustered, each side of the street, all the stores and shops of the place, save one.

That shop was my own ; for there I both lived and labored, the " Only and Original Cooper of Dundee."

This shop was the farthest of any from the business center of the village, and stood just back of, and facing, the main highway upon the crest of a fine hill, about three hundred yards distant from the bridge. It was my home and my shop.

I had straggled out here a few years before, and by industry and saving had gradually worked into a comfortable business at my cooper's trade, and now employed eight men. I felt proud of my success because I owed no man, had a cheery little home, and, for the early days when it was pretty hard to get along at all, I was making a comfortable living.

My cooper-shop and house were one building—a long, one-story frame building with a pleasant garden about, some fine old trees near, and always stacks of staves and hoop-poles quite handy. At one end we lived, in a frugal, but always cheery way, and at the other was the shop, where, as nearly all my hands were German, could be heard the livelong day the whistled waltz, or the lightly-sung ballad, now in solo, now in chorus, but always in true time with the hammering of the adz and the echoing thuds of the "driver" upon the hoops as they were driven to their places.

This was my quiet, but altogether happy, mode of life in the beautiful village of Dundee, in the summer of 1847, at which time my story really begins ; but, to give the reader a better understanding of it, I will have to further explain the existing condition of things at that time.

There was but little money in the West, which was then sparsely settled. There being really no markets, and the communication with eastern cities very limited, the producer could get but little for his crops or wares. I have known farmers in these times "hauling," as it was called, wheat into Chicago for a distance of nearly one hundred miles, from two to five streams having to be forded, and the wheat having to be carried across, every bag of it, upon the farmer's back, and he not then able to get but three shillings per bushel for his grain, being compelled to take half payment for it in " truck," as store goods were then called.

There was plenty of dickering, but no money. Neces- sity compelled an interchange of products. My barrels would be sold to the farmers or merchants for produce, and this I would be compelled to send in to Chicago, to in turn secure as best I could a few dollars perhaps, and anything and everything I could use, or again trade away.

Not only did this great drawback on business exist, but what money we had was of a very inferior character. If one sold a load of produce and was fortunate enough to secure the entire pay for it in money, before he got home the bank might have failed and the paper he held have become utterly worthless. All of these things in time brought about a most imperative need for good money and plenty of it, which had been met some years before where my story begins, by several capitalists of Aberdeen, Scotland, placing in the hands of George Smith, Esq., also an Aberdonian, sufficient funds to found a bank in the Great West.

Milwaukee, then a city of equal importance with Chicago, was chosen as the point, and the Wisconsin Legislature, in 1839, granted a charter to the institution, which was known as The Wisconsin Marine and Fire In- surance Company, which, in its charter, also secured banking privileges.

But a few years had elapsed before the bills of this in- stitution gained a very wide circulation throughout the Northwest. Branch agencies were established at Chicago

and various points in the West, as also an agency for the
redemption of the bills at Buffalo ; and at the time of
which I write, Chicago, having taken rapid strides to the
front, had in reality become the central office, although
the Wisconsin organization and Milwaukee headquarters
were still retained.

Many reasons obtained to cause these bills—which
were of the denominations of one, two, three, five, and
ten—to be eagerly sought for.   The company were known
to have large and always available capital at command ;
its bills were always redeemable in specie ; and with the
personal character of George Smith, who stood at the
head of the concern, there was created an almost unequaled public confidence in it and its management.   In
fact, the bills soon became known far and wide as " George
Smith's money," and " as good as the wheat," the farmers
would say.

Smith himself was a Scotchman of very decided and
even erratic character ; and the old settlers of Chicago
and the West have many an interesting incident to relate
of his financial career.   One, serving for many, to give
an idea of the peculiarities of the man, and showing how
he gained a great reputation in those times and that section, is as follows :

The almost immediate popularity of " George Smith's
money " caused considerable envious feeling ; and the officers of several other western banking institutions sought
as far as possible by various means to prevent the en
croachment upon their business.

At one time a small bank near the central part of Illinois, in order to assist in the depreciation of this particular money, began the policy of refusing to receive the Wisconsin Marine and Fire Insurance Company's bills at par, which for a time caused in certain sections considerable uneasiness among the holders of those bills.

The quiet Scotchman in Chicago said never a word to this for some time, but at once began gathering together every bill of this bank he could secure. This was continued for several weeks, when he suddenly set out alone and unattended for Central Illinois, being roughly dressed and very unpretentious in appearance.

Reaching the place and staggering into the bank, he awkwardly presented one hundred dollars in the Fire and Marine bills, requesting exchange on Buffalo for a like sum.

The cashier eyed him a moment and then remarked sneeringly :

"We don't take that stuff at par."

"Ah ! ye dinna tak it, then ? "

"No," replied the cashier ; "'George Smith's money' is depreciating rapidly."

"Then it's gaun down fast, is it ?" responded Smith, reflectively.

"Oh, yes ; won't be worth fifty cents on a dollar in six months ! "

"It'll be worth nae mair than fifty cents ? An' may yours be worth a huner' cents on a dollar, *noc* ? "

"Certainly, sir, always. If you should happen to have

ten thousand dollars' worth about you at the present time,'
replied the cashier, as he gave the stranger another super
cilious look, "you could get the gold for it in less than
ten seconds."

"Then," said the travel-stained banker, with a very
ugly look in his face, as he crashed down a great package
upon the counter containing twenty-five thousand dollars
in the bills of the opposition bank, "Mister George
Smith presents his best respects tae ye, and would be
obleeged tae ye if ye wad gie him the specie for *this !*"

This shrewd stroke of business policy had its legitimate
effect.   The bank in question could not instantly redeem
so large a sum, and opposition of an unfair character in
that and other directions, through the notoriety given this
practical humiliation, was effectually ended.

In countless other ways this early Western financier
established credit and compelled respect, until, as I
have said, "George Smith's money" was as good as the
gold throughout the entire western country, and this fact,
in time, caused it to be taken in hand by eastern counter·
feiters.

This brings me again to the main part of my story.

Just afternoon of a hot July day in the year mentioned,
a gentleman named H. E. Hunt, then keeping a small
general store in, and now a wealthy merchant at Dundee,
sent word to my shop that he wished to see me imme·
diately at his place.

I was busy at my work, bareheaded, barefooted, and
having no other clothing on my body than a pair of blue

denim overalls and a coarse hickory shirt, my then almost invariable costume ; but I started down the street at once, and had hardly reached Hunt's store before the proprietor and myself were joined by a Mr. I. C. Bosworth, then another storekeeper of the village and now a retired capitalist of Elgin, Illinois, the place previously referred to.

" Come in here, Allan," said Mr. Hunt in a rather mysterious manner, leading the way to the rear of the store, while Bosworth and myself followed; " we want you to do a little job in the detective line."

" Detective line ! " I replied, laughing ; " why, my line is the cooper business. What do I know about that sort of thing ? "

" Never mind now," said Mr. Bosworth, seriously, " we *know* you can do what you want done. You helped break up the ' coney men ' and horse-thieves on ' Bogus Island,' and we are sure you can do work of this sort if you only will do it."

Now the reference to breaking up the gang of " coney ' men and horse-thieves on " Bogus Island," calls for an explanation.

I was actually too poor to purchase outright a wheel-barrow-load of hoop-poles, or staves, and was consequently compelled to cut my own hoop-poles and split my own staves. In the pursuit of this work I had found a little island in the Fox River, a few miles above Dundee, and but a few rods above the little post-town of Algonquin, where poles were both plentiful and of the best qual ity, and one day while busy there I had stumbled upon some smouldering embers and other traces indicating that the little island had been made quite common use of There was no picnicking in those days—people had more serious matters to attend to—and it required no great keenness to conclude that no honest men were in the habit of occupying the place. As the country was then infested with coin-counterfeiters and desperate horse-thieves, from the information I gave, the sheriff of that county (Kane) was able to trace the outlaws to this isl-and, where subsequently I led the officers who captured the entire gang, consisting of men and women, securing their implements and a large amount of bogus coin; while, in honor of the event, the island ever since has been known as "Bogus Island."

Upon this faint record Messrs. Hunt and Bosworth based my claim to detective skill, and insisted on my winning new laurels, or at least attempting to do so.

"But what is it you wish done?" I asked, very much preferring to return to the shop, where my men and their work needed my attention.

Mr. Hunt then explained that they were certain that there was then a counterfeiter in the village. They both felt sure he was one, although they had no other evidence save that the party in question had been making inquiries as to the whereabouts of "Old man Crane."

Old man Crane was a person who from general reputa tion I knew well. He lived at Libertyville, in the adjoin-ing county of Lake, not more than thirty-five miles dis

tant, bore a hard character generally, and it was sus
pected that he was engaged in distributing for eastern
counterfeiters their worthless money. Nearly every
blackleg that came into the community invariably in
quired for "Old man Crane," and this fact alone caused
the villagers to give him a wide berth. Besides this fact,
but recently counterfeits on the ten-dollar bill of the Wisconsin Marine and Fire Insurance Company's bank had
made their appearance, and were so well executed as to
cause serious trouble to farmers and country dealers.
Pretty positive proof had come to light that Crane had
had a hand in the business; and the fact that a respectable appearing man, a stranger well mounted and altogether mysterious, and also well supplied with money,
had suddenly shown himself in the village, to begin
quietly but searchingly making inquiries for "Old man
Crane," seemed to the minds of my friends to be the
best of evidence that the stranger was none other than
the veritable counterfeiter who was supplying such old
reprobates as Crane with the spurious ten-dollar bills on
George Smith's bank.

But this was curious business for me, I thought, as protesting against leaving my work for a will-'o-the-wisp
piece of business, which, even should it happen to prove
successful, would pay me nothing, I said : "Now, see
here, what do *I* know about counterfeiting ? "

"Oh, we *know* you know enough about it !" they both
urged anxiously.

"Why," said I, laughing at the absurdity of the idea of

turning detective, "I never saw a ten-dollar bill in my iife!"

And neither had I. There I stood, a young, strong, agile, hard-working cooper, not exactly green, perhaps,— for I consider no man verdant who does well whatever he may have in hand,—barefooted, bareheaded, dressed, or rather, almost undressed, in my hickory and denims, daring enough and ready for any reckless emergency which might transpire in the living of an honest life, but decidedly averse to doing something entirely out of my line, and which in all human probability I would make an utter failure of. I had not been but four years in America altogether. I had had a hard time of it for the time I had been here. I had *heard* of all these things I have mentioned concerning banks and money, but I had positively never seen a ten-dollar bill!

A great detective I would make under such circumstances, I thought.

"Come now, Allan," urged Mr. Hunt, "no time is to be wasted. The man is down there now at Eaton Walker's harness-shop, getting something done about his saddle."

"But what am I to do?" I asked.

"Do?—Well!—*do* the best you can!"

I suddenly resolved to do just that and no less; although I must confess that, at that time, I had not the remotest idea how to set about the matter.

So I began by strolling leisurely about the street for a few minutes, and then, villager-like, sauntered into the saddlery shop.

Eaton Walker, a jolly, whole-souled, good-hearted fellow, was perched upon his bench, sewing away, and when I entered merely looked up from his waxed-end and nodded, but made no remark, as my being in his place was a very common occurrence.

There was the usual quota of town stragglers loafing about the shop, and looking with sleepy eyes and open-mouthed at the little which was going on about the place.

I passed, as I entered the shop, a splendid horse hitched outside. It was a fine, large roan, well built for traveling; and in my then frame of mind I imagined from a casual glance that it was a horse especially selected for its lasting qualities, should an emergency require them to be put to a test. The owner of the animal, the person who had caused so much nervousness on the part of Messrs. Hunt and Bosworth, was a man nearly six feet in height, weighed fully two hundred pounds, was at least sixty-five years of age, and was very erect and commanding in his appearance. I noticed all this at a careless glance, as also that his hair was dark, though slightly tinged with gray, and his features very prominent. His nose was very large, his mouth unusually so, and he had a pair of the keenest, coldest small gray eyes I have ever seen, while he wore a large, plain gold ring on one of the fingers of his left hand.

I made no remark to him or to any person about the place, and merely assumed for the time-being to be a village loafer myself. But I noticed, without showing the fact, that the man occasionally gave me a keen and searching glance. When the work had been completed by Walker, I stepped outside and made a pretense of being interested, as any country gawky might, in the preparations for the man's departure; and was patting the horse's neck and withers as the stranger came out with the saddle and began adjusting it, when I carelessly assisted him in a free-and-easy country way.

There were, of course, a number of people standing about and a good deal of senseless chatting going on, which the stranger wholly refrained from joining in; but while we were both at work at the saddle, he said, without addressing me, but in a way which I knew was meant for my ears : " Stranger, do you know where old man Crane lives ? "

I took my cue from the manner in which this was said, and followed it to the best of my ability. I was now as certain as either of my friends that the man was a black-leg of a dangerous order, whatever his special line of roguery might be. We were both busy at the saddle on the side of the horse where there were the fewer loungers, and being close together, I replied in the same tone of voice :

" Cross the river to the east, take the main road up through the woods until you come to Jesse Miller's farm-house. Then *he* will tell you ; but if you don't want to ask "—and I put considerable meaning into this—" hold the road to the northeast and inquire the direction to Libertyville. When you get there you will easily find the old man, and he is as good as cheese ! "

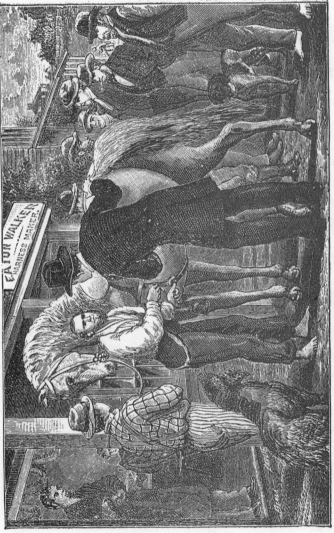

"Do you know where old man Crane lives?" — Page —

He then said in the same cautious voice as before:

"Young man, I like your style, and I want to know you better. Join me over the river in some ravine. I want to talk to you."

" All right," I rejoined, "but you better let me go ahead. I'll have to go up to the shop first and put on my boots and hat. I'll be as quick as I can, and will start on first. Then you follow on, but not too closely. I'll be up in some of the gorges, so we can talk entirely by ourselves. But I'll tell you the truth, stranger," said I, rather indifferently, " upon my word, I don't care very much about going, because I've already lost too much time at the shop to-day."

He had by this time finished saddling his horse, but he continued adjusting and readjusting things so as to gain time to say what he wished ; and to my intimation that I cared very little about leaving my work, he responded :

" Don't fail to join me. *I'll make it worth something to you !* " He then added flatteringly : " You're as good a man as I've met lately."

I then moved forward to fasten the reins, and he edged along towards me, asking carelessly : " Do you know John Smith, of Elgin ? "

"I know all the Elgin John Smiths," I replied. " Do you mean the gunsmith ? "

" Yes," he answered tersely.

" Well I know John," I continued ; " that is, he has re paired my rifle and shotgun several times ; but he might not remember me, I never had much talk with him."

"He's a square man," replied the stranger. "*I'm* his uncle. I came up from Elgin this morning. Smith didn't know just where Crane lived. He told me that he traded here and that the boys were over here a good deal, so that I would be likely to find somebody here who could readily direct me to his place."

"Well," I said rather curtly, "we've talked too mucl already. It won't do. I'll join you over the river soon."

With this I carelessly walked away towards my shop, and at some little distance turned to see the stranger now engaging Eaton Walker in conversation with an evident purpose of gaining time.

"Well," I thought, as I hastened on, "there's no doubt now. This man is certainly a counterfeiter. John Smith is always loaded down with it. He gets it from old Crane ; and this man at Walker's is the chief of the gang traveling through the West to supply these precious rascals. But then," it suddenly occurred to me, "what business of mine is all this ? Good gracious ! I've got a lot of barrels to make, my men need attention, and everything is going to the old Harry while I am playing detective !"

But having got this far my will had been touched, and I resolved to carry the matter through, whatever might be the result. While putting on my hat and boots hastily, Hunt and Bosworth came in, and I quickly related what I had learned.

Looking down the hill, we could see the stranger slowly moving across the bridge, and as I was starting in the same direction my friends both urged :

" Now, Pinkerton, capture him sure ! "

"Oh, yes," I replied, " but how am I to get at all this ? "

" Why, just get his stock, or some of it, and then we'll have him arrested."

"Oh, yes," said I, "but, by thunder ! it takes money to buy money ! I've got none ! "

" Well, well, that's so," remarked Mr. Hunt ; " we'll go right down to the store. You drop in there after us, and we'll give you fifty dollars."

All this was speedily done, and I soon found myself over the bridge, past the horseman, and well up the hill upon the highway.

It was a well-traveled thoroughfare, in fact, the road leading from all that section of the country into Chicago ; but it was in the midst of harvest-time, and everybody was busy upon the farms. Not a soul was to be seen upon the road, save the stranger and myself, and almost a Sabbath silence seemed to rest over the entire locality. The voices of the birds which filled the woods in every direction were hushed into a noon-day chirping, and hardly a sound was to be heard save the murmuring of the rills issuing from the sides of the hills and from every nook in the gorges and glens.

I confess that a sense of insignificance stole over me, originating doubtless from the reflection caused by this silence and almost painful quiet ; and I could not but realize my unfitness for the work before me. There I was, hardly more than a plodding country cooper, having

2

had but little experience save that given me by a life of
toil in Scotland and my trip to this country, and no
experience of things in this country save that secured
through a few years of the hardest kind of hard work.
For a moment I felt wholly unable to cope with this
keen man of the world, but as I was gaining the top of
the hill I glanced back over my shoulder, and noticing
that the horseman was following my instructions to the
letter, I reasoned that, from *some* cause, I had gained an
influence over this stranger, or *he* thought he had secured such a one over me, as would enable me, by being
cautious and discreet, to obtain a sufficiently close intimacy with him to cause the disclosure of his plans and
possibly ultimately result in his capture.

I had now reached the top of the hill, and taking a
position which would permit of my being seen by no
person save the horseman, I waited until he had approached near enough for me to do so, when I signaled
him to follow, and then struck into the woods over a
narrow trail about two hundred yards to a beautiful
little opening on the banks of a purling brook, leaping
down the descent towards the river from a limpid spring
a few feet above the spot I had chosen for the interview.

But a few moments elapsed before the stranger, dashing in over the trail in fine style, leaped from his horse
with a good deal of dexterity for a man of his age, and
carelessly flinging the bridle-rein over the limb of a small
sapling, passed me with a smile of recognition, proceeded
to the spring, where he took a long, deep draught, and

then returning to where I was seated upon the velvety greensward, threw himself carelessly down upon the ground beside me.

There we two lay—the stranger with his keen, sharp eyes, and his altogether careless, but always attentive manner, closely regarding me and looking me over from toe to tip ; while I assumed an equal carelessness, but was all intent on his every movement. I saw the handles of two finely-mounted pistols protruding from inner coat-pockets, and I did not know what might happen I was wholly unarmed, but I was young, wiry, powerful, and though I had nothing for self-protection save my two big fists and my two stout arms, I was daring enough to tackle a man or beast in self-defense at a moment's warning.

After a moment's silence, he said :

"Well, stranger, I'm a man of business from the word 'go.' What's your name and how long have you been about here ? "

"My name's Pinkerton. I've been here three or four years, coopering some, and harvesting some ; but coopering's my trade. You'd have seen my shop if you had come up the hill. I manage to keep seven or eight men going all the time. But times are fearfully hard. There's no money to be had ; and the fact is," said I, looking at him knowingly, "I would like to get hold of something better adapted to getting more ready cash out of—especially if it was a good scheme—so good that there was no danger in it. But what's *your* name and where did you come from?" I asked abruptly.

He scarcely heeded this, and, Yankee-like, replied by asking where *I* came from before locating in Illinois.

"From Scotland," I replied, "from Glasgow. I worked my way through Canada and finally found myself here with just a quarter in my pocket. What little I've got has been through hard work since. But, my friend," said I smiling, "the talk is all on one side. I asked *you* something about yourself."

"Well," he said, still looking at me as though he would read me through and through, "they call me 'Old man Craig.' My name is Craig—John Craig, and I live down in Vermont, near Fairfield; got a fine farm there. Smith, down here at Elgin, is a nephew of mine; and old Crane, over at Libertyville, and myself, have done a good deal of *business* together."

"Oh, yes," said I nodding, "I understand."

"But, you see," resumed the counterfeiter, "this part of the country is all new to me. I've been to Crane's house before, but that was when I came up the lakes to Little Fort,* and when I got through with my visit there I always went into Chicago on the 'lake road.'"

"And of course you both stopped at the Sauganash," I said meaningly.

"Certainly we stopped there," replied Craig musingly.

* The city of Waukegan, in Lake County, Illinois, was called "Little Fort" by the early settlers.

" I *know* that Foster's a man that can be depended on," I remarked with considerable meaning upon the word "know."

" He's a square man, Foster is," rejoined the counterfeiter; "and, Pinkerton, I believe you're the right sort of a man too. I sold Foster a big pile the last time I was in Chicago." And then quick as thought he said, looking me in the eyes: " Did you ever ' deal' any ? "

" Yes, Mr. Craig," I replied, " but only when I could get a first-class article. I frequently 'work off' the stuff in paying my men Saturday nights, when traveling through the country, and on the merchants here in Dundee, who have all confidence in me. But I wouldn't touch anything like it for the State of Illinois, unless it was as good in appearance as the genuine article. Have you something really good, now ? " I concluded indiffei ently.

" I've got a ' bang up' article," said the stranger, quietly.

"But I don't know *what* you've got," I persisted " I thought you were going over to old Crane's ? "

" Well, so I was, Pinkerton ; but I believe you're a good, square man, and I don't know but I had as soon sell to you as him."

" I think you had better see Crane," said I indiffer ently. " He's probably expecting you, and as it's after-noon now, it would be a good idea for you to make the best time you can there."

" How far is it ? " he asked.

"Oh, thirty-five miles or thereabouts, and as you've got a good horse, you can make it by dark or before."

He rose as if undecided what to do, and without making any further remark at the time, took his horse to the spring and watered it.

He then returned, and again throwing himself down beside me, remarked carelessly :

"But I haven't yet showed you what I've got. Here are the 'beauties;'" and he whipped out two ten-dollar bills, counterfeits on the Wisconsin Marine and Fire Insurance Company's money.

I looked at them very, very wisely. As I have already said, I had never seen a ten-dollar bill in my life ; but I examined them as critically as though I had assisted in making the genuine bills, and after a little expressed myself as very much pleased with them.

They were indeed "beauties," as the old rascal had said, and in all my subsequent detective experience I have hardly seen their equal in point of execution and general appearance. There was not a flaw in them. To show how nearly perfect they had been made, it is only necessary to state that it was subsequently learned that several thousand dollars in these spurious bills had been received unhesitatingly at the bank and its different agencies, and actually paid out and received the second time, without detection.

"Come now, Pinkerton, I'll tell you what I'll do," continued Craig earnestly ; "if you'll take enough of this I'll give you the entire field out here. The fact is

Crane's getting old ; he isn't as active as he used to be ; he's careless also, and, besides all this, he's too well known."

"Well," said I thoughtfully, "how much would I have to take ?"

" Only five hundred or a thousand," he replied airily.

" On what terms ? " I asked.

" Twenty-five per cent. cash."

" I cannot possibly do it now," I replied, as though there was no use of any further conference. " I haven't anywhere near the amount necessary with me. I *want* to do it like thunder, but when a man can't do a thing he can t, and that's all there is about it."

"Not so fast, my man ; not so fast," answered the old rogue reassuringly. " Now, you say these lubber-heads of merchants down at the village trust you ? "

" Yes, for anything."

"Then can't you make a raise from them somehow ? You'll never get such another chance to do business with a square man in your life ; and you can make more money with this in one year than any one of them can in ten. Now, what can you do, Pinkerton ?

I assumed to be studying the matter over very deeply, but, in reality, I had already decided to do as the man wished ; for I knew that Messrs. Hunt and Bosworth would be only too glad to have the matter followed up so closely. Finally I said : "I'll do it, Craig ; but it won't answer for you to be seen hanging about here. Where shall we meet, and when ? "

"Easy enough," said he, grasping my hand warmly "I won't go over to old Crane's at all. If he wants any of the stuff after this, he'll have to come to you. I only let Smith have about one hundred dollars in the bills, and that out of mere friendship, you know. When he wants more, I'll make him come to you too. Now, I'll go right back down there, and you can meet me at Smith's this evening."

"Oh, no; no you don't, Craig !" I answered with an appearance of deep cunning. "I'm willing to take the whole business into my hands, but I don't propose to have every Tom, Dick and Harry understand all about the business from the beginning. I'll find my own customers," I concluded, with a protesting shake of my head.

"Well, that *is* best. You're right and I'm wrong. Where'll we meet ? " he asked.

"I've a capital place," I replied. "Do you know where the unfinished Baptist Church and University are, down at Elgin ? "

"Let me see," he said, smiling. "I ought to know. I'm a splendid Baptist when I'm in Vermont—one of the deacons, as sure as you live ! Are they up on the hill ? "

"Yes, the same," I answered. "It's a lonesome enough place to not be likely to meet anybody there ; and we can arrange everything in the basement."

"All right," he acceded, laughing heartily, "and the next time I write my wife, damn me if I don't tell her that I dedicated the new Baptist Church at Elgin, Illinois ! "

I joined in this little merriment at the expense of the Elgin Baptist Church; and then Craig, who had begun to feel very cheerful and friendly, went into quite a lengthy account of himself and his mode of operations.

As before stated, he said that he was located in Fair-field, Vermont. This location was chosen from the ready facility it offered for getting into Canada, should danger at any time present itself. He owned a large and fine place, and was legitimately engaged in farming, was wealthy, and had been a counterfeiter for many years, keeping two first-class engravers constantly employed, and he warmly invited me to visit him, should I ever happen that way, although it was morally certain at that time, to him as well as myself, that it would be a very long time before I began traveling for pleasure, and I received all this for what it was worth, but fervently promised him a call while mentally observing : " Ah ! my man, if everything works right, maybe that the call will come sooner than you are expecting it ! "

What chiefly interested me, however, was what he told me concerning his mode of operations.

He said that he never carried any quantity of counter-feit money upon his person. This twenty dollars which he had shown me was the largest sum he ever had about him. This was simply and only a sample for use, as it had been with me. Should he be arrested not one piece of paper which would not bear the most rigid inspection, although he had always upon his person about two thou-sand dollars in genuine money, chiefly in eastern bank

2*

bills.   No person, understanding the condition of things
at that time, could be persuaded to condemn a stranger
in a new country and unfamiliar with its money, for having twenty dollars of spurious money in so large a sum as
two thousand dollars.

I asked him why he did not pad his saddle with the
bills and carry them with him, in this manner, for convenience.   I made this inquiry, more than anything else, to
draw from Craig his manner of supplying parties, and I
was successful, for he immediately replied :

"No, that wouldn't do.   To begin with, the horse
would sweat the pad and badly discolor the bills, and, in
the next place, somebody might be as curious as yourself,
and rip open the saddle.   Oh, no, no ; I've got a better
scheme than that.   I've got a fellow, named Yelverson, as
true as steel and as shrewd as a man can be made.   He
follows me like a shadow, but *you* will never see him.
He is never seen by any living person with whom I have
business.   I simply show my samples and make the
trade.   I receive the money agreed upon from the buyer,
and then tell him that I *think* he will find the speci-
fied sum in my money in a certain place at a designated
time.

"He goes there, and never fails to find the bills.   But
Yelverson is not seen in the transaction, and, in the
meantime, I have hidden my samples, as well as the
money received by me, which *might* be marked, so that
if there should be any treachery, nothing could be proven
against me.   I have a good deal of Canada trade, and it

is all effected in this manner. Old John Craig is nevei
caught napping, young man!"

The last remark was evidently made by the counter
feiter to give me to understand that though he had given
me, or pretended to give me, very freely, his valuable con
fidence, that he was not a man to be trifled with in any
particular, and I fully believed this of the man already.

I was satisfied that he had a good deal of the honoi
which is so frequently referred to as existing between
thieves. There is no doubt but that this man always
kept his word. In that sense he was honorable. This
kind of honor was a necessity to his nefarious business,
however, and I fail to perceive, as many sentimentalists
do, where the criminal deserves the credit for being hon
orable when that peculiar quality is only used for the
worst purposes, and is as much required by the criminal
as the bread he eats.

It was now fully half-past one o'clock, and I suggested
to the counterfeiter that we conclude our interview, as
some stragglers might happen that way.

"You will be on hand, Pinkerton?" asked Craig as he
rose from the grass.

"There's my hand on it," said I quietly.

"And you'll bring enough money to take five hundred?"

"I'm certain I can raise that much," I replied. "But
see here. Don't you come down throug'i the village
again. It will cause talk, and couple you with myself in
the village gossip in a way that won't do for me at all."

He agreed with me in this, and I then directed him to take what was called the "upper road," past General Mc-Clure's old place, and having got this well fixed in his mind, agreed to meet him at the designated place in Elgin, at about four o'clock, bade him good-by and took my departure.

I hastened towards the village, and saw on my way, just as I was descending the brow of the hill, my counterfeiter friend well along the upper road, halting his horse to wave me a good-luck, or good-by, as it might be taken, to which I merely nodded a reply, and then made all possible speed to Mr. Hunt's store, where I quickly reported the result of my interview to Messrs. Hunt and Bosworth.

They were very gleeful over my success in working into the confidence of the counterfeiter, but both were rather apprehensive that the money *was* in the man's saddle, that Yelverson was a myth, and that possibly we had lost an opportunity of securing either. But I felt pretty certain that Craig would be on hand at Elgin according to appointment, and securing the required amount of money, one hundred and twenty-five dollars, and a bite of lunch, I set out on foot for Elgin. The place was only about five miles from Dundee, and five miles for me then was as nothing ; so that, a few minutes before four, I was within the deserted structure.

I looked into every conceivable corner and cranny, but could discover the counterfeiter nowhere.

I passed outside and looked in every direction, but

still he was not to be seen. Tired and worried about the whole matter, I retired within the basement, and had been sitting upon one of the loose timbers there but a few minutes, brooding over the loss of my day's work, and disgusted with the whole business, when Craig suddenly entered and smilingly greeted me.

" Why, helloa, Pinkerton, you're ahead of time."

"I told you I would be here," I replied.

" Well, did you bring the money with you ? "

"Certainly I did. Here it is," said I, counting out one hundred and twenty-five dollars as carelessly as though accustomed to handling comfortable sums of money.

He looked it over more carefully than suited me exactly. The act seemed to hold a faint trace of suspicion, but he found it to be in eastern bills and correct in every particular.

" Coopering must be pretty profitable work ? " he remarked with a light laugh.

" Oh, fair, fair," I answered, indifferently. " Does pretty well when one can do some other quiet business along with it."

" Oh, I see," he said pleasantly. " Now, Pinkerton, you go outside for a few minutes, and keep a sharp lookout, lest somebody may be watching. Remain outside four or five minutes, and if you see no one by that time, come back."

I went out as directed, but I could not but feel that I had placed myself in the man's power completely, as fa' as giving him a fair opportunity to abscond with my friends' money was concerned, and though a new hard at this kind of bellows, I determined to be as keen as he was shrewd. So, instead of leaving the building alto gether, for the time mentioned, I started off for a little distance, and, quickly returning up through a small ravine, took a position near an open window, just in time to observe my Baptist friend from Vermont placing something beneath a wide, flat building-stone in one corner of that portion of the basement where we had been together.

This much seen, I got away from the place as speedily as I could, and at once sought a small eminence near the building, and made a great pretense of keeping a close watch on the locality.

While thus occupied, I observed, out of the corner of my eye, that Craig had appeared at one of the entrances and was closely watching my movements. Apparently satisfied at last, he gave a low whistle, attracting my attention, of course, when he then motioned me to join him.

As I entered I told him that I had looked everywhere, but was unable to see any person about.

"That's all right," he replied pleasantly, and then looking at me in a quizzical sort of a way, asked:

"Pinkerton, what would you think if I told you that Yelverson had been here during your absence outside, and left the five hundred in my bills?"

"Well, I don't know," I answered; "I'd *almost* think you'd got old Nick working along with you!"

"Perhaps I have, perhaps I have," he returned quietly "Look under that stone over yonder."

I went to the place indicated, and, lifting the stone which from the outside I had seen him busied with, I picked up a neatly-made package.

"I *think* you will find what you bought inside it," remarked Craig.

I opened the package, and found that it contained fifty ten-dollar bills. They were the counterfeits, but, as I have already stated, were most handsomely executed.

I make this open confession to my readers:

For a moment the greatest temptation of my life swept over me. A thousand thoughts of sudden wealth and a life free from the grinding labor which I had always known, came rushing into my mind. Here in my hands were five hundred dollars, or what professed to be, every one of them as good as gold, if I only chose to use it. The purchasing power of five hundred dollars then, the use which could be made of it, the large gain which would accrue from its judicious investment, were one and all ten times what they are now. What would it not purchase? Why, to my mind then it was a great fortune!

All this and more pressed upon me with such weight—the first and last time in my whole life—that with this struggle in my memory, while I have always been unshaken in my determination to never lose sight of a criminal when it once becomes my duty to pursue him, I can never think of one undergoing the first great temptation to crime

whether he has resisted or fallen, without a touch of genuine human sympathy.

I am satisfied that this showed in my face somewhat,
but was taken by him to indicate cupidity and eagerness
at the prospect of large profits as his "wholesale agent"
in that section, and soon after probably stood me in good
service.

We sat down upon one of the timbers and chatted
pleasantly for a time, during which he informed me that
Yelverson had at once returned to Smith's, where his
horse was stabled, and ere then was on his road toward
Chicago, where he, Craig, should rejoin him on the next
day, after passing the night at his nephew's.

My thought was to get the two together and nab their
both, if it were in my power.   I saw that I had no possible
opportunity to do this in Elgin, for, according to Craig's
statement, Yelverson was well on the road to Chicago
out of all danger of pursuit ; and even should I cause
Craig's arrest, from what I already knew of his character
and habits, his conviction on my unsupported evidence
would prove difficult.

Accordingly, while sitting there and chatting away with
Craig, all these things were playing back and forth like
a swift shuttle through my mind, with the following
result .

"Look here, Craig," said I, "if you wouldn't be in
too big a hurry about getting back home, I'll tell you
what I'll do.   I believe I could make arrangements to
buy you out altogether."

"Well, now, that's a good idea, Pinkerton," returned the counterfeiter thoughtfully, but evidently pleased at the proposition.

" How much have you got ? " I asked.

" I haven't any, " he answered with a sly look. " Yelverson has about four thousand dollars in the stuff, I believe."

" All right, " I replied. " Craig or Yelverson, it's all the same so I get it. Now I've been thinking that I could take a trip out to Naperville, in Du Page County, and St. Charles, Geneva, Batavia, Aurora, and Oswego, in this county, and work off the greater part of what I've got, and while at Oswego see Lawyer Boyd, who, I am certain, will take a share with me."

" How long will this take you ? " inquired Craig.

" I can't tell," said I ; " not more than three or four days at the outside, I think."

"Well, try and see what you can do. I would like to sel. my horse and my entire outfit too, and go back by the lakes, if I can."

" All right, Craig," said I. " I'm pretty sure that I can buy everything. I'll try hard, and think that if I can see Bill Boyd, at Oswego, there'll be no doubt about our being able together to take everything you have."

" Good-by, then," said the counterfeiter, shaking my hand warmly. " I'll spend the night with Smith, go into Chicago to-morrow, and wait there at the "Sauganash" for you four or five days. But, mind you, be discreet ! "

With this we parted, Craig going over the hills into

the woods behind the town, to make some slight detour before rejoining the gunsmith, and I, with my five hundred dollars in counterfeit bills on the Wisconsin Marine and Fire Insurance Company's Bank, starting on foot for home, where I arrived just as the sun was setting behind the grand hills of Dundee, upon what I then felt was the most exciting and eventful day of my life.

Messrs. Hunt and Bosworth were on the *qui vive* of expectation, and listened to my recital with the greatest interest ; but they both seemed apprehensive that the counterfeiter would not keep faith with me, and had probably set out from Elgin for some distant point as soon as I had started for home, and would leave us all in the lurch with five hundred dollars in counterfeit money on our hands for all our trouble and officiousness.

I confess that, being new to the business, I had something of a like fear, or distrust ; but still, in revolving the matter in my mind, I could not but always come back to the first impression I had gained of my Vermont friend, to the effect that, criminal though he was, he was a man who, when he had passed his word, would be certain to keep it.

With a view of allaying the anxiety of my friends, and also satisfying my own curiosity concerning the matter, I promised that early the next morning I would take some measures to learn definitely the whereabouts of the counterfeiter. And so, tired, partly discouraged, and fully satisfied in my own mind that I was not born to become a detective, I went home, and sought my bed with a feeling that the little cooper-shop, my good wife, and our plain homely ways, were, after all, the best things on earth and, altogether, better than any other sort of life or attainments possible for man to secure.

Prompt to my promise, I was up betimes the next morning; and, after a hasty breakfast, secured a horse, and was soon rapidly cantering off in the direction of Elgin, where I arrived by the time the villagers of the little town were stir.ing about their several avocations. I proceeded directly to the house of John Smith, the gunsmith.

Before I had reached the same, my spirits were measurably raised to observe, sitting there upon the rough porch shaded with roses and honeysuckles, the veritable gentleman from Vermont who had given us all so much uneasiness.

He was smoking his pipe and enjoying the morning as composedly as any man well could, and, as I approached, looked up with a pleasant smile of greeting.

He advanced quickly to the gate, and grasped my hand heartily, saying quietly :

" Helloa, Pinkerton, what's up ? "

" Only myself," I answered jokingly.

" Have you got started out on your trip this early ? " he inquired.

" Yes, I believe if anything's worth doing, it's worth doing quickly and thoroughly. I'm on my way down the river to take in the towns I mentioned yesterday. I'll see Boyd to-morrow, get back as quick as can, and meet you as agreed at the 'Sauganash, in Chicago."

"You'll do, you'll do," said Craig encouragingly.

"I just thought I'd call on my way, shake hands with you, and show you I was at work carrying out my part of the agreement."

"Glad you stopped; glad you stopped. Make as good time as possible, for I want to get through here and get back east. The church interests always languish while I am away," he added laughing.

And so, with a cheery good-by, we again parted.

I rode away ostensibly for St. Charles, but, after getting some little distance from Elgin, took a detour, and, riding through the little post-town of Undina, reached Dundee some time before noon.

The information secured through this little ruse satisfied both myself and my Dundee friends that dependence could be placed upon meeting Craig in Chicago. This was what I most desired; for, alone in the country, and not knowing what secret companions he might have near him ready to spring to his aid at the lifting of his finger, made an attempt at his capture, with my then inexperience, simply foolish and something not to be thought of.

Three intervening days were passed in frequent consultations with Messrs. Hunt and Bosworth, very little attention to my casks and barrels, and a good deal of nervous plotting and planning on my own part; and before daybreak on the fourth morning I had caught the last glimpse of the little village of Dundee, nestling like a bird by the gleaming river, and was speeding my horse at a brisk pace over the winding highway toward Chicago.

I arrived in that then thriving, but little city, during the early forenoon, and my first move was to procure warrants for the arrest of both Craig and Yelverson, as I had high hopes of now being able, by a little good management, to get the two men together ; and I easily secured the services of two officers, one of whom I directed to follow and watch the movements of Craig, which would undoubtedly, if there was any such person as Yelverson, bring the two men together. My idea was to then wait until they had separated and were so situated that immediate communication would be impossible, and thus capture Yelverson ; while, after this had been effected, myself and the second officer would attend to Craig. But, as fine as all this looked in a plan, it was doomed, as the reader will observe, to prove *merely* a plan.

After all these arrangements were perfected, I went to the Sauganash Hotel. The officers were merely constables, and one was stationed outside the house, to follow Craig wherever he might go, or whoever might come in contact with him, should he be observed to meet any person with whom he might appear to have confidential relations ; while the other officer was located inside the hotel, to cause Craig's arrest whenever the proper time arrived.

I wanted to bring things about so that I could capture

the men with the money upon them, or in the very act of passing it; but circumstances and my own youth and inexperience were against me.

I had been seated in the office of the hotel but a few minutes when Craig entered, smoking a cigar. He saw me instantly, but several minutes elapsed before he saw fit to approach me, and I observed by his manner that he did not wish me to recognize him. He sauntered about for a time, apparently like one upon whose hands time hung heavily, and, finally securing a newspaper, dropped into a seat beside me.

Some minutes even elapsed before he in any manner recognized my presence, and then he said, with his attitude such that no one could imagine him otherwise than deeply engaged with his paper:

" Have you got the money? "

" Yes," I replied, quite as laconically.

" Well, I've an even four thousand now. The horse is sold; so you pay me one thousand dollars, and in the course of an hour I will see that you have the package."

" Craig," I said, " Lawyer Boyd, from Oswego, is here with me, and you know these lawyers are sticklers for form. Now, he don't want to pay the money until we see the bills."

" Why, he has seen what you had, hasn't he? *You* know that old John Craig's word is as good as his money, and that's as good as gold! " he replied with some warmth, and evidently nettled.

" If it was wholly my own affair, Craig, you *know* it

"Have you got the money." —Page—

would be different. You know I would trust you with ten times this sum," I replied reassuringly ; "but I've placed myself in this damned lawyer's power in order to keep my word like a man with you, and he insists like an idiot on having the thing done only in one way."

"Well, I'll think the matter over, and see you here a half-hour or so later," returned Craig.

We then adjourned to the bar, and partook of sundry drinks ; but I observed, without showing that I did so, that Craig was very careful in this respect. We soon parted, and I must confess that I began to have a presentiment that matters were beginning to look a little misty. I could not imagine what the outcome would be ; but that Craig had become suspicious of something, was certain.

I could not of course then know, without exposing myself, what was done, or how Craig acted, but I afterward learned that he seemed perplexed and doubtful about what he should do. He started out rapidly in the direction of the lake, suddenly halted, returned, started again, halted again, and then walked aimlessly in various directions, occasionally giving a quick look back over his shoulder as if to determine whether he was being followed.

Whatever he might have thought about this, at last he returned to the hotel with the air of a man who had determined upon something, and entered the office.

Not making any move as though he desired to see me, I soon moved toward him, and finally said :

"Well, Craig, are you going to let me have the money ? "

He looked at me a moment with a puzzled air of sur prise, the assurance of which I have never since seen equaled, and replied quietly :

"What money ?"

I looked at him in blank amazement, and finally said : "The money you promised me."

With a stolidity that would have made a Grant or a Wellington, he rejoined :

"I haven't the honor of your acquaintance, sir, and therefore cannot imagine to what you allude."

If the Sauganash Hotel had fallen upon me, I could not have been more surprised, or, for the moment, over-whelmed.

But this lasted but for a moment. I saw that my fine plan had fallen to the ground like a house of straw. Yelverson had not been located ; probably no counterfeit money could be found upon Craig ; and there was only my own almost unsupported evidence as to the entire transaction, as the reader has been given it ; but I also saw that there was only one thing to do, and that was to make Mr. Craig my prisoner. I therefore said :

"All right, John Craig ; you have played your game well, but there are always at least two at a really inter-esting game, and I shall have to take you into custody on the charge of counterfeiting."

I gave the signal to the officer, and Craig was at once arrested ; but he fairly turned the tables upon me then by his assumed dignity and gentlemanly bearing. Quite a crowd gathered about, and considerable sympathy was expressed for the stately, gray-haired man who was being borne into captivity by the green-looking countryman cooper from Dundee.

Not a dollar in counterfeit money was found upon Craig, as I had feared. He was taken to Geneva, in Kane County, lodged in jail, and, after the preliminary examination, admitted to bail in a large sum. While awaiting the arrival of friends to furnish the required bonds, he was remanded ; and it was soon noticed by the frequenters of the place that Craig and the sheriff, whose apartments were in the jail building, had become very intimate. He was shown every courtesy and favor possible under the circumstances, and the result was that the community was suddenly startled to learn that the now famous counterfeiter had mysteriously escaped—leaving, it was said, the sheriff of Kane County considerably richer in this world's goods from the unfortunate occurrence.

This was the outcome of the matter ; but though this great criminal, through the perfidy of an official, had escaped punishment, the affair was worth everything to the Wisconsin Fire and Marine Insurance Company in particular, and the entire West in general—it having the effect for a number of years to drive counterfeiters entirely from our midst.

But I cannot resist relating, in connection with the termination of the case, another incident characteristic of George Smith.

With all his business success, like Dickens' "Barkis,
he became considerably "mean," and finally obtained the
sobriquet, among his friends and acquaintances, of old
"Na!" on account of the abruptness and even ugliness
with which he would snap out his Scotch "na!" or no,
to certain applicants for banking or other favors.

As soon as I had got Craig safely in jail, Messrs. Hunt
and Bosworth, who had expended nearly one hundred
and fifty dollars in the matter, saw that they had nothing
left for their pains save the counterfeit five hundred dollars, and that even was deposited in the hands of the
Kane County Court clerk; so it devolved upon me to
go into Chicago, see George Smith, and get from him,
if possible, so much money as had been expended, and a
few dollars for my own services.

So I took my trip, after a vexatious delay was admitted to the presence of the mighty banker, and tersely
stated my errand.

He heard me all through, and then remarked savagely:
"Have ye nae mair to say?"

"Not anything," I replied civilly.

"Then I've just this tae speak: ye was not author
ized tae do the wark, and ye have nae right t' a cent.
I'll pay this, I'll pay this; but mind ye, roo," and he
shook his finger at me in no pleasant way, "if ye ever do
wark for me agin that ye have nae authorization for, ye'll
get ne'er a penny, ne'er a penny!"

In fact, it was hard work for the close-fisted Scotchman
to be decently just in the matter, and I am certain the

incident has been of service to me during these later years in causing prudence in all such undertakings.

The country being new, and great sensations scarce, the affair was in everybody's mouth, and I suddenly found myself called upon, from every quarter, to undertake matters requiring detective skill, until I was soon actually *forced* to relinquish the honorable, though not over-profitable, occupation of a cooper, for that of a professional detective, with the result and a career of which the public are fully acquainted; all of which I owe to "Old John Craig" and this my first detective case.

CHAPTER II.

JACK CANTER.

THE subject of this sketch, who is still living and occupying a felon's cell through the efforts of my detectives, has been one of the most brilliant of professional criminals.

I am unable to give my readers any idea of the circumstances leading to his becoming what he has been, which to me, of all criminals and especially those of the better class, as studies of human experience and the yielding to human temptations, always prove intensely interesting.

Canter is supposed to be of American parentage, and, as nearly as I am able to learn, was born in some little

village of Central New York. He is, at this writing, forty
five years of age, is five feet seven inches in height, of
slight, spare frame, has a dark complexion, dark hair and
black beard, usually worn after what is termed the "Burn-
side" fashion, and altogether is possessed of a remarkably
distingué appearance. He is probably one of the oldest
counterfeiters and forgers in the United States, and has
served nearly twenty-five years of his life in various pris-
ons, principally at Sing Sing, where he has been incarcerated during three terms, one of which was for fourteen
years.

I wonder if any of my readers ever endeavored to impress their minds with the actual duration and effect of
such a period and kind of existence.

Whatever Jack Canter might have been before his first
prison experience, when he passed out from the walls of
Sing Sing he was a confirmed criminal, and never since
has seemed to have an aspiration for any other course of
life.

He has been arrested by the Secret Service authorities,
under Colonel Whitley, numberless times, on the charge
of counterfeiting; but whenever apprehended he invariably
had one or more engraved plates, generally valueless,
which he would turn over to the Government authorities
on the condition that he secured his liberty, which was
too frequently accorded him.

His acquirements, for one who had passed so many
years in a prison, were really of a brilliant nature, and
certainly show him to have had an exceedingly thorough

education in his youth, or to have been one of those singularly constituted persons that can instantly acquire and always retain whatever they get their minds upon.

He is a great linguist, a very perfect and correct one, having the French, German, Spanish, Italian, and many other languages at thorough command. He is a splendid phonographer and an expert penman; is a well-informed chemist, and graduated with high honors as a physician, is, or has been, one of the most exact and artistic line-engravers in America, and line-engraving requires the highest nicety and proficiency in the art; and is a man of so general good attainments and fine ability that he has very frequently given the press scientific articles of rare vigor and merit. When one considers how great the possibilities of such an able man are, and then see to what base uses these accomplishments are put, it causes a genuine pang of regret in the heart of every well-wisher of society.

Canter was always received at Sing Sing as a distinguished guest, and granted favors to an unlimited extent.

Concerning his service there, it is related that he was made book-keeper of the prison, and, through his expert use of the pen and extensive knowledge of chemicals, drove a thriving trade with convicts who were fortunate enough to have wealthy friends. His system of "raising the wind" was to hunt up the antecedents of notorious professional criminals there incarcerated, and boldly offer to reduce their term of service for a certain stipulated sum of money.

For instance: a convict had received a ten years' sen
tence. Canter would ascertain how much ready cash the
prisoner's friends could or would advance for a reduction
of the term for one or two years or from one to five years,
and then, after securing the money—which rumor alleges
was generously divided among certain prison officers—he,
by and with the aid of certain chemicals, would alter the
prison records, so that paying parties would be able to
secure a discharge on a greatly reduced term.

Through these favors and irregularities, which the
prison officials must have been cognizant of, Canter carried a "high hand" at Sing Sing. He supported several
"fast" women ; went out and in the prison as he liked ;
drove the fastest team in the place ; and it is alleged, on
the best of authority, was frequently seen at New York,
where he mingled with his friends at leisure.

In other words, while he was at Sing Sing he was
"boss" of the prison ; and he either carried so high a
hand on his own account, or had so many of the most
influential officials there mixed up in his counterfeiting
affairs, that he had everything his own way

But his star of success waned when he fell under the
influence of honest detectives, as represented by my
Agency.

He was arrested by my officers, in 1874, for his connection with the gigantic forgeries committed in September
of that year ; and those influences he had been enabled to
make use of whenever he so wished were wholly withdrawn when I had secured his committal to the Eastern

Penitentiary of Pennsylvania, at Philadelphia, for one or
the shrewdest forgeries he had ever been known to
commit.

In February, 1873, an insurance company was formed
in Philadelphia, under the name of the "Central Fire
Insurance Company," of which W. D. Halfman, a gentle
man said to have been worth nearly a million dollars, was
elected president, and W. F. Halfman, a convenient rela-
tive, as treasurer. The secretary and directors were
John Nicholson Elbert, W. J. Moodie, C. A. Duy, P.
Thurlow, W. H. Elberly, and others.

It was represented by this company to the Insurance
Commissioner of the State of Pennsylvania that they had
a capital of two hundred thousand dollars, invested in
various railroad and other securities, and that their
stock had been subscribed for as follows :

P. Thurlow,	900 shares, representing.		. . . .$45,000
C. A. Duy,	200 "	"	 10,000
W. H. Halfman,	100 "	"	 5,000
W. D. Halfman,	800 "	"	 40,000
W. J. Moodie,	200 "	"	 10,000
Moodie, Gross & Co.,	40 "	"	 2,000
W. D. Halfman,	1,560 (in trust)	"	 78,000

All of the above officers and stockholders were well
known citizens of Philadelphia, reputable business men
and capitalists of moderate resources, and, as far as
could be publicly known, were able to purchase and own
the stock, as listed for inspection by the Insurance Com
missioner,

The company opened out in fine style, had elegant offices, and were supposed to be doing a very prosperous business; but, in time, J. M. Foster, one of the Insurance Commissioners of the State, becoming suspicious that the concern was not all that it purported to be, caused an overhauling of its business.

This examination developed the fact that all of the assets of the company consisted of forged railroad stocks as follows :

    500 shares Phila. & Reading R.R. Stock.
    500   "   Lehigh Valley.
    500   "   Delaware, Lackawanna and Western Stock.
    300   "   Central Railroad of New Jersey   "
    100   "   Pennsylvania Central   "
    4,000 "   Lebanon Paper Company   "
    130   "   Westend Railroad of Phila.   "

All of which the company claimed to own absolutely.

Investigation developed the fact that all of these stocks, so far as their assumed value was concerned, were forgeries. They had originally been issued for one or two shares, and afterward, by a chemical process, their numbers had been erased, and they were each then made to represent three hundred or five hundred shares, as occasion required.

This alarming condition of things leaked out, and the Philadelphia and Reading Railway Company, in order to protect its stockholders, secured my services to thoroughly ventilate the matter. After considerable trouble,

1

I caused the arrest of one J. H. Elbert, from whom I secured a confession to the effect that he had employed a man named Charles Ripley, of New York, to make the alterations on the certificates. He had been introduced to this Ripley at a hotel in Jersey City, by a person named Louis W. French (afterward convicted in New Jersey for the frauds committed by the "Palisade Insurance Company" of Hoboken, N. J.).

Elbert had paid Ripley twenty-five thousand dollars for making the alterations. The former also stated that he addressed letters to Ripley at a saloon, No. 303 Bridge Street, Brooklyn. Inquiries by my most careful operatives at this place developed the fact that the letters addressed to Charles Ripley, at that number, had been delivered to a man known by the name of Charles Ostend. Upon securing this much, I placed men so that every person arriving at or leaving this place, if not then known, could be followed and their identity established. The result of this was that I had shortly effected the arrest of Ostend, whom I immediately recognized as the notorious Jack Canter.

He was at once removed to Philadelphia, where he and W. D. Halfman, the president of the bogus company, were tried, and on January 2, 1875, Canter was sentenced to nine years and six months' solitary confinement in the Eastern Penitentiary, at Cherry Hill, Philadelphia, and Halfman to seven years and six months' imprisonment at hard labor.

At the time of my arrest of Canter, he had been

3*

out of Sing Sing only about two years. A curious illustration of the negligence of the police surveillance is
shown in the fact that, when I captured the fellow, he
had been living *within one block* of the First Precinct
Brooklyn police-station; and, on searching the room there
were found a very fine nickle-plated press for counterfeiting purposes, a full set of the finest quality of en-
graver's tools, and a fine plate for use in counterfeiting
two cent bank-check stamps—a perfect imitation of the
genuine.

There were also found in his room several poems
which this strange man had written while a convict at
Sing Sing. Many of these possessed rare merit, not
showing, perhaps, the fine polish of eminent writers, but
still indicating the great degree of natural ability and
poetic genius which were certainly his.

Probably the most pretentious of these poems was
one called the "Tale of a Cell," which I have reason to
believe is a partial history of the man himself, and an
impulsive, passionate outpouring of his own bitter prison
reflections.

Some portions of the poem are only mediocre, many
grammatical and metric errors exist; but there are frequently seen the indications of real genius, while occasionally there occur passages worthy of the best author.
The following is the poem complete:

TALE OF A CELL.

Ah, me ! how many years have flown,
  My wearied mem'ry scarce can tell,
Since, piece by piece, and stone by stone,
  They wrought me in this dismal cell.
Through storm and calm, and sun and rain,
  Six thousand years since I had birth,
On yonder hillside I have lain,
  Soft in thy bosom, Mother Earth !

But rude men sought my resting-place,
  And with a sudden, fearful shock,
They tore me from thy strong embrace,
  The wreck of a once mighty rock.
They formed me in this living grave,
  A thing abhorred, a loathsome den ;
Here am I now, man's wretched slave,
  To guard and grind his fellow-men.

I recollect the time as well
  As if it were but yesterday,
When I was but a new-made cell.
  My naked walls were cold and gray,
For then I had not been o'er-reached
  By sad and never-ceasing care ;
Long years of misery have bleached
  My sombre sides like whitened hair.

'Twas summer time, and hill and dell
  And plain with loveliness were strown,
When my first inmate came to dwell
  Comparion of my silence lone.

The earth was redolent with life
　Of all that's beautiful and fair,
With birds and flowers and foliage ripe
　That sang or bloomed and budded there

The setting sun's departing ray
　Just pierced the darkness lone and drear,
When strange men came from far away
　And brought the trembling captive here.
He was a stripling still, and one
　Who ne'er had tasted grief till then ;
Poor child ! he had but just begun
　To live his three-score years and ten.

Upon the threshold of the door
　He shrank as if from touch of death ;
His heart beat faster than before,
　And hot and hurried was his breath.
I saw him shudder and grow pale
　When clanged the door—poor captive bird !
He sighed, and then a low, sad wail
　Of speechless agony was heard.

He leaned upon his prison-bars
　And gazed until the sun went down,
While one by one the twinkling stars
　Glowed bright in night's imperial crown
But the broad sky was shut from view ;
　A glance upon the rippling wave
And one small strip of heaven's blue,
　Were all his narrow window gave.

Yet there one little star appeared
  On which he gazed until it wore
The semblance of a face endeared
  By ties that he could know no more—
The ties of mother and of son ;
  No stronger ties on earth are riven ;
Perhaps it was this same dear one
  That beckoned her lost child to heaven.

A recollection sad, but sweet,
  Stole o'er his senses like a thief,
While he, unconscious of the cheat,
  Forgot his shame, forgot his grief.
His thoughts were far away from here,
  'Mid scenes where once he used to roam
With friends and kindred fond and dear,
  Within his childhood's happy home.

There were his sisters young and fair,
  And there his brothers stout and tall,
And there his aged sire, and there
  His mother, dearest of them all.
Again he lived his childish hours,
  So gay, so good, and yet so brief,
So strewn with pleasure's blooming flowers,
  He scarcely saw the thorn of grief.

Where'er he moved, whate'er he saw
  His mother's form was ever there ;
With her, in reverential awe,
  He knelt at morn and evening prayer.

With her, each holy Sabbath day,
    He listened to God's sacred word;
'Twas she who taught his lips to pray,
    And his young heart's devotion stirred.

And when he stretched his weary form
    Upon the couch he used to share,
That little bed, so soft and warm,
    Was made by that fond mother's care.
He saw her wasted, wan and pale,
    But with that faith that never dies,
Admitted, through Death's shadowy vale,
    To life eternal in the skies.

Before the last of life had fled,
    As he stood weeping by her side,
" I'm going home, my child ! " she said,
    And bade him meet her there, and died.
He saw her borne to her last bed,
    By fellow-travelers to the grave,
The sweet " City of the Dead, '
    Where mourning yew and cypress wave.

And ere he well could comprehend
    A mother's love, a mother's worth,
He saw her coffined form descend—
    " Dust unto dust," and " earth to earth."
He saw his home deserted, bare,
    Bereft of all that made it dear ;
His kindred gone ; no thing was there
    Of all he used to love, revere.

And then he wandered forth, apart
   From all that blessed him when a **child—**
Untutored in the world's black heart,
   Temptation his young heart beguiled.
The crime, arrest, confinement, shame,
   The trial, sentence, felon's cell,
Passed through his mind like withering **flame ;**
   'Twas conscience—first crime's fiercest **hell.**

Dim grew the little star's bright beam,
   A dark cloud o'er the heavens crept ;
The captive started—'twas no dream ;
   And then he turned aside and wept.
'Twas his first crime, and guilt and fear
   Had pressed him deeply, darkly down ;
No penitential grief could cheer
   No tears his crying conscience drown.

Though night advanced and darkness stole
   With midnight blackness o'er the skies,
No hope had soothed his troubled soul,
   No sleep had closed his weeping eyes.
A sudden thought his bosom thrilled,
   A hope by memory long delayed,
His grief subdued, his passion stilled,
   And on the ground he knelt and prayed.

And ere he could that prayer repeat,
   " Or echo answer from the hill,"
" A still, small voice," divinely sweet,
   Said : " Peace! thou troubled soul, *he* still !

He slept—the tranquil sleep of those
  Who feel no guilt and fear no hell—
The weary sinner's sweet repose,
  When danger's past, and all is well.

He woke when morning's purple beams
  Along the hill-tops richly glowed ;
And, as he rose from his sweet dreams,
  And gazed around his grim abode,
O'er his fair face there came a shade,
  And in his eyes a strange light burned.
He looked bewildered, lost, afraid,
  Till, one by one, his thoughts returned,

Bringing his terrors back again
  In all their darkest hues arrayed ;
But faith and hope sustained him then.
  Again he wept, again he prayed,
And then, unseen by mortal eye,
  In that bright morn serene and still,
With heart and hand uplifted high,
  He vowed to do his Maker's will.

And when they took him forth that day
  Among his brotherhood in sin,
To toil with them he went his way,
  Cheerful without and calm within ;
And night, returning, brought no change—
  He knew the justice of his lot,
And to its mandate, harsh and strange,
  He meekly bowed and murmured not.

Thus day by day, each morn and night,
  Sad, but resigned, he went and came;
Still mourning o'er his wretched plight,
  He buried hopes and early shame.
Thus months, like ages, passed away;
  A change came o'er the convict lad:
Sometimes his heart was almost gay,
  And sometimes very, very sad.

And often by the night-lamp's flame
  I saw his youthful features wear
A vengeful look that ill became
  The face of one so young and fair.
I knew not what it was that made
  His heart grow colder day by day;
I knew not why his hope decayed,
  Nor why at length he ceased to pray.

But, sometimes in his absent moods,
  With flashing eye and actions strange,
He muttered long, like one who broods
  O'er bitter wrongs and sweet revenge.
At length he came not back again—
  One winter's evening black and chill
I watched and listened all in vain—
  The doors were closed, and all was still.

The morning went and came again,
  And went and came for five long weeks,
Ere he returned sick and in pain,
  With sunken eye and sallow cheeks,

His haggard face and matted hair
    With dungeon and with damp defiled—
The hate, the anguish, and despair
    Seen in his glances fierce and wild;

The muttered curses deep and long,
    That bubbled up at every breath
And told a tale of ruthless wrong,
    Of smothered ire, revenge, and death.
Again he knelt, but not in prayer,
    And called on God, but not for grace,
But with blasphemous oaths, to swear
    Undying vengeance on his race.

Calmly he laid him down, as lies
    The weary tiger in his den;
Calmly in sleep he closed his eyes,
    O'er his fell purpose brooding then.
But, even while he slumbered there,
    His injured spirit scorned repose,
And other scenes, in form of air,
    Around the restless sleeper rose.

That night the mystery which draped
    The convict's fearful fate was broke,
And, in his feverish sleep, escaped
    From lips that all unconscious spoke.
I saw the secret of his heart
    By slow and sure degrees unfold,
As, night by night, and part by part,
    His sad and cruel tale was told.

The slave of men* who bought and sold
    Their brother fellows for a price;
Whose creed is gain, whose god is gold,
    Whose virtue is another's vice;
Who live by crime, and rave and storm
    At those who hate their hellish lust,
Curse God, religion, and reform,
    And all that makes men good and just;

Who seemed to 'think him born to be
    The slave of a contractor's will,
To doff the cap and bend the knee
    To keeper's manner, viler still.
In vain he sought by gentle tones,
    Respectful speech and humble air,
To please the pompous, senseless drones
    Employed to drive him to despair.

In vain he toiled with all his might
    His grinding masters to appease;
In vain he wrought from morn till night,
    Heart-sick and wasted by disease.
He could not sate their thirst for gain,
    And when exhausted nature's store
Of strength and health began to wane,
    They never ceased to cry for more;

But dragged him forth, I know not where,
    To scenes from which the thoughts recoil.
Till death should free, or strong despair
    Should lend him energy to toil;

       * Contractors.

Or torture's keenest, fiercest pains
　Should grind his very soul away,
To swell a grasping miser's gains
　Or swell a tyrant jailor's sway.

He spoke of dungeons where no light
　Can ever pierce the noisome gloom,
Whose icy chill, and long, long night
　Outlive the horrors of the tomb;
Where time appears so loth to leave,
　Each moment seems an age of care,
And noon and night, and morn and eve,
　Are all alike to dwellers there;

Where the lone wretch in terror quaked
　While madness darkened o'er his brain,
And naught the deathless stillness waked
　Save the dull clank of his own chain,
As, blindly, fearfully, he groped
　In solitude complete, profound;
Or, half-unconscious, sat and moped
　Upon the cold and slimy ground.

He spoke with agonizing cries
　Of tortures pen can ne'er depict,
That none but demons could devise,
　And none but hell's foul fiends inflict;
Now writhing as in mortal pangs,
　Now gasping hurriedly for breath,
Now trembling like the wretch that hangs
　Suspended o'er the brink of death.

Defiant now, and now dismayed,
  Now struggling with an unseen foe,
He smiled and frowned, and cursed and prayed,
  In accents piteous and low.
So day by day, and week by week,
  His bed the grave-cold granite stones,
While hunger gnawed his pallid cheek
  And almost bared his aching bones.

Debarred the sweet, reviving air,
  The shining sun and azure sky,
The pale, pale victim, in despair,
  Outlived the death he longed to die.
Thus, often, when the night unrolled
  Its sable screen o'er land and sea,
The all-unconscious dreamer told
  His cruel wrongs to God and me.

And while he muttered in his sleep
  His tale of sorrow and distress,
I knew he suffered pains too deep
  For pen or pencil to express.
I knew it by the sunken eye,
  Distorted face and blood-stained lip,
The sweat, the tear, the groans, the cry,
  Convulsive grasp and death-like grip.

I knew it by the heart's hard beat ;
  I knew it by the bursting brain;
I knew it by the fever heat
  That burned and blazed in every rein ;

I knew it by the fearful lines
　That mortal woe and anguish wear;
I knew it by the thousand signs
　Of great and measureless despair.

How changed since they brought him here,
　A timid, trembling, weeping boy—
No foes to hate, and none to fear,
　No friends to grieve, and none to joy!
Respectful, willing, meek, benign,
　He toiled as for a royal crown—
Rejoiced by an approving sign,
　Disheartened by an angry frown.

As pliant as the potter's clay,
　They might have moulded him at will
For honored happiness, had they
　The wish, the justice, or the skill;
But those who should have taught his mind,
　By precept and example loud,
Were stone-blind leaders of the blind,
　Base, overbearing, lawless, proud;

Exacting, cruel, harsh, and grim,
　In Christ no hope, in heaven no share,
They went not in, and hindered him
　Who gladly would have entered there,
With no kind, Christian friend to steer
　His drifting bark to ports above,
No eye to pity, tongue to cheer,
　Or loving, kindred heart to love.

Condemned to herd with those who sought
  His purer nature to defile,
Whose every word, and deed, and thought,
  Was vile, the vilest of the vile;
To them, the vicious and depraved,
  In his extremity he turned;
With them he sought the cheer he craved,
  The sympathy for which he yearned.

They welcomed him to darker shame,
  A baser life, a deeper fall;
And the once child-like youth became
  The vilest, sternest of them all—
Rebellious, scornful, fierce, profane,
  Vindictive, stubborn, void of fear:
Well might I marvel and exclaim,
  How changed since first they brought him here!

Time went as time has always went—
  In pleasure swift, in sorrow slow;
And soon, unfettered and unspent,
  He would be free to come and go.
Enraptured thought!—ah, would it be?
  He scarcely dared believe it so.
But time rolled on, and he was free;
  Was he then truly happy?—No!

No! life had nothing left for him;
  No joy to lend, no boon to give;
He could not sink, he could not swim,
  But struggling, dying, doomed to live!

Yes, live, though life's bright sun had set;
  He cared not how, he thought not why;
He knew that he must live, and yet
  Forget, alas! that he must die.

I saw him, when, in after times,
  With nothing left of sin to learn,
He came again, for darker crimes,
  A bearded ruffian, hard and stern.
He mocked at those who brought him back,
  And laughed to scorn their idle threats.
What torture from his frame could rack
  The sum of his unmeasured debts?

He laughed to think how many times
  He sinned unpunished and uncaught;
What nameless and unnumbered crimes
  That red right hand of his had wrought.
He laughed when he remembered how
  His wrongs were soothed in human woes,
And he but one lone captive now
  To his ten thousand thousand foes.

He cursed the faithless hopes that first
  His too confiding heart beguiled;
He cursed his innocence, he cursed
  The dreams that mocked him when a child
He cursed his lonely prison den,
  And death, hell, and the grave defied;
He cursed himself and fellow-men;
  He cursed his Maker, God—and died.

The world will never know the wrong
That drives its erring children back
To deeper crime and those who throng
Destruction's broad and beaten track.
'Twill never know the trusts betrayed,
The worth its wolfish tools devour;
'Twill never know the prices paid
To sate the cruel pride of power !

JACK CANTER.

SING SING, Oct. 31, 1870.

CHAPTER III.

THE GHOST OF THE OLD CATHOLIC CEMETERY.

IT would be a surprise to the general public if the records of all my offices could be thrown open for inspection, so that it might be observed what a *wide range* has been covered by investigations which I have been called upon to undertake—the mysteries to unravel, or crimes to prevent or unearth. It must not be supposed that the services of my agencies are wholly devoted to criminal matters. Some of the most important legal contests of the times have been decided in accordance with the irresistible array of evidence which a small army of my men have quietly, keenly, and patiently secured; while the operation of immense business interests, like banking, insurance, and railway matters, have often been interrupted by seemingly inextricable confusion and com-

4

plexity, which threatened great loss, until my services were asked ; and by my thorough and complete system, through which almost general and instant communication and information can be secured, I have been enabled to bring order out of chaos, and prevent what might have otherwise resulted in commercial ruin to my patrons. As the individual detective's notice must be brought to everything great and small upon any investigation he may be conducting, so is it true that the principal of a large system of detective agencies must be so situated that he may consider and receive every possible variety of business—always excepting that which is disreputable—and then have means at his command to carry each case, may it be great or insignificant, to a successful issue.

In the pursuit of these cases there is frequently both tragedy and pathos ; they are always full of deep and fascinating interest to myself and my operatives, and quite frequently they bring to the surface all phases of ridiculous humor, which I frequently enjoy to the greatest possible degree.

In the summer of 1857 there was located, along the shore of Lake Michigan, within the limits of the city of Chicago, a high, narrow, sandy strip of land, then occupied as a cemetery, known as the "Old Catholic Burying-Ground," or the "Old French Cemetery," from the fact that within it reposed the remains of hundreds who had died in the Catholic faith, as well as large numbers of the early French settlers and their half-breed progeny.

Quaint inscriptions and devices were there seen, and

everywhere upon the great cenotaph or monument, or upon the most modest of graves, the cross. in every manner of design, somber with black paint or bright with fanciful colors, or still white in chiseled marble, could be found.

The old cemetery has since been removed; and where once stood, in silence and mournfulness, the city of the dead, now are seen splendid mansions of the rich, with magnificent gardens and conservatories, or, in that portion which has been absorbed by Chicago's beautiful Lincoln Park, handsome drives, fine fountains, exquisite lawn or copse; and over all the old-time somberness has come an air of opulence, beauty, and healthful diversion. Scarcely could a greater change anywhere be noted than from the former solemnity and desolation to the present elegance and artistic winsomeness.

In the time of which I write Chicago was much younger than now. Twenty years have made the then little city the present great metropolis. All the great enterprises which now distinguish the city were then in their infancy. Particularly were all institutions of learning having a hard struggle to creep along; and the medical schools, then just started, were put to every possible shift for the funds necessary to an existence; and there being often no legal provision for securing "subjects" for dissection, the few students pursuing their course of study were compelled to secure these essential aids to their work by grave-robbery, that greatest and most horrible desecration imaginable.

The old French cemetery being situated less than a mile and a half from the river—which then as now was called nearly the geographical center of the city—the temptation to steal newly-buried bodies from so convenient a locality proved irresistible, and the city was soon startled by a succession of grave-robberies which excited general indignation and alarm. Coupled with this indignity to the dead and the friends of the dead, some malicious persons had entered the cemetery and wantonly desecrated graves from which subjects had not been taken.

Some held that this had been caused through religious ill-feeling, others that it was the result of pure mischief or the part of such persons as had been concerned in other impudent and graceless grave-robberies ; but the result of it all was that so much public wrangling and excitement occurred that a committee of prominent gentlemen, including some of the city officials, called upon me, and desired me to take such measures as would cause a cessation of the outrages, and bring to punishment whoever might be found to have been the perpetrators of the same.

While such was the result of the operation, it is only my purpose here to relate a single incident of the many interesting ones which transpired, and one which, while it illustrates the ridiculous length of absurdity to which an inherent superstition and a hearty fear will lead their possessor, I can never recall without almost uncontrollable laughter.

My plan of operations was as follows :

I detailed eight men from my force, under the charge of Timothy Webster, one of the most faithful men ever in my service—who, it will be remembered, was executed at Richmond as a Federal spy during the late civil war. These were so stationed that every entrance to the cemetery should be guarded, as well as all the new-made graves thoroughly watched. As no word could be spoken lest it might frighten away any culprit before he could be captured, I found it absolutely necessary to devise some simple, though silent and effective means of communication. To effect this I decided upon using several sets of heavy chalk-lines, such as are generally used by carpenters in laying out work. The ends of each line were attached to small stakes driven in the ground about three feet apart. The operatives' station was between these stakes ; and, in order that every man should be forced to not only remain at his post, but remain continually awake and vigilant, I required the line to be gently pulled three times, beginning with a certain post, and extending rapidly, according to a pre-arranged plan, and the same signal repeated after a lapse of about one minute, in reverse order. This was the general signal that everything was as it should be, and nothing new had transpired. This was repeated every fifteen minutes, so that by no possi-bility could any dereliction of duty pass undetected.

Aside from this, the system of signals comprised means of communicating the presence of any outside party, at whatever point the intruder should make his appearance, and such other necessary information as would lead to a silent, swift, and certain capture of any person who might, for any cause whatever, enter the cemetery.

I had detailed men for this work whom I felt I could rely upon. Simple as it may seem to one who has never had such an experience, remaining all night in a grave-yard, with every nerve and faculty on the constant *qu vive* of expectation, is not such pleasant work as it may be supposed ; and though the novelty of the affair, coupled with all manner of outlandish jokes upon the situation, kept up an interest which lasted a few nights, I began to notice signs among a few of my men indicating that the solemnity and dread of the situation were taking the place of its original romance.

Coupled with this, there were among these eight, as there always are among any like body of men the world over, a few who, like myself, began to notice these indications of weakness on the part of the more susceptible among them. These braver fellows immediately commenced, with solemn tones and long faces, to relate hob-goblin tales of ghosts and materialized spirits which came from their silent resting-places for unearthly strolls among them. Although I put a stop to this as much as possible, what had already been done had had its desired effect, and a few of the watchers showed well-defined evidences of genuine fear, and to such an extent that I was finally compelled to relieve some men, and fill their places with others.

Among the cemetery detail was one young fellow

named O'Grady, a genuine son of the Emerald Isle, who had come to me almost direct from Ireland, and who, though he had been in my service but a few months, had shown native traits such as gave promise of improvement and advancement. He was the very life and soul of the detective rooms, and the wonderful tales he related of himself, his ready wit, his true bravery in all places wherever he had been previously used, and his quick generosity toward his fellows, had given him an exalted place among them.

I saw that O'Grady was weakening.

He tried hard not to show it. He endeavored to look bright and spirited, but it was all up-hill work. He began to get thin on this grave-yard duty. It was very reflective work. From eight to ten hours utterly alone, and surrounded by everything which could fill one's mind with fear and dread, had its effect. His natural superstition suddenly developed into an abnormal and unnatural dread, which to the ignorant fellow seemed to become almost overwhelming. Had he not been such a hero in his own eyes, I am certain that I could not but have relented ; but, under the circumstances, I confess that I heartily enjoyed his forlorn appearance as he dejectedly left the Agency to take up his all-night's vigil, which undoubtedly soon became a genuine terror to him.

Having carried the matter so far, the spirit of innocent mischief and practical joking, which has always been strong within me, as many of my personal friends long ago discovered, prompted me still further.

I determined to play ghost for one night, show O'Grady a genuine goblin, and put his often-told tales of personal bravery to a practical test.

Accordingly, giving out at the Agency that I should be absent at a neighboring town for the night, before sundown I secured a private conveyance which took me to a point along the lake shore, about a mile beyond the old Catholic Cemetery ; and then, before the time for the detail to go on duty came, disguised all that was necessary to prevent recognition by any chance stroller, I hastily returned to the cemetery through the heavy copse of scrub-oak and willow that then lined the shore at that point, and, entering the place unobserved just as the twilight began to gather heavily, secreted myself within a heavy clump of *arbor vitæ* ornamenting a family lot, not over twenty feet from the point where I had previously learned that O'Grady was stationed each night.

I had no time to spare, for I had thus hardly become one of the cemetery watchers before, one by one, and all in stealth, the men began coming in from every direction, but so secretly and carefully that they might have been mistaken, by one not informed of their purpose, for ghosts or grave-robbers themselves, while Timothy Webster noiselessly sped from point to point, stretching the line which held the men silently to their work.

I could have touched the fellow as he passed me. In fact, an almost irresistible desire seized me to play Puck, as he sped by, and trip him among the damp, dark weeds

Pretty soon O'Grady came to his station, groaning and muttering.

As soon as the dark came down upon the old cemetery I left my hiding-place and got in line with the tell-tale string.

O'Grady was busy saying his prayers, and of course did not hear me rustling about in the long grass.

My first impulse was to grab a cross from some old-time grave, and toss it, over the stones, in upon him; but by great effort I suppressed this, and soon found myself sitting in a hollow between two mounds, with my hand upon the line.

"One, two, three!"—jerk, jerk, jerk, went the line: the first signal was being given.

My hand touched the line as lightly and yet as knowingly as the telegraph operator's fingers touch his well-known instrument; but I made no sign of my presence.

O'Grady answered the signal loyally; but scarcely was his duty done in this respect before he began a sort of a low, crooning wail, half like a mother's lullaby, half like a "keen" at a wake.

"Why did I lave ye, ye green ould sod? Why did I lave ye, ye dear old bogs? Why did I lave ye, ye blue-eyed swateheart? Feule I am that I came to the divil's ould boy, Phinkerton! Feule I am that I sit here by the blissed crosses av the dead, waitin' for the ghouls to rob! Och, murther! happy I'll be if the whole blissed place is tuk away!"

"One, two, three!"—jerk, jerk, jerk, came the signal

4*

again, while O'Grady answered it, as I could feel, with an impatient response.

After this, for a time, the brave Irish guardsman weaved back and forth upon the grave where he was sitting; when suddenly, to my horror, he lighted his pipe and began smoking.

I knew the man had become desperate in his loneliness, and had arrived at a point of feeling where he was utterly regardless of the success of the operation; and if I had felt sure of this when he recklessly lighted his dudheen, I could not but realize it to my sorrow when, in the glow of his roaring pipe, I could see that he followed his solace of tobacco by a more substantial quieter of superstition and fear from a black bottle, which the bold O'Grady had conveniently set, after each passage to his lips, upon the base of the monument above the grave where he was sitting.

I was indignant, and yet interested. I felt like dragging the brave O'Grady from his comfortable quarters to give him a good drubbing for his utter carelessness of the interests of the operation, and I am certain that in my then state of mind I would have done so if my desire to nearly scare the life out of him had not been uppermost.

Outside of the fussing and wailing of the O'Grady, there were no other but unpleasant surroundings in the old Catholic Cemetery. Now and then the ghostly hoot of the owl sounded weirdly from the surrounding tree-tops. From the low copses beyond came the mournful cry of the whip-poor-will. And down along the silvery beach of the shore, which gleamed and darkened as the new moon appeared, or was obscured for a time behind the darkening clouds, floated up and over the dreary place the sad and ghostly beating of the waves upon the beach.

It *was* a lonesome place, and it began to occur to me that I would not care to pass many nights in such a manner myself; but, under the circumstances, I saw that Mr O'Grady had fixed himself about as comfortably as it well could be done. Every time the signal was given, Mr. O'Grady would respond, when he would immediately recollect that his good bottle stood idle beside him. After a little he seemed to become so lonesome and dejected that he began a sort of conversation, in a low tone, with himself, in which he compelled the bottle, by proxy, to join, all after the following fashion :

"An' it's a big feule ye are, O'Grady. If it were not for mesek that's thakin' pity on yez, ye'd be dead enthirely."

"Ah, faith!" Mr. O'Grady would reply, with a sigh, "thrue for ye, thrue for ye! If I ever get out of this divel's own schrape, ould Phinkerton 'll never get me in the loikes again!"

"So ye say! so ye say, O'Grady; but yer always and foriver resolvin', and ye come to nothin' in the ind!"

"Don't be worryin' and accusin' me, me dear boy. This schrape wid the graves will be me last. By the rock of Cashel! phat's that?"

This last exclamation from Mr. O'Grady, which was in

a tone of great alarm, was caused by my displacing a small foot-stone, which fell from the elevation of the graded mound with a sharp crash upon the graveled walk below.

I had got my sheet well adjusted, and had intended moving upon the scared Irishman at one rush ; but his terribly frightened manner and the unfortunate falling of the foot-stone caused me to change my plan and decide to bring on the climax in a gradual accumulation of horrors. So I gave a well-defined moan, and watched for the results.

Mr. O'Grady listened for a moment, as if hoping that he had been deceived; but I could see in the faint light, to which my eyes had become accustomed, that he was trembling violently. He applied his bottle to his lips, and its mouth rattled against his teeth as he did so.

Another prolonged and blood-curdling moan came from the cluster of *arbor vitæ.* This caused Mr. O'Grady to industriously begin crossing himself, and at the same time mutter some prayers as rapidly as his half-drunken lips could dole them out.

I saw that this should not be too far prolonged, for the poor coward might give the danger signal, which would at once bring a half-dozen stalwart fellows upon us ; and so, while in his abject fear he was pleading with all the saints in the calendar for protection, I suddenly rose in my ghostly attire and in a moment was upon him, waving my arms and gesticulating very savagely for any sort of ghost that was ever manufactured, but never uttering a word.

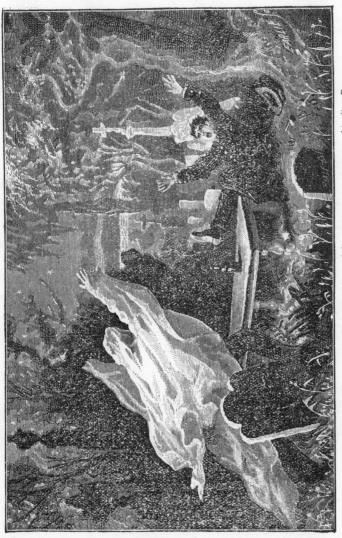

"I suddenly arose in my ghostly attire and in a moment was upon him."—Page—

" Holy mother of Moses!" yelled O'Grady, springing wildly into the air, and turning a complete back somer- sault over the base of an uncompleted monument while I sprang after him.

"Murther! Help! Murther!" howled O'Grady, re- covering, and bounding like a deer over four graves at a leap; while I could see, as I flew after him, that my oper- atives were hastening to the rescue.

I could not help but know that grave consequences might follow my unusual action; but a wild, boyish, and uncontrollable desire to pursue the flying O'Grady sud- denly possessed me, and for the time overcame all other motives.

And so away we went together!

Mounds, headstones, clumps of evergreens, newly-dug graves, wheelbarrows, and grave-diggers' litters were cleared as though we two were fox-hounds at a chase. Some sort of instinct for safety seemed to direct the wild O'Grady toward the western boundary of the cemetery; and away he went, howling and yelling at every jump, but increasing his speed at each terrified glimpse of the relentless ghost behind him.

Over the fence he went at a bound, cursing and pray- ing at every gasp. I was younger then a score of years, hardy and agile, and I now saw a two-fold reason for keeping pretty well upon the heels of O'Grady. My operatives were in full pursuit, and "Halt, halt, halt!" was heard on every side; and so, making a running jump of it, although my ghostly toggery impeded me

somewhat, I managed to get over the fence with quite at
much grace and agility as the wild Irishman in advance.
It was well that I did so, for at that moment I could see
the flash of several pistols lighting the sky behind, and
instantly after heard the whispering of several bullets
within dangerous proximity to my person. Over the
fence scrambled my men in hot pursuit, but swift on the
wings of terror and fear sped the horrified O'Grady ; and,
never for an instant relinquishing what were certainly unusual exertions on my own part, I sped on wildly after him.

We soon outdistanced my operatives so much that I
could see, as I ran, that they were compelled to give up
the chase and return defeated ; but the witless O'Grady
and his vengeful ghost still swept on and on. That part
of the city, then containing but a few scattering residences, was soon passed, and O'Grady and the ghost
continued the trial of speed out across the open prairie,
still to the northwest. This was traversed in the most
remarkable time ever made, O'Grady still yelling and
cursing and praying, but the ghost, ever silent and relentless, not far behind ; when suddenly we came to the north
branch of the Chicago River, then hardly more than a
creek, into which, with a wild cry of despair, the Irishman
plunged, swimming and scrambling to the other side just
as I had reached the shore, where I gave another spurt
to his speed by an unearthly yell, which seemed to send
the man on still faster, if it could be possible ; and the
last I heard of O'Grady he was tearing and bounding
through the hazel brush like a mad bull beyond

So far as I know, O'Grady is still running.

He has never been heard of by me or any of my many employees. Though I advertised for him repeatedly, no answer ever came ; and if any one of my readers, whose eyes may chance to fall upon this sketch, can prove that he is the veritable O'Grady, he can have the small amount of salary still standing to his credit on my books, which has so far been wholly unclaimed.

After a hearty laugh on the shore of the North Branch, I cast my ghostly attire upon the prairie, and, utterly tired and exhausted, plodded back, through the darkness, to the city, taking lodgings at an out-of-the-way hotel for the balance of the night, and was ready for business as usual at my office in the morning.

Never were there seven more perplexed men than those who reported the mystery of the night previous at the Old Catholic Cemetery.

O'Grady was gone—that was certain. His cries for help had been heard. His wild flight, pursued by a veritable ghost, which could be vouched for by those who had attempted its capture, was related. There, at the mound of the uncompleted monument, were found a nearly empty whisky-bottle and a still smoldering pipe. But this was all that was known by the honest fellows, or will be known, until this sketch is given to he public, of the Ghost of the Old Catholic Cemetery.

CHAPTER IV.

BURGLARS' TRICKS UPON BURGLARS.

CRIMINALS not only are very ingenious in their schemes against the general public, but they frequently show considerable skill and a certain grade of quiet humor in well-laid plans against each other.

An instance of the kind happened in this wise :

In 1875, Scott and Dunlap—the famous bank robbers who robbed the Northampton National Bank of nearly a million dollars, and who are now behind the bars of the penitentiary of that State, through the efforts of my Agencies—had laid their plans to rob a certain up-town New York city bank.

George Miles, *alias* Bliss, *alias* White, the notorious Max Shinburne's old partner, and his party were concocting a like operation for relieving a down-town bank of its capital.

Now it was found by the Miles party that both banks were to be robbed in like manner, by that very popular method of "bank-bursting," which consists of renting a room or rooms above those occupied by a bank, and then, if possible, tunneling through into its vaults or into the bank offices, and then breaking into the vaults in the regular manner.

Miles saw that, if the Scott-Dunlap gang should happen to first complete their job, the publicity given the method employed would set every bank officer in New York investigating the possibility of a like misfortune, and thus defeat his own purpose. He accordingly took two of his men, who were wholly unknown to the other party, provided them with complete police uniforms and clubs, and, at a suitable time after nightfall, stationed them in hiding behind the up-town bank, and when the members of the Scott-Dunlap party approached the building "to pipe it off," or take observations, they were of course recognized by Miles' policemen, who drove them away.

The Scott-Dunlap party were now in utter consternation. They felt certain that their scheme had been discovered, or at least that the officers of the bank had had their suspicions in *some* manner awakened, and certainly to that extent which would make their project impossible.

To put the matter to further test, on the succeeding night other of their men were instructed to "pipe off" the place still more cautiously. But these too were discovered by Miles' vigilant but bogus police, given chase to, and unmercifully clubbed.

This delayed matters with Scott and Dunlap until Miles and his party, the chief members of which consisted of George Miles, "Pete" Curly, and "Sam" Perris, *alias* "Wooster Sam," got everything ready for their attack on the down-town bank, which was located within one block of the First District police-station and within the same distance of my New York office, at No. 66 Ex change Place.

In the meantime, it is thought, the Scott-Dunlap party had learned of the down-town scheme, and caused information to be given, and before the Miles party had got fairly at work they were pounced upon by the police.

A lively fight ensued, and, although considerable shooting was done, the entire party of burglars escaped, so that two great bank burglaries, where very probably hundreds of thousands of dollars in cash and bonds would have been secured, were prevented through nothing more or less than what was hoped to be a very excellent trick by one notorious set of rogues upon another.

CHAPTER V.

SHERIDAN, THE FORGER.

THERE was born, near Sandusky, Ohio, in the year 1838, an adventurous lad named Walter Eastman Sheridan. His people were plain but intelligent farmers, and, while not possessed of an over-supply of means, had considerable pride in the boy, gave him a liberal education, and destined him, as fond parents usually do, for some very bright career in life.

He remained at home until about fourteen years of age, when its restraints became too irksome, and full of

Sham police charge upon the rival Bank burglars.—Page—

an adventurous spirit, and feeling able to take care of himself in the world, he did what thousands of boys did before him with various results—he "ran away" from home to seek his fortunes in the then brilliant and fascinating city of St. Louis.

Here he secured employment ; but, being without a home and its healthful influences, soon fell into bad company. He was a bright, pleasant-faced fellow ; but as he was "too independent" to return to his friends or accept their advice, little tricks were soon resorted to, and the boy readily saw that it was an easy matter to win the confidence of those with whom he came in contact, and before he had become eighteen years of age he was an adept in the art of living genteelly from forced public contributions of a varied character.

His first crime, or rather the first crime for which he was tried, was for horse-stealing at St. Louis, in 1858. He was convicted, and, while awaiting sentence, broke jail and escaped to Chicago.

Being a dashing, rosy-cheeked fellow of elegant address, after he had been in that city for a time, he became the pupil of Joe Moran, a noted confidence man and hotel thief, the couple doing a neat and thrifty business from the beginning.

Sheridan proved so pat about everything he did, and exhibited such aptness and delicate judgment in everything he undertook, that the pair continued in partnership nearly three years, working the hotels of Chicago and neighboring cities, but in the early part of 1861 were arrested in the act of robbing the guests' rooms at the old Adams House in that city. They were both convicted, and given three years each at the Illinois Penitentiary, then located at Alton.

The two men, after serving this term, returned to Chicago together, Moran soon dying of some disease brought on by prison exposure, while Sheridan resumed the same class of operation with the then notorious men of the same ilk, Emmett Lytle, Matt Duffy, and John Supple.

But Sheridan, being a young man of good mind, somewhat cultivated tastes, and large ambition, notwithstanding his reprehensible calling, soon tired of the low associations necessary to this standard of villainy, broke with his old companions, and took a step higher in the profession, becoming the "brains" and leader of "bank-sneaks," consisting of the notorious Joe Butts, Tom Parrell, *alias* "Pretty Tom," and others, and for some time the party did a very successful business, the elegant and refined Sheridan acting as "stall."

As many of my readers may not be very familiar with criminals and their modes of procedure, I will explain what a "stall" is in connection with the neat work of "bank-sneak gangs."

To begin with, the "gang" is the party generally consisting of about three to five persons working together. As a rule, these persons are gentlemen of elegant leisure, secure large plunder, and have plenty of time to devote to becoming acquainted with the workings of a bank, famil iar with the faces and habits of its officers, as also of many of the heavier depositors; and when ready foi work have quite as much knowledge of the interioi arrangements of the bank as many of its employees. Though there are numberless modes of accomplishing the same thing, the following instances will serve as illustrative of them all.

A gentleman who has business stamped in every line of his face and article of his clothing, steps into a bank about noon, when the officers and several of the clerks are generally at lunch, and either presents a forged letter of introduction or in some other manner compels the respect ful attention of the cashier, or teller, as the case may be.

He will very probably produce a figuring-block or tablet upon which are various memoranda and figures, and, while asking questions very rapidly and interrupting them quite as abruptly, conveys to the teller, who has already become somewhat distracted, the information that he, as the trustee for something or somebody, has, we will say twenty thousand dollars in five-twenty bonds to invest in different securities, and desires five thousand dollars in gold, five thousand dollars in seven-forties, five thousand dollars in ten-twenties, and five thousand dollars in some railroad stock or other.

This affords the cashier, or teller, a series of delicate, if not difficult, calculations, and all this time the business-like "trustee"—who is none other than the "stall"—is annoying him with questions, suggestions, and *probably* other Orders as to the character of the investment desired.

so that the teller's whole attention is absolu.ely requited to follow the customer's whims and his own calculations.

This is exactly what has been striven for by the "stall," and his eminence in his profession is in just the proportion to his ability to accomplish this, whatever be the means he may employ in doing it.

But before this "stall" begins playing the "trustee," or other game, three of his companions, or pals, called "pipers," are on the look-out for the approach of any of the bank officers or employees, and are ready to sound a signal at the approach of the slightest cause for alarm ; and sometimes other "stalls" are stationed in the bank wherever necessary ; while, at a given signal, the "sneak," who is generally a nimble little fellow, slips behind the partition through some open door, or sometimes through open windows, and thence into the bank-vault, where he secures his plunder, which is usually large, because the thieves have taken time to make the operation a success.

After the "sneak" is well away, the "stalls" draw off, so as not to excite suspicion, and the "trustee," after thankfully receiving the teller's calculations and agreeing to return with the bonds to effect the desired exchange before the close of banking hours, takes his departure. The entire job is done in ten or fifteen minutes, and fre quently the loss is not discovered for days.

Another game of the "bank-sneak gang," but one whicn requires far more nerve, assurance, and personal bravery though far less tact and skill, is to become cognizant of parties making heavy, deposits at a late hour, when every thing is rushing about the bank and the check desks are crowded.

In this instance, the sneak, with a bogus bank book in his hand, and with a business-like air about him, taps some gentleman with a flush deposit in his hand lightly on the shoulder, and politely calls his attention to the fact that he has dropped some money. Looking upon the floor, the latter sees a genuine ten-dollar bill (which the sneak has dexterously dropped there, of course), and bends over to pick it up, leaving his book and deposit upon the check-desk.

In an instant the polite gentleman has the money left upon the desk and is upon the street, while the robbed and astounded depositor recovers himself and gives chase ; he is apparently accidentally, but very effectually, impeded by other gentlemen (all pals of the sneak), who run into him and beg his pardon in the most natural manner possible, giving the party—who had invested merely a ten-dollar bill and a little politeness, and who may have secured several thousand dollars—ample time to escape.

I could fill pages with instances of this kind, but will only mention a few of the heavier robberies of late years, which were all committed in this manner, all of which are probably still fresh in the public mind. They are :

The noted Lord bond robbery, where a million and a half dollars were taken ; the Royal Insurance Company robbery, over a half-million dollars being taken · Cambering & Pine, New York brokers, robbed of two hundred thousand dollars ; Litchmere Bank, East Cambridge,

Mass., seventy-five thousand; the recent robbery of James H. Young, of New York, by the " Little Horace " Hovan party, of five hundred thousand; the Canal Bank, of New Orleans, in 1872, sixty-five thousand; paymaster's office of the Grand Trunk Railway, Montreal, twenty-five thousand; Adams Express Company's office, at Cincinnati, ten thousand; First National Bank, of Council Bluffs, Iowa, twenty thousand; and so on, *ad infinitum*.

Sheridan and his party worked this line of business— robbing banks at Chicago, Cincinnati, Louisville, St. Louis, and other large cities—until 1865, when he separated from these fellows, seeking more high-toned companions, and was taken on by George Williams, *alias* " English George," a widely-known thief and bank-robber. Williams had had his eye upon the young criminal for some time, and, admiring his shrewdness, audacity, and tact, took him into his Eastern operations, where he did such good work that in 1867 he was known to be worth fully seventy-five thousand dollars.

A little later he participated in the robbing of the Maryland Fire Insurance Company, of Baltimore, acting as " stall " when his party crowded the office and secured upward of seventy-five thousand dollars in money and negotiable bonds.

Not one cent of this money was recovered, nor were any of the robbers captured.

One of the neatest robberies Sheridan ever engaged in was that of United States Judge Blatchford, at an apple-stand in New York city.

The Judge was sauntering along the street, and feeling like partaking of some fruit, he stopped at a little apple-stand, at the corner of Nassau and Liberty Streets, and in a fatherly manner purchased a few apples of the old apple-woman there. Sheridan accosted him, and so interested him for a moment that, when he turned to take up the wallet, which he had carelessly laid upon the stand, he found that it was gone. A suspicion flashed across his mind that the handsome stranger had had something to do with its disappearance ; but he too was gone. The wallet contained seventy-five thousand dollars' worth of bonds, and but a small portion of the plunder was recovered.

One of his first exploits, after becoming a professional, was at Springfield, Illinois, where he was not so fortunate. After the Baltimore robbery, he had come West with Charles Hicks, a Baltimore sneak-thief, and Philip Pierson, *alias* " Baltimore Philly," and their initiatory move was upon the First National Bank, at Springfield.

Sheridan called at the bank, and as usual proposed some complicated business, lucrative to the bank, which completely engaged the cashier's attention ; while Hicks " piped," and Pierson sneaked into the bank, securing packages containing thirty-two thousand dollars, passing the money over to Hicks.

As Hicks was leisurely leaving the bank the president entered, and observing the huge package peeping out from under his summer overcoat, which was not large enough to cover them, grabbed him, and demanded where he got so much money. He replied that he had just

5

drawn it out. But the president suggested that they had better step into his apartment until he could see about it. The cashier at once saw what had been nearly accom plished, and on some pretext handed a card into the president's apartment without exciting Sheridan's notice, instructing the president to send two men to the front of the bank to detain the person conversing with him, which was done, and which resulted in Sheridan's cap- ture, though Pierson escaped.

Sheridan and Hicks of course claimed that they had never seen each other before, but they were put in differ- ent cells and given separate trials. Hicks pleaded guilty, and was sentenced to eight years' imprisonment in the Illi- nois penitentiary at Joliet; but Sheridan played the high moral dodge, gave bail to the amount of seven thousand dollars, which sum he deposited and subsequently for- feited, when the District Attorney set this sum aside tow- ards securing his apprehension, and immediately em- ployed me to use *all* the means at my command to effect his recapture.

I soon ascertained that Sheridan was communicating with Hicks at Joliet, through the latter's brother, who vis- ited him with unusual frequency; and I therefore detailed my son, William A. Pinkerton, with an assistant, to follow out this clue and see what it was worth.

In keeping unremitting watch over this Hicks, my son one evening found himself in the pretty city of Hudson, Michigan, having arrived there on the same train with Hicks.

The latter at once proceeded to the best hotel in the city, still followed by William, who was not long in learn ing to his surprise that Sheridan owned the hotel, which was being conducted by his brother-in-law, as also a fine fruit-farm in the vicinity of St. Joe, and large tracts of pine and farming lands scattered throughout the State.

Hicks directed the hotel clerk to call him at seven o'clock the next morning, and my son accordingly was put down on the call-book for six.

As great care was necessary to be exercised, lest Sheridan or his friends might learn that he was being so closely followed, William could make only sparing inquiries ; but he did succeed in learning enough to convince him that he was not then at Hudson, and, on awakening bright and early in the morning, he decided on making an attempt to accomplish something which might be of the greatest possible assistance in the future.

Although Sheridan had already become famous as a criminal, no picture of him had ever fallen into the hands of the authorities. The public may not be aware of how much service a good picture of a criminal is to the detective. It will do good duty in a hundred places at one time. Accordingly William ascertained the location of the landlord's family rooms, and, while the occupants were at breakfast, committed a small and under the circum- stances quite excusable burglary, resulting in securing a capital photograph of Sheridan, which has for several years adorned the rogues' galleries at my different agent cies. This picture undoubtedly effected the eventual recent capture of this great criminal, as it was the only picture extant, and was placed in the hands of my almost numberless correspondents both in this country and in Europe.

On this particular occasion spoken of, however, it was of no great importance save to familiarize its possessor with the handsome features of Sheridan, who returned to Hudson the same day.

William wisely concluded that it would be foolish to attempt his arrest in the midst of so many friends, who, if they could not effect his forcible escape, would undoubt-edly use every possible effort to secure his legal rescue upon some trivial technicality ; and consequently followed him for several days, finally capturing him at Sandusky, Ohio.

As it was, my son had a difficult time in getting the criminal to Chicago, as the splendidly-appearing fellow strongly protested to the passengers that he was being kidnapped, and appealed for aid and rescue in the most impassioned manner possible. Finding this of no avail, although it came pretty nearly being successful, he then shrewdly pretended complete acquiescence, and when for a moment left alone with the operative who had im-mediate charge of him, offered that person ten thousand dollars in cash merely for the opportunity of being per mitted to jump through the window of the car saloon, although well ironed, so that both men were necessarily watched every mile of the remaining distance.

Even after he had been brought to my Chicago Agency

preparatory to being forwarded to Springfield, a little instance occurred illustrative of the daring character of the
man.

For convenience he had been given a seat temporarily
in my private office—he being perfectly secure there,
and it being necessary for my son to step outside the
door for a moment. Scarcely had he done so, when
Sheridan espied my snuff-box, and, instantly grasping it,
placed himself in a position to fling its contents into
William's eyes as he re-entered, with the intention of
bounding by him in the confusion which would follow and
attempting to escape—which, however, would have been
utterly impossible, owing to constant safeguards in use at
my offices to cover similar cases.

But his intention was just as determined, notwithstanding all this, of which he of course was not aware.

My son re-entered the room slowly—feeling that there
might be danger, and knowing his man—with the grim
muzzle of a splendid English "Trauter" revolver in
front of him ; and Sheridan, seeing that his captor was as
wary as he was daring and inventive, resumed his seat
with the manner of a French courtier, took a pinch of
snuff. as he replaced my box, and with airy politeness
remarked :

"Billy, that snuff of your father's is a d—d fine
article ! "

" For the eyes? " asked William quietly.

" Eyes *or* nose," he retorted. " But I'm very sorry to
say that the *noes* have it this time ! '

I succeeded in having the man safely conveyed to Springfield; but Sheridan made his money count in another way than upon my detectives. He had the case fought on every legal technicality which could be brought forward, secured a postponement of trial for nearly a year, and finally a change of venue to the city of Decatur, where, after retaining the very best lawyers in the State of Illinois, and—what was quite as useful—a portion of the jury, he was eventually acquitted, expending altogether for this manner of acquiring liberty the snug little sum of twenty thousand dollars, as he subsequently admitted.

After this affair, Sheridan, who was inordinately ambitious to become noted as one of the most successful thieves in America, went East, and organized a party of "bank-bursters," or bank-robbers, consisting of Frank McCoy, *alias* "Big Frank," James Brady, James Hope, Ike Marsh, and others, the crowd becoming a terror to the East, until so closely hunted there that its members were compelled to disband; when he assisted at a robbery of a Cleveland bank, where forty thousand dollars were taken. This was followed by a raid upon the Mechanics' (Hawley's) Bank, of Scranton, Pennsylvania, where Sheridan and ".Little George" Corson appropriated thirty-thousand dollars' worth of negotiable bonds.

His next exploit of note, and one which struck a very tender chord in the hearts of several citizens of Louisville, Kentucky, was his planning of and participation in the I al:s City Tobacco Bank robbery at that city in 1873 when upward of three hundred thousand dollars were secured.

The robbers rented an office immediately over the vault of the bank, and carried on a legitimate business therein for some months before the robbery occurred. My readers will remember the circumstances of the great Ocean Bank robbery, in New York, where Max Shinburn's party robbed that bank by renting an insurance office immediately *below* the president's apartments, and then sawed through the floor into the bank and blew open the safe. The same kind of tactics were used here, only the robbers went into the bank from above instead of from beneath, and tumbled into the vault direct, instead of blowing open the vault door.

The gang were divided into regular reliefs, and while one party were digging away through the night, the other were posted in a front room over the St. Charles restaurant immediately opposite, from which point a fine but strong silk cord was stretched to the robbers' windows. Attached to the end of this cord, next the windows over the bank, was a pendant bullet, so that the confederates located over the St. Charles restaurant—whose business it was to watch for any signs of approaching danger—could signal the same on their immediate discovery. In this manner the thieves had an abundance of time and leisure, and finally effected an entrance to the vault early in the night, when they carried away almost everything of value the vault contained.

It was Sheridan's generalship and even bravery, if one

has the right to apply that term to a person of this char
acter utterly devoid of fear, that caused the retirement
of this large amount of capital from Louisville circula
tion ; and these instances, showing his wonderful genius
for schemes requiring skill, patience, and personal courage, could be multiplied almost beyond number; but
those I have already given will serve to illustrate his
marked ability, and also the almost exceptional instance
of a criminal beginning among the lowest of associates, and
by the tact, skill, and frugality which would have made
him a millionaire in respectable life, gradually climbing
higher and higher in his grade of crimes with his companions as stepping-stones, until he arrives at the very
pinnacle of his criminal calling, and has acquired in that
profession everything which men ordinarily seek for—respect, admiration, and hosts of friends, as well as great
wealth ; for Sheridan was worth in 1874 fully a quarter
of a million of dollars, while during these later years of his
crimes he maintained most respectable social and business relations.

All of this eminently fitted the man for becoming, as
he really was, the author of the gigantic Bank of England
forgeries, although the very caution, ability, and skill
which first made the scheme possible eventually led to
the work being done by other parties ; and it is safe to
say that if Sheridan had had the management of the affair throughout it would have proved a success instead of
a failure.

The members of the original party subscribing to this

Bank of England scheme were Sheridan, George Wilkes, Andrew J. Roberts, and Frank Gleason, while McDon nell and Bidwell, now serving life sentences for the crime, were to conduct the English branch of the opera tion. Sheridan discovered that the two last named men were lacking in discretion, as afterward proved true, and ne consequently withdrew from the scheme altogether. He then organized a party—consisting of Roberts, Glea-son, Spence Pettis, and Gottlieb Engels—for a series of the most gigantic forgeries ever known in America, and finally issued bonds, to the extent of five million dollars. on the following institutions and corporations : New York Central, Chicago and Northwestern, New Jersey Central, Union Pacific, and California and Oregon Rail-roads, the Erie Water Loan Bonds, the Western Union Telegraph Company, and other similar great corpora-tions. The floating of these forged bonds ruined scores of Wall Street brokers as well as private investers. Their execution was almost absolutely faultless, and an instance is given where some of these forged bonds of the Buffalo and Erie road were taken to the president of the company for examination, having been offered sus piciously low, when he not only pronounced them genu-ine, but purchased thirty thousand dollars' worth for an in-vestment.

At least half the amount issued was disposed of.

Sheridan now assumed a new character. He became Ralston, nephew of the once great San Francisco banker who committed suicide after his financial downfall. With this name and plenty of money he became a member ol the New York Produce Exchange, and at No. 60 Broad·way carried on a successful business as agent for the Belgian Stone Company, dealing largely in all manner of fancy marbles.

On the eventual discovery of the forgeries, Sheridan quietly gathered his assets together, and sped to Belgium —that fashionable retreat for Americans having too little honesty and too much brains.

It is not known just how large an amount Sheridan succeeded in disposing of, but it must have equaled all that of the other large operators. "Steve" Raymond sold ninety thousand dollars' worth, and Charles Williams, *alias* Perrin, one hundred and ten thousand, while the American public was mulcted fully two millions in excess of the amount secured from our English cousins in the Bank of England forgeries.

When I sent my son, William A. Pinkerton, to Europe to capture and return Raymond, which he accomplished, he met Sheridan in Brussels, where he was then living like a prince, with the avowed determination of never return-ing to America. But he did return here ; and that mistake eventually led to my capturing him. He could not live without the excitement of scheming, speculating, crimi-nal adventure, and what was to him the genuine pleasure of transacting business on a large scale.

He slipped back to America, and, under the name of Walter A. Stewart, suddenly appeared at Denver, where he established probably the largest and most expensive

"*Robert A. Pinkerton, arresting Sheridan, the forger.*" —*Page* —

hot-house in America, did an immense business in supplying that market with vegetables and rare plants, was elected a director of the German National Bank of that city, and soon established a bank of his own at Rosita, in the Colorado mining districts. Here his spirit of speculation took possession of him again, and he began the wildest kind of gambling in mining stocks, which resulted in his losing every dollar he possessed on earth.

About this time I again got upon Sheridan's trail, and, following him from point to point, learned that he contemplated a trip to the East, to discover his old companions and inaugurate some new and brilliant scheme of robbery. In trusting matters at New York to my son, Robert A. Pinkerton, Superintendent of my New York office, I gradually caused the lines to be drawn in about him ; and on the night of March 23, 1876, at eleven o'clock, as Sheridan, *alias* Ralston, *alias* Stewart, was landing in New York city from the Pennsylvania ferryboat, at the foot of Desbrosses Street, my son Robert slipped his arm through that of the criminal's, and quietly said :

"Sheridan, I want you to come to the Church Street police-station with me. I have a bench warrant for your arrest."

He made no resistance, but seemed to give up all hope and courage at once.

As he was without money, the legal fight made for his liberty was not so bitter as had been anticipated, and in consideration of this, and the sympathy created on account of his rapidly failing health, and though he came into New York with eighty-two indictments hanging over his head, his trial and conviction only resulted in a sentence for five years in the penitentiary ; which, under the circumstances, will serve all the ends of justice, as undoubtedly before the expiration of that term he will pass from an infamous life to an infamous grave in the little cemetery just above Sing Sing.

CHAPTER VI.

A GIGANTIC CONSPIRACY DEFEATED.

HOW apt and true are many of the sayings put into the mouths of the marvelous characters created by Charles Dickens !

Notice how much is contained in the eloquent passage spoken by " Obenreizer " to " Vandale " in the Christmas story of " No Thoroughfare," where the former, when the moral conviction of his great guilt sinks down upon him like a fall, remarks : " What did I always observe when I was on the mountains ? We call them vast, but the world is *so* little. So little is the world that one cannot keep away from persons. There are so few persons in the world, that they continually cross and recross. So very little is the world that one cannot get rid of a person ! "

Neither can dishonest men get rid of the consequences of their guilt ; and sometimes it seems inexplicable to me that men possessed of good intelligence, surrounded by pleasant associations, which could be held to the sunniest level that life affords, and with the countless examples before them of fatal errors and their most fatal results, will so far forget themselves as to enter a criminal career with the vain hope that some pressing necessity can *be* relieved and their honor remain unsullied and intact.

But the terrible greed that often overwhelms men to suddenly become possessed of vast wealth, or even a moderate competence, without patiently striving for and earning it, has, and ever will, create criminals, who must be hunted down and punished.

The instance which I am about to relate shows the frustration of one of the most deliberate conspiracies to commit a gigantic robbery of and swindle upon a great business corporation that has ever come under my notice, and illustrates forcibly the truth of the statement that the world *is* very small, in the sense that, when modern detective methods and appliances are thoroughly employed, it is not big enough to permit the criminal to escape, however certain he may be that his schemes are perfect, or whatever way he may turn when the desperation of failure stares him in the face.

Some time in 1866, one James C. Engley was at the head of what was known as the Neptune Express Company, at Providence, Rhode Island. At the time the Merchants' Union Express Company was organized and started, a proposition was made by the latter to buy up the former, which was accepted, and the Neptune be came absorbed in the Merchants' Union.

In the arrangements for the transfer of business, Eng ley insisted upon the stipulation that he should be the Providence agent. This was objected to, but finally it was agreed that he could have the position as nominal agent.

Among the articles transferred was the office safe , but before the transfer was wholly consummated, Engley, having conceived a plan for swindling the new company on a gigantic scale, had duplicate keys made which fitted most admirably, enabling him to open and shut the safe quite as easily as with the original keys. These duplicate keys he reserved for use when the proper time should arrive.

Engley moved in the best social circles of Providence, notwithstanding attacks had been made on his character, on account of several questionable transactions of his dur- ing the war. He had been charged with defrauding a regiment of colored volunteers out of their bounties ; but an examination of the case by the Rhode Island Legisla- ture resulted in his favor, which was said to have been owing to the complicity of some high officials with Engley in the alleged irregular transactions.

Having acquired a large amount of money, he purchased a controlling share of the stock of the Neptune Express Company, already mentioned, and continued apparently to enjoy the confidence of the best men in Providence, occasionally passing his note with them for considerable amounts, but never meeting his engagements except with brilliant promises for the future.

At length his financial condition became so precarious that he was compelled to do something to sustain himself; and it was at this juncture in his affairs that he determined to reveal his plan to some one upon whose ability and secrecy he could rely with unshaken confidence. He visited Boston, and there met an old acquaintance, named C. A. Dean, to whom he related his plan for becoming suddenly wealthy at the expense of others.

Mr. Dean happened to be a man of Engley's ilk, and fell in with the plan rapturously, lauding Engley and his genius most unsparingly.

At Engley's subsequent suggestion, the arrangement first settled on was altered, and I only give my readers the plan finally decided upon.

Engley said he had keys with which he could open the safe in the office of the Merchants' Union Express Company at Providence whenever he so liked; that when the Neptune was sold out to the Merchants' he had conceived the idea of making a little fortune at some future date, for which purpose he had insisted on remaining agent for the new company; that he had carried his point; that he was not held responsible for the contents of the safe; and that, therefore, any depredation he might commit by taking funds from it would cause others to be suspected, and was besides fully protected by his powerful social relations; that his idea was to have three hundred thousand dollars sent from New York to Providence by the Merchants' Union Company; that the said amount should disappear in Providence by his hand; that the company, being responsible, would of course refund the whole amount to the sender ; that the money so refunded should be divided into three equal shares between himself (Engley), Dean, and whatever third party they should take into the conspiracy in order to raise the sum to be sent ; that the amount should be made up at some bank of good standing before being forwarded, so that there should exist the most undoubted evidence of its having been shipped; that he, in his capacity as agent at Providence, would receive and receipt for it; that he could subsequently make affidavit, if necessary, that he had so received it and receipted for it ; that at night, while an evening party should be in full blast at his house, he would slip out for a few moments unobserved by the guests, and return again, so that every guest might, if called upon, prove an *alibi* in his favor; that in the interval of his absence from the party at his house, he should enter the office of the Express Company, abstract from the safe the three hundred thousand dollar package, and retire unnoticed and unsuspected by any one.

Such was the plan, its only other details being as to who might be suspected. The tradesman who kept the store adjoining the Express Office, which was only separated by a very shaky wooden partition, a fruit-seller, who occupied a basement adjacent to the office ; Mr. Charles R. Dennis, responsible and acting agent for the Merchants' Union Express Company, and the cashier—these were the par ies whose reputations were to be uined for the benefit of Mr. Engley and his co-conspirators, should his plans work as smoothly as he calculated.

The next step in this nice little game was to find some party who was the possessor of three hundied thousand dollars, or who could secure the possession of so large a sum of money temporarily, and who would permit himself and his money to be used in this manner even for the possible great benefit to accrue from the same. This, of course, caused another canvass and search. Speculators in New York and Boston, known to both parties, were named, and the probabilities of their being willing to enter into any such feasible plan as they had plotted were dis cussed.

A Mr. C. W. Fitch, of New York, was finally selected as a possible party to the enterprise. He is a respect able man, so far as I know, but was understood by these fellows to be "available." He is a man of means and a genuine speculator, but, as subsequently transpired, was not in the habit of speculating in just this kind of a way.

But a letter was written to him by Dean, who had conveniently assumed the *alias* of Drew, and whom I will hereafter call by that name. Mr. Fitch was informed by Mr. Drew that the latter had some business proposition of great importance to communicate to him, and was also requested on the strength of this to make an appointment for an interview.

Mr. Fitch, who was naturally open for ary chance to increase his fortune, replied, inviting Mr. Drew to pro ceed to New York. Drew went there, and a preliminary talk occurred, during which Mr. Fitch had some trouble to understand just what the Boston gentleman's plan was, as he only spoke of it in general terms, apparently to test Mr. Fitch's fitness for the particular work before the party. This meeting not proving altogether satisfactory, an appointment was made for another to be held in Boston.

Mr. Fitch went to Boston, and met Drew at the Parker House, where, being a gentleman of an inquiring turn of mind, he soon discovered that a certain Mr. Engley occupied a room, to which apartment his friend Mr. Drew seemed to have a peculiar fondness for frequently retiring ; and, on further finding that Engley's name corresponded on the hotel register with that of an Engley he knew considerable about, he felt rather chary of coming to anything definite in a scheme which promised extra perilous results.

On returning to New York, he therefore laid the matter before a legal friend, informing him of Engley's connection with the scheme, which he already suspected to be one of robbery of the express company, from certain supposed operations which had been submitted to him for his consideration. The lawyer properly advised him to go on and ascertain all he could of the plan, as though he were acting in good faith, and, if he discovered that the matter looked to the injury of the express company, it would then be his immediate duty to communicate all the particulars of the matter to the officers of the company in New York.

Mr. Fitch readily agreed to this, and again met the conspirators in Boston, when they unfolded the whole plan to him. He apparently accorded his hearty support to it, and returned to New York ostensibly for the purpose of preparing himself for his part of the enterprise ; but instead of doing this, he immediately communicated the entire facts obtained to Mr. J. D. Andrews, then agent of the company in New York.

Mr. Andrews at once submitted all the information to me, at my New York offices, and I at once arranged a counter-plan, which, though Engley had repeatedly boasted that he had " thought his scheme over and over, and found that there was not a flaw in it," I felt certain would eventually rather astonish the two embryo swindlers.

Several subsequent meetings were held by Drew, Engley, and Fitch.

On one of these occasions, in order to test the ability of Engley to carry out his design, should he remain unmolested, I directed Mr. Fitch to inquire of him how he intended to account for the shipment of so large a sum as three hundred thousand dollars to Providence.

" Why, I have arranged for that already. I tell you we can't be beaten. You know we need a hotel at Providence, a big hotel—one worth at least half a million. Well, it has, some way, got into the papers," continued Engley, with a knowing wink, " that we *are* going to have one. So the minds of our Providence people are amply prepared for the reception of even a million dollars through the banks, through the express company, or any other way it can get there ! "

Another circumstance also occurred, which proved beyond doubt Engley's intentions to become both a robber and a swindler.

One day Engley, while transacting some business in the express office, thoughtlessly laid his pocketbook down upon the desk. As he turned away to some other part of the office, Mr. Dennis, the responsible agent, noticed that a small paper package slipped down the inclined surface of the desk away from the pocketbook. Mr. Dennis, who did not, for some reason, have the highest possible confidence in his superior, opened the package quickly, ascertained that it contained a set of safe-keys the perfect duplicate of his own, and, applying them to the safe, found that they also worked quite as well as his.

With commendable presence of mind he took a file and reduced such portions of both keys as would destroy them from operating on the combination of the safe.

After this very sensible precaution was done, he returned the keys to their place in the paper package, and laid the latter on the desk beside the pocketbook. He had hardly accomplished this when Engley returned, picked up the pocketbook and piece of paper, not suspecting that either had been molested, put them in his pocket, and went out.

When this was first reported to me, it flashed into my mind that perhaps this was a clever ruse on Engley's part to ascertain definitely whether he was suspected; but from other moves made by the man, and the conviction that this might prove too daring a risk for a man of his calibre, I satisfied myself that he was serenely awaiting the realization of his fond hopes.

Everything being ready, the package of three hundred thousand dollars was made up at the company's offices in New York, under my direction, but it did not contain that large sum of money. It was *marked* " $300,000," but really contained only three thousand five hundred and ninety-four dollars, so arranged with five hundred dollar bills at top and bottom as to deceive a nervous, hasty, and adventurous observer. I arranged matters so as to have the package arrive in Providence on Thursday evening, December 19; but one of the heaviest snowstorms of the year suddenly set in, and delayed all the trains, so that the package and other goods did not reach that place until Friday evening, and the reception at Engley's residence, which could not be postponed, and which proved a very fashionable affair, could not be very well used as planned, for *alibi* purposes.

I very well knew the high standing of the man we had to deal with, and consequently realized the impossibility of showing him in his true light in Providence unless what was about to occur was participated in to some extent and actually witnessed by some of the best people of the place; and I accordingly secured the co-operation of a few of the most reputable business men of Providence, who were detailed to quietly watch Engley at the time of the arrival of the package as well as his subsequent movements, and also to occupy the store-room adjoining the express office, through the partition of which all movements of Engley might be observed.

The package had arrived at about eight o'clock. **Mr.** Dennis suggested, in the hearing of Engley and one or two respectable gentlemen, that, as a package so valuable was in their safe, it would be well to have a watch placed upon it ; but Engley nervously pooh-poohed the suggestion, saying that the safe was a solid institution, had ever defied burglars, and could never be opened. Dennis seemed to fall in with the idea that the safe could be trusted, and at nine o'clock closed the office and went home.

It was a bitterly cold night, and my operatives on duty had a slight taste of the actual hardships which are often meted out to the honestly faithful and persistent detective ; while the gentlemen stationed at different points throughout the city, and particularly those in the store next to the express office, on account of the rigor of the night, came near deserting their posts. Nothing but inordinate curiosity held them.

At about ten o'clock a phantom-like object left Engley's residence, and could have been observed moving cautiously toward the express office, followed at a little distance by a very faithful attendant, who never permitted the distance between them to grow less or become greater. There were also several unobserved observers, silent watchers of the night, who never made a useless movement, but every one of whom did what they had been detailed to do mechanically and noiselessly.

The leading figure, passing down the now deserted streets, was none other than Engley, who had left "the best society of Providence" for a few minutes, to take a quiet stroll on one of the coldest nights of the winter of 1867 and 1868.

Arriving in front of the express office, he stopped, quickly and searchingly looked up and down the street, and then peered long and anxiously within. The usual lights were burning, and the window-blinds were sufficiently low to permit everything inside to be seen.

In a moment more Engley walked past, suddenly turned a corner, came back, crossed over in the snow, went up an alley; after being out of sight for a while, appeared at an unexpected point, turned another corner, dodged a policeman who was just emerging from the cheery glow of a saloon, and at length returned swiftly to the express office. It was a singular fact, too, that the party before referred to would have reminded one, who could have observed all, of "Mary's little lamb," at least in one particular, for everywhere that Engley went that man was sure to go. He had a happy faculty of almost understanding what Engley's next cutting of corners, dodging up alleys or doubling his route, would be, and seemed to be on hand, but always invisible to Engley, wherever that gentleman's peculiar movements led him.

Engley entered the office, locked the door behind him,

and. in another instant, had raised the window-blinds so that no person could look into the place from the street. The parties in the adjoining room were all agog now, and a half-dozen pairs of eyes were applied to a half-dozen crevices in the thin partition.

After thoroughly searching the place, as if to ascertain that no person could be hidden in the office, Engley took the keys from a vest-pocket, stepped quickly to the safe, and applied them. The lock refused to respond. Again he tried, and again failed. With an oath he stepped to a gas-jet, and carefully examined the keys. In his haste, excitement, and nervousness he could see nothing wrong about them.

Again he tried the safe. No, it could not be opened. The work of Mr. Dennis upon them a month previous had been effectual.

"My God! it can't be got!" he muttered; stood looking at the safe a moment, as if half tempted to try some desperate method of breaking the great iron recep-tacle open, and then swiftly left the place.

He had scarcely finished locking the door, when a heavy hand was laid upon his shoulder, and the voice of the mysterious follower of the robber sternly said:

"Engley, you're my prisoner!"

A moment more and the door of the store had opened, and a crowd of the best business men of Providence had surrounded the officer and his prisoner; and Engley, looking into the faces of his old friends, only said, with a kind of moan:

" Gentlemen, I'm ruined ! Be as merciful as you can
to me ! "

Dean, *alias* Drew, was arrested the next day in Boston,
and though the two men never received the just deserts
for their infamous attempt at robbery and their more infamous and heartless scheme to ruin for life the charac
ters of honest men in order to shield their guilt, had not
its consummation been prevented, they were given such
penitentiary sentences as undoubtedly impressed, irrevocably, upon their minds the principle laid down by Dickens, that, " So little is the world that one cannot get rid
of persons," and, I would add, especially if those persons
happen to be honest detectives.

———•———

CHAPTER VII.

MAX SHINBURN.

MAXIMILIAN SHINBURN, *alias* Mark Shinburn, *alias* Mark Baker, *alias* Zimmerman, with
half a hundred other *aliases*, is a very brilliant and exceptional instance of a professional criminal having won
considerable fame from a series of masterly bank and
bond robberies, marvelous prison escapes, and the like,
in America, and then crowning all by a final escape,
sound and safely, to Belgium, where he has since lived
an active, and, as far as can be learned, an honorable
business life, being favored with luxury and the pleasantest of life's surroundings.

6

He is now about forty years of age, and, whethei born
in America or elsewhere, is a German Jew, and has a
fluent command of the English, German, French, Spanish, and Italian languages. One account has it that he
was born in Europe, and received his superb education
there, leaving his native country on account of some wild,
boyish escapade, and coming to America when he was
about eighteen years of age, proceeding to St. Louis,
where he became very proficient in the locksmith's trade ;
but finding this a slow way to secure the elegancies of
life, turning the knowledge thus gained to criminal pur-
suits, and after being arrested, and while awaiting trial,
effecting the liberation of himself and seventeen other
prisoners.

Again, some of his old associates in crime state that he
was born of German parents, near Germantown, Pennsylvania, and was spoiled by a rich mother, who lavished
her wealth upon his education and accomplishments ;
and that, after graduating from college as a highly
finished scholar and gentleman, he was placed in a large
mercantile establishment, and, after securing a thorough
knowledge of business there, was given a position in a
bank, where he familiarized himself with monetary affairs,
but where he grew so extravagant in his habits and disso
lute in his mode of life that at last he became hopelessly
in debt, when he duplicated the keys of the bank vaults
and for a long time pursued a system of "weeding" the
packages of notes in the vaults, and making its loss cor-
respond by false entries in the ledgers. This was con-

tinued for nearly a year increasing in amount until the annual settlement, when the loss was discovered. So artfully had the thing been done, that both tellers were arrested on suspicion, as the alterations in the books were exact imitations of their handwriting; but as they lived honest and respectable lives, nothing could be ascertained derogatory to their characters, and the charges were subsequently withdrawn. At length suspicion was thrown upon young Shinburn by his reckless life generally, and, while no absolute proof of his guilt could be gathered, he was eventually discharged in disgrace.

These same old companions also relate that the stigma of his crime rested heavily upon Shinburn, and, after a night's carouse, he suddenly resolved to become a professional criminal. Hardly had the idea seized possession of his mind, than he proceeded to carry it into execution. Securing what money he could command, he attired himself magnificently, and departed on the Camden and Amboy road for Boston.

His adventures here were attended, as they always seemed to be, with fine success. Registering himself as Walker Watterson at the Revere House, he soon, by his engaging conversation, elegant manners, and liberal expenditure of money, rendered himself the favorite of all the gentlemen of the house. After a good standing had been secured, he laid siege to the heart of a prepossessing daughter of a cultivated Boston banker, and in this way became intimate at the banker's house, the bank itself, and with many of the bank officers and clerks—of course all this time keeping a keen eye out for the main chance, and gradually acquiring possession of all information in reference to the character of the locks and the location of the vaults; and early one morning, when returning from a fashionable party, amidst a terrific storm, he forced an entrance to the building. He then retired from the place, changed his clothing, and returning, passed inside of the bank, and immediately began operations upon the vaults. Here was occasioned his first great trial, as the locks at first baffled his attempts; but after a half-hour of patient work he had the satisfaction of seeing the entire contents of the vaults at his command. But instead of taking a large sum of money, which would immediately raise a hue and cry, he only took several thousands of the money, closed and locked the vault-door, and then, after taking a wax impression of the locks, decamped from the place, arriving at his hotel safe and sound before the milkmen had made their morning calls.

However much truth there may be in all this, the adventure is wholly characteristic of the man. He was a zealous student of everything that might fit him for a most complete, safe, and perfect success in his nefarious calling; and wherever and at whatever time he secured his mechanical knowledge, it is certain that he was most splendidly skilled in all that pertained to the locksmith's trade and intricate work in iron and steel. He was a constant reader of the *Scientific American,* and devoted

much time and money in keeping posted on the intrica
cies of every new patent or novelty that in any way per·
tained to appliances for bank protection.

His keenness in this regard is illustrated by the fact
that at one time there was not a Lillie lock in existence
of which he could not secure the combination and which
he could not pick. His genius was also as inventive as
it was inquiring.

He purchased a Lillie safe simply for the purpose of
"operating" on the lock. Every part and portion was
studied with an assiduity and zeal truly remarkable. He
shut himself up with it until he was the complete master
of it. But though he had acquired as much knowledge
of it as its inventor, there was one thing still to be over·
come. He could never be certain of the combination.
Here his inventive skill was exhibited in a brilliant manner indeed. He actually constructed a delicate piece of
mechanism by which he could secure the combination of
any Lillie safe, providing he could only get access to the
outside of it.

This was when the dials of the Lillie lock were secured
by screws on the outside, and could be taken off.

It was usually no trouble for him to secure entrance to
a bank, for he could manufacture a key to its doors without the least trouble. When this much was gained he
had a sure thing on a Lillie safe or any vault guarded by
that kind of a lock. His apparatus was a delicate affair,
a handsomely finished ratchet, which, when placed under
the dial, would make no mark or indication if moved in

one direction, but when the dial was stopped and at attempt made to move it in an opposite direction, it made a little puncture in a sheet of paper or other light substance which would retain it, and which was properly placed to receive such puncture.

Shinburn would enter a bank at night, insert this under the dial of the lock, and the next night on his return he would have discovered the first feature of the combination. Then he would set his register for the reverse motion, which he would secure the second night, and so on until he had just as perfect a knowledge of the combination of the safe or vault as any officer of the bank.

In this way he robbed the New Windsor Bank, of Maryland. Some of his confederates proved traitorous subsequently, and he was arrested by John Young, then chief of detectives of New York city, since deceased, who, or securing a portion of the stolen money, permitted Shinburn to go free ; and following this Young resigned.

He also in this manner committed a robbery at Norwalk, Connecticut, where he obtained nearly two hundred thousand dollars, as also the robbery of a bank at Binghampton, Vermont ; while a large number of the same class of depredations were done by him which never came to light.

After his Boston adventures, already related, Shinburn arranged a regular system of bank depredations throughout New England, which should apply in its operations to all banks of importance. In pursuance of this scheme be made regular tours of that section of the country, for the purpose of securing information in reference to the location of these banks and the means necessary to enter them successfully. Having secured this indispensable knowledge, he prepared the keys and implements requisite to carry his plans into execution. Then the raid began and continued for several years, in which he was from first to last undetected, and was at length arrested only through the treachery of some of his false friends, after he had stolen and recklessly spent hundreds of thousands of dollars in the most extravagant manner.

His adventures during this period were as remarkable as his criminal successes. During the summer of '64 he had secured a very handsome sum from several banks in the section of country referred to, and he determined to pass a gay season at some of the fashionable watering-places. Procuring a magnificent outfit, he proceeded from New York to Saratoga, and, registering a romantic *alias* on the books of the Union Hotel, soon became one of the leaders of the fashion in that summer hot-bed of dissipation and frivolity.

His appearance was particularly agreeable : well-proportioned and finely-cut, expressive features, his form attired in the latest style of clothing, with a magnificent solitaire diamond glittering in his shirt-front, small hands and feet, with altogether a *distingué* air, he presented every external appearance of a gentleman. His intellectual ability, of a high order, was rendered more conspicuous by his fluent command of the foreign languages, already referred to. With these combined qualifications and a plentiful supply of greenbacks, which he expended most lavishly, he speedily made his way into the very best society, and was everywhere courted as a desirable acquaintance Flirting with handsome young ladies and playing the heartless Lothario, betting at the race-course, mornings at the springs and night divided between faro and the hops, he led a life of reckless extravagance, vile deceit, and crim inal pleasure.

During the time he favored the Grand Union with his presence, he courted and was under promise of marriage to the daughter of a prominent western politician, which of course was never consummated. After paying visits to Newport and Long Branch, he passed through the summer, and devoted the winter to his regular practice of bank " weeding " with varying success, until, emboldened by his hitherto good luck, he determined, in concert with several noted bank-thieves, among whom was his criminal partner, George White, *alias* George Bliss, to rob the Concord (New Hampshire) Bank, which was most brilliantly executed, and from which they succeeded in securing over two hundred thousand dollars. With the plunder the thieves separated with their shares, when one of the gang was captured, and disclosed the names of the depredators, chief among whom was that of Max Shinburn. Upon this information the hunt commenced, and Shinburn was captured, tried, convicted, and sentenced to the Concord state prison for ten years.

His arrest was effected while he was holding one of his orgies of pleasure at Saratoga ; and a most profound sensation was caused there at the sudden retirement of the gorgeous leader of fashion ; but the social waters soon quieted, to be disturbed by the next ripple, while Shin-burn went behind the great gray walls of the prison.

But he was too much of a genius in his line of life to sit down meekly and waste his time brooding over his misfortunes. While others of the common sort might give themselves up to the despair of a life in the living tomb of a prison, his being in such a place at all was only preliminary to getting out of it. His first move was to make friends with everybody ; and as he always man aged to keep a good supply of money on hand, this was not difficult to accomplish. Being a wonderful burglar, he was treated with distinction, and of course everybody knew him. His keepers came to think that Shinburn was one of the cleverest fellows in the place. He was an exemplary prisoner, and, as he always had a cheery smile for his fellows and an occasional substantial " tip " for the officer, he soon had everything his own way, and had acquired a degree of familiarity with his keepers that made the bold and daring act he had so long planned, possible.

One night he called the keeper to his cell, and entered into conversation with him over some trivial matters which were made very agreeable and entertaining on Shinburn's part, for some little time, when suddenly he asked the keeper to step inside for some purpose which the shrewd fellow made seem an important one. The unsuspecting guardian did as he was requested, when

6*

quicker than lightning, Shinburn overpowered the keeper took his revolver from him, threatening, if any alarm was given, he would blow his brains out, took his keys from him, locked the unfortunate keeper in his own cell, and coolly let himself out of the prison and regained his liberty.

Great astonishment and alarm was created at the time in New Hampshire at this daring and bold escape, and a large reward was offered for the recapture of the reckless criminal; but for twelve months he eluded the most vigilant search, until one evening a private citizen, traveling on the cars from Binghampton, recognized Shinburn amongst the passengers—the citizen having been in court at the time of his trial and conviction.

With commendable presence of mind, the gentleman, well knowing the desperate and dangerous character of the man, immediately went into another car and inquired if any sheriff's men or other officers of justice were on the train.

It so fortunately happened that four deputy-sheriffs, who were returning from the State prison, to which place they had conveyed some convicts, were on the train, and they returned to the car in which Shinburne was quietly sitting, and with drawn revolvers pounced upon him and made him their prisoner.

He was conveyed to his old quarters, and an extra watch and guard set over him; but he soon disarmed suspicion, and a want of caution supervened, which, as the sequel shows, resulted in a second escape. Shinburn, with the potatoes that were served with his food, took an impression of the cell-lock, and from his iron spoons made a key to fit it. Think of the patience, perseverance, and real ability requisite to such a purpose. After a painfully long time he found himself provided with the means to reach the corridor; and after all was still for the night he would leave his cell and proceed to the outer barred gate, where, with a delicate steel saw that had been conveyed to him by an accomplice, by being imbedded in the fore-piece of a light silk cap, he would saw the massive iron bars until they would just hold, but would be broken off by any sudden contact of a heavy object. The slight trace of this work would be completely removed by filling the interstices made by the slender saw with portions of a potato mixed with soot.

It was the rule of the prison to march the prisoners around the yard every day; and Shinburn, having by perseverance so cut the bars that they would give way upon a quick pressure, on one of these occasions, when the prisoners were taking their daily circuit, the daring fellow made a sudden rush at the then apparently secure bars, which yielded as if by magic, and Shinburn went through them like a flash of light, and while the keepers were struck dumb by what appeared a miracle, the bold thief sprang into a wagon in waiting for him, and was again at liberty. He immediately changed his clothing, and with his companions set out for Plymouth. They were hotly pursued by the prison watch and a large posse of citizens, who came up with the fugitives in a dense piece of woods. Here they were ordered to halt; but their only answer was a well-directed volley from their revolvers; and finding that the desperate men were determined to surrender only after a conflict, in which many of the pursuing party would undoubtedly meet their death, the latter retired, and Shinburn was free to again pursue his brilliant career, to eventually be recaptured and again make his escape in a manner which for a time turned the laugh upon me, as he had so often upon others, and which I will not neglect to record, at the risk of a joke upon myself, with the reflection that he is about the only criminal that ever escaped me in my nearly a third of a century's active and exciting detective's career.

On the night of July 9, 1868, the office of the Lehigh Coal and Navigation Company, at White Haven, Pennsylvania, was entered, the vault and safe opened by means of false keys, and fifty-six thousand dollars, in bank-bills, currency, and bonds, stolen.

The entrance to the building had also been effected by means of false keys; and while no clue to the robbers remained, it was evident the job had been carefully planned, and that professionals were concerned in it.

The case was put in my hands; and from certain evidences of the style of work which are as marked in noted criminals as are the brands on goods of different manufacture, I at once concluded that whoever had suggested the robbery, it was Max Shinburn's master-mind that had planned it and brought it to a successful execution.

In pursuance of these convictions, I soon had run down the entire party, among which was the redoubtable Shinburn. It then came to light that the robbery had been suggested by one Starks, then proprietor of the White Haven Hotel, in White Haven, who had let two other parties, named Spencer, *alias* Griffin, and one Sinclair, into the scheme; but none of them being accomplished criminals, Shinburn's services had been secured.

The robbery had been planned as early as March previous, and the scheme was to enter the place while it contained a large amount of currency for the monthly payment of the company's hands. On arrival at White Haven, and receiving such information as the conspirators there were able to furnish, Shinburn daringly entered the agent's house at night, and then, in the bed-chamber, took from the pockets of the sleeping man all the keys of the safe, vault, and compartments, of which he took impressions in wax, and, having returned the keys and removed all signs of his visit, departed. When Shinburn had manufactured such keys as he desired, he returned to the place, and at night entered the coal company's office, opening the various doors and the vault. One key was found imperfect; but this defect was subsequently remedied. The thieves now only awaited the arrival of the money to do their work; but although they were ready for operations in April, it was not until July that circumstances favored them.

On July 5th Griffin hired a team in Dunmore, representing that he would be absent for a number of days and leaving a deposit for the value of the turn-out. A short distance out of town he met Sinclair and Shinburn, to whom he surrendered possession of the team, returning to town himself and going into retiracy. Sinclair then drove to a rendezvous in the woods, near Wilkesbarre, where they remained until the 9th, when, after dark, they drove to White Haven, arriving there at midnight. Shinburn entered the office, opened the safe, abstracted the money, and within twenty minutes they were dashing away toward Scranton, fifty-six thousand dollars richer for their nocturnal visit.

I had already captured all the lesser game, and had just succeeded in laying my hands upon Shinburn, after an exciting chase, when my clients urgently advised that Shinburn should be held in custody by my officers until he had been relieved of the lion's share of the plunder which it was known he had carried off. Though strongly objecting to this course—as it is a thorough principle with me to immediately turn prisoners over to the regularly con-stituted anthorities—I at last reluctantly yielded. This deviation from my rule in such cases cost me my prisoner, for Shinburn's matchless cunning, which always seemed to be equal to any test, came to his rescue again, and he here made one of the most remarkable escapes for which he has become so notorious.

Knowing the slippery character of the man, I had every precaution taken to prevent the execution of any of his brilliant schemes. I shut him up in a oom at a Wilkesbarre hotel, and put my most trustworthy men in charge of him, handcuffing them together, so that there could be, as was thought, no possibility of escape. In this way they passed the time, eating, drinking, and sleeping together, seemingly as inseparable, on account of the handcuffs, as the Siamese twins, while the men were relieved often enough to keep them wakeful and vigilant. At night extra precautions were taken, and the guard and prisoner were compelled to sleep together.

But all this did not avail ; for Shinburn, one night, after countless trials which would have unnerved and dismayed any less wonderful a man, using his *left hand*, picked the lock of the handcuff with the shank of his breast-pin, stole softly, silently, and breathlessly from the side of the sleeping officer, and fled. All pursuit was useless. He in some manner shipped as a sailor, and finally reached Belgium, from which country he could not be taken by an American officer.

But Shinburn could not resist the temptation of returning to a field where his abilities made him so successful ; and it is quite probable that he came back to America with the fixed determination of securing enough plunder to give him a competence for the remainder of his life. He worked for nearly six months with the greatest secrecy and good fortune, finally crowning all by his masterly planning and execution of the famous Ocean Bank robbery, at New York, in June, 1869, in which over a quarter of a million dollars in securities and currency was taken.

This robbery was done in the following manner : Par

ties in the scheme rented a portion of the basement
under the bank, at the corner of Fulton and Greenwich
Streets, for the ostensible purpose of opening a branch
office of the Chicago Life Insurance Company, but announced to Mr. Okell, the lessee of the entire basement,
that they would not be ready for business for some weeks,
as they would have to comply with the insurance laws of
New York, which required a deposit from foreign insurance agencies.

After this much was done, every little item of information concerning the bank was gradually secured, until a
favorable time had arrived, when the burglars began
work after the closing of business on Saturday evening,
and probably within twenty-four hours had secured all
that they wanted, departing with the utmost leisure, and
leaving not the slightest clue behind them. They had
made most accurate calculations, and had sawed a large
hole through the ceiling of the basement and the bank
floor, enabling them to come up through within the private office of the president of the bank. Having thus
gained access to the bank floor, they hung black glace
and oiled silk over the windows and doors, and went to
work. In some mysterious manner the combination to
the locks of the main vault was known—which showed
Shinburn's genius again; and when the vault was entered, the small safes and compartments were easily
opened with a massive jack-screw and other well known
burglars' appliances. Thirty thousand dollars in gold was
left—that evidently being too heavy for transportation—

but altogether upward of a quarter of a million in money
and securities was captured. The adventurous fellows
left behind them probably the finest "kit" of tools ever
got together. It must have cost at least three thousand
dollars, and comprised a jack-screw capable of raising
the side of the bank building, six large and powerful
"jimmies," an assortment of finely-tempered steel
wedges and copper-headed sledge-hammers, also patent
drills, braces and bits, augers, compasses, saws, small
hand-saws, brad-awls, two large pruning-knives, putty-
knife, powder-flasks, patent fuse, a cleverly contrived
and constructed funnel with an India-rubber tube attached for inserting powder into holes drilled in the doors
of the safes, a pair of handcuffs, coils of rope, dark-
lanterns, rubber shoes, overalls, and a large quantity of
oiled silk used for deadening the sounds of the blows
from the heavy sledge-hammers, and a large number of
cold-chisels, screw-drivers, gimlets, and other small tools
too numerous to mention in detail. The "kit" comprised over two hundred pieces, and was the largest and
finest ever seen.

Immediately after this magnificent capture, Shinburn,
who probably secured a large portion of it, at once
escaped to Europe, and settled in Belgium. It is
thought that he must have saved from two to three hundred thousand dollars. With a portion of this he purchased a title from some wretchedly impecunious Belgian,
and is now living in luxury and ease from the proceeds
of his villainies in America.

Altogether, Maximilian Shinburn may be considered
one of the most remarkably successful criminals of the
present century, and is almost the single instance on
record where such a character has escaped a violent
death, a convict's career, and cursed end, or a final dragging out of a miserable existence in wretched poverty
and disgrace, which may yet be his end, as the old adage,
that "a fool and his money are soon parted," is no less
rue than that "a thief and his plunder soon separate,"
rhen the old daring, the old temptations, and the great
shadow of old crimes prove the irresistible power that
propel to the certain fate of the professional criminal.

CHAPTER VIII.

MR. BLUFFER AND THE MONTE-MEN.

I HAVE at present in my employ, and have had for a
great number of years, at the head of one of the de-
partments of my business, a now elderly man, who is a
genuine character. His fidelity and ability in my service
have given him the right to my utmost confidence and
respect; but he possesses traits of character that have
created at different times, for myself, my officers, and
large number of employees, almost infinite merriment.

He is known far and wide, as well as among my peo
ple, as Mr. Bluffer, which *sobriquet* was bestowed upov

him some years since, by being deputized at Chicago to make the arrest of a notorious criminal who was at that time claiming a large share of public attention, and who had come under my surveillance for capturing.

Although then past the prime of life, and already gray and grizzled, he was determined in whatever he undertook ; and though that kind of work was outside of his department, he accomplished his mission successfully, and with such vigor and spirit, that, when the prisoner was brought to my office, he laughingly remarked that his captor was a " cranky old bluffer, and no mistake ! " and in honor of the exploit he came to be called " Mr Bluffer."

The most striking characteristics of Mr. Bluffer, which gave everything he said or did a marked individuality, were a disposition to speak out plainly about anything and everything that came under his attention—and but little escaped it—and then, if there was anything which he fancied wrong about the matter, he would set it right, if the very dead had to be raised in doing it. This, coupled with an abruptness and occasional ferocity which often provoked the most disastrous results to himself, caused him to be in hot water most of the time, always gave his tormentors the keenest enjoyment, and frequently resulted in his being handled without gloves.

Some time since I had occasion to send Mr. Bluffer from New York to Albany on a rather important mission, and on his return he met with an adventure in which he came out victorious, but which, at the same time, nearly upset the old gentleman from the terrible " canary " which his indignation and rage threw him into.

The train left Albany at half-past eight in the morning, and, after an hour's delightful companionship with an an- cient and odorous pipe, which Bluffer keenly enjoys and which is his inseparable companion, he returned to the ladies' from the smoking car, and with a copy of Mark Twain's " Tom Sawyer " seated himself comfortably in a seat with a friend for the remainder of the trip.

He had not been long thus engaged when his attention was attracted from his book to an individual " made up " for a Texan—homespun suit, sombrero hat, cowhide boots, etc.—who began a rambling conversation, in a high falsetto voice, with one or two of his neighbors.

The gist of his remarks was that in the North wonderful sights were to be seen by the unsophisticated Southerner, and lucky is the man who gets back to his country home without being robbed and in a sober condition from the great metropolis of the West, Chicago, which great city he had just left.

The peculiar voice, the well-imitated Southern dialect, and his *tout ensemble*, had amused the passengers for some ten or fifteen minutes, when he suddenly bent forward and shouted in the ear of a gentleman who was quietly reading a paper in front of him :

"Say, stranger, that ar' Chicago's a buster anyhow, ain't it ? "

" Did you address your question to me, sir ? " said the gentleman rather testily.

"Ya-as, 'n no bad meanin' with it either. How do *you* like Chicago ?"

"I'm a resident of Chicago, and it's good enough for *me !*" This with an expression of contempt for the questioner.

"Wall, all I've got ter say is just this," resumed the Texan, not at all disconcerted, "Chicago is the gauldurndest town I ever struck. They tell me New York is about half as big as Chicago, and I'm going to see the show thar too. These cities is big sights fur us cattleraisers. Was you ever in Texas, stranger ? "

"No, and have no desire to go there either."

"Then you *do* live in Chicago, eh ? Ar' you travelin fur ? "

"I am going to New York on business, simply," answered the Chicago business man, evidently very much bored.

"Wall, now, you Chicago fellers are right smart. Some of the boys played it on me a couple of days ago ; but I'm agoin' to get even on 'em, gauldurned if I don't. I'll tell you how it was."

At this point the passengers' attention, ladies and all, had been attracted by the eccentric appearance and language of the "Texan," and all were listening.

"You see," continued the Texan, " I was walkin' along the street, when a feller asked me if I wanted to buy a gold watch. 'Wall, I reckon not,' says I. 'I can't stand the press.' 'I know where you can get a good watch for a dollar,' says he. 'You *do ?*' says I

'I'm your man. 'Come along with me,' says he. And
stranger, we just measured mud right smart, you can bet
'Here you are,' says he; and we walked into a nice·
looking doorway, and went up-stairs into a room whar a
gang of lads was chuckin' dice. 'Step right up and beat
twenty-five, and you can git one of these elegant gold
watches,' a feller says to me as was standin' behind a bar
like; 'it's only a dollar a throw.' I got up and I
throwed, but I didn't beat twenty-five. 'You're in bad
luck not to beat twenty-five,' says a young feller to me;
'I jist won a watch, and I beat thirty-six!' 'Hold on
thar,' says I to the man behind the bar; 'I'll try that
agin.' But I slipped up on it, stranger, and I'll be gauldurned if I didn't try it twenty-five times. I couldn't
fetch it once, and it cost me twenty-five dollars for my
fun. But, by and by, I smelled a right smart-sized mice
and I says: 'Gentlemen, I've had enough!' and gaul-
durn me if I didn't get eout o' that right quick—I
reckon!"

"Why didn't you complain to the police?" kindly inquired a gentleman who was sitting behind him. This
individual had been chatting with an elderly lady about
the decadence of steamboat travel on the Hudson, and
praising the good cheer of the olden times, when there
were such life and gayety "on the river." He was a pom-
pous-looking person, and had let slip several remarks so
worded that a stranger would easily understand that he
was a member of some Legislature, and appeared to
have plenty of money in his well-filled pocketbook, judg-

ing from its appearance when he displayed it as he gave his ticket to the conductor.

"Complain to the police? Why I didn't want my friends to know I'd been such a gauldurned sucker. My friends read the papers—they do, stranger. And then I expected to get beat anyhow, somehow afore I got eout of Chicago, and so I jist said nothin' to nobody."

The roar of laughter had scarcely subsided, when Mr. Bluffer, whose ears had been pricked up for a time, and whose suspicious disposition had shown him that the car contained a first-class "monte" crowd, whispered to his companion: "I say, friend, that fellow ought to be an actor. He plays that very well."

"What do you mean?" was the reply.

"Hold on—let's wait; he's got another yarn;" and just then the Texan, apparently flattered by the attention he was receiving, resumed his yarns about Chicago.

"But the worst beat I got was in losing five hundred dollars in the slickest way you ever seed."

"How was that?" said the Chicago merchant, at length becoming interested, and unbending from his former dignity.

"Why, a feller come up to me and showed me three cards. He says: 'I'll bet you ten dollars you can't tell me which one is the "old woman,"' and he mixed 'em all up an' laid 'em all down on a little board he had in front of him. 'No, you don't play that on me,' I says; 'I jist got bit on one game.' 'Here, I can tell you,' says a young feller what was lookin' on; and he did tell him.

'Do you want to try it again?' says he. 'Well, I don't mind,' says the young feller. 'I'll bet you fifty dollars, all I've got with me,' and I'll be gauldurned if he didn't win. 'Here,' I says, 'I'll go you on that thing.' You see, I had been a watchin', and I knew the card jist as well as the feller that won. 'How much?' says the feller with the cards. 'Two hundred dollars,' I says. 'All right,' says he, 'I'll bet you.' I put my finger on the old woman, but he turned up the card, and it wasn't her—not much: it was the Jack, and I got beat. Now you jist calkerlate my eyes stuck out. I couldn't see how I made such a mistake, and I offered him to go just once more for three hundred. He took it; but, stranger—well, don't you ever try that game—that's all. You'd get beat!"

And the Texan leaned back with a sigh.

"Then you lost?" asked the senator.

"Yes, you bet I lost. The feller offered to bet me just once more, to give me a chance to git even, but I told him I was tired and wanted to go home!"

Another roar of laughter followed this story and the Texan resumed:

"But I tell yer what I *did* do. I give that Chicager skunk ten dollars for them three keerds, and I'm goin' to take 'em down to Texas and clean all the cow-boys out of their stamps. I kin do it, sure. Why, I've got 'em right here," said he; "I'll show 'em to you," and he went down into an inner vest-pocket, produced a red bandana handkerchief, which he carefully unfolded, and showed three playing-cards—the knave, queen, and king.

"There's the jokers," he said triumphantly, displaying them awkwardly to the Chicago merchant.

All this time Mr. Bluffer had been bristling up. Here were some villains aboard a coach full of respectable people—many of whom probably had large sums of money with them—who were now playing the prelude to the little drama of robbery. It was a shame, Mr. Bluffer thought; and, like a valiant knight, he determined to distinguish himself. He confided to his friend what was really going on under the appearance of rural simplicity, and expressed a purpose of denouncing the parties there and then; but he was finally persuaded to let the matter rest until there was really some danger of a swindle being perpetrated.

"Why," said the solid Chicago business man to the Texan, "that's the game they call 'three-card monte.' It's a shame," he continued, addressing a gentleman whose curiosity had drawn him near, " that such rascality cannot be prevented. The manner in which these poor, ignorant countrymen will allow themselves to be swindled is pitiable in the extreme. Something should be done to stop it. The penalties upon those convicted should be more severe than they are."

"That's true," remarked the senator warmly. "We are thinking of introducing a bill at the coming session of the legislature at Albany making it an offence punishable with imprisonment ten years in the penitentiary. Gambling *must* be stopped!"

By this time Mr. Bluffer was in a very fever of virtu-

7

ous indigration, and low mutterings from time to time escaped him, and were given in very strong language. He'd be dashed if *he'd* see such goings on. Very decided adjectives affirmed that *others* might permit such damnable work, but old Bluffer, true to his pugnacious disposition, would be blanked if he would allow it. In fact, he began to attract considerable attention in his part of the car; but his friend, who had some curiosity to see how the matter would end, coupled with some apprehensions that the deputy's violent temper might precipitate trouble should he interfere in his brusque manner, quieted him down somewhat for the time being.

The Chicago business man had noticed this; and after eying Mr. Bluffer for a moment, he beckoned him to follow him to the extreme end of the car, where, although the former evidently endeavored with a most winning argument to calm my old employee down, from the indignant snortings, the savage shaking of his head, and the demonstrative manner of his entire person, it could be seen that it was an entirely one-sided argument.

While this by-play was going on, the Texan and his confederate, the senator, were losing no time. The former proceeded to show his amused and interested listeners just how he had been beaten. He shuffled the cards in a bungling manner, eliciting a remark from the senator to the effect that he must do better than that or he would never get even on the Chicago sharks by beating his friends in Texas on that game, because any man could tell which card was the "old woman."

" Wall, now, stranger, I doubt it. I kinder think *you* can't turn her over ! "

" Oh, yes ; any one can tell," responded the senator airily.

" Look a-here : I'll just bet yer a ten-dollar note yer can't, stranger ! "

" Done ! Here it is ! " And the senator picked up the right card, which was apparent to every bystander, from the clumsy manner in which the cards had been shuffled.

" Wall, you *did* beat me, didn't you ? " ejaculated the Texan, with a look of stupid simplicity and unaccountable astonishment. I reckon I'll have to practice this thing a little afore I can hide it ; but I'll be gaul-danged ef I don't git even ! "

Down at the end of the car, where the virtuously indignant Mr. Bluffer and the Chicago business man were having their one-sided argument, the former was shaking his head furiously, and exclaiming :

" No, sir—never ! That's all very fine ; but I can't see it ! I wouldn't be found dead with any of your money on me ! If I was to carry it about me in Chicago, I'd be arrested for handling counterfeit money. You've got hold of the wrong man for a bribery ! " and the like ; and then Mr. Bluffer, snorting and puffing, returned to his friend, muttering and fussing, and showing many symptoms of a near explosion.

In the meantime the senator had been solicited to bet once more, and had done so to oblige the Texan ; and again won—-this time fifty dollars.

Among the spectators stood a young man, with a Jewish cast of countenance, whose hand had been going in and out of his pocket for some time, as though he were anxious to try his luck. The fire of excitement was in his eyes, and his cheeks were flushed—a gambler in inclination, young as he was, and evidently unsophisticated.

"I'll bet you ten dollars I can show you that card," said he ; and he was laying down a ten-dollar bill on the improvised table, consisting of an overcoat upon the Texan's knee, on which he was showing how the "little game" was played, when suddenly Mr. Bluffer, in a burs⁺ of indignation, seized the young man's arm.

"No, you don't!" he exclaimed, pushing him away ; "no, you don't! Don't be a fool, young man!" he continued, while the bystanders looked surprised, and an ugly light scintillated from the Texan's eyes as he looked up at the intruder.

"Let him bet. I'll take my chances. Let him bet," said the Texan.

"You'll take your chances, will you?" burst forth old Bluffer ferociously. "A nice chance that would be for *him*, wouldn't it?"

The young man paused for a moment bewildered, while the Chicago business man, smiling pleasantly and reassuringly, beckoned him to bet ; and the senator urged him to try his luck : why, he could beat him certainly, just as easy as *he* had done. The young Hebrew was reaching his hand down, when a sign from Bluffer and his friend restrained him again.

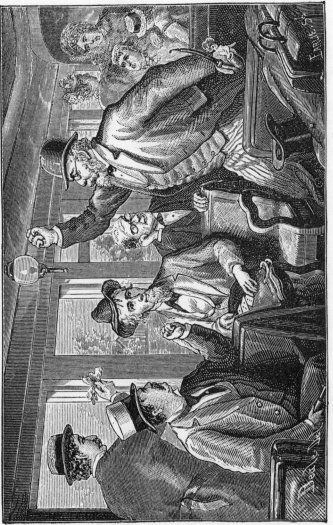

"That's all very fine!—That's all very fine!" snorted Mr. Bluffer.—Page—

"You're a nice gang, ain't you?" blurted out Bluffer notly, eying the Chicago merchant with a look of contempt as his fists began to double up. "I want you to get out of this car as quick as ever you can go!" and he made a step in the direction of the latter, while that sleek individual assumed an indignant attitude and turned very red in the face.

"What do you mean, sir?" he exclaimed, bridling up. "Do you know to whom you are speaking? I demand to know what you mean by insulting me in this manner."

The passengers stared from one to another in astonishment, and the ladies began to look frightened.

"I am a respectable merchant from Chicago, sir, and I demand an apology instantly, sir, or you must answer for this insult!"

"That's all very fine! that's all very fine!" snorted Mr. Bluffer, weaving back and forth from a very excess of contempt and rage. "Oh, you do it very well—*very* well. You ought to be an actor! A respectable merchant from Chicago, eh? Why, ladies and gentlemen, these scamps are an organized gang of three-card-monte gamblers, who have come here to rob: yes, rob—and be damned to you!" he added savagely, as "Texas" jumped up, muttering threats and curses, and placing the cards in his pocket. "And what are you going to do about it? Yes, ladies and gentleman," said old Bluffer, in a high tragedy voice, "and this fellow here" (pointing to the "business man") "does the genteel business. That one over there" (referring to the senator) "is pal

No. 2, and always wins to encourage the victims, in order that that scoundrel " (pointing to the Texan) " may fleece them. Why, that Chicago business man ! "—and here the brave old Bluffer shook his trembling finger very close to the nose of that individual—" not five minutes ago offered me twenty-five dollars to keep my mouth shut and say nothing. It's all pretty well played, but I object to their presence here, and, damn me, but they'll go out of the car, or I will ! "

At this the "business man," boiling with rage, suddenly put his hand into a convenient valise, drew forth a revolver, which he cocked. This was followed by shrieks from the ladies, while an ominous and painful silence ensued among the bystanders, who shrank out of the way. The ugly eyes of the baffled Texan gleamed, the " senator," in a ridiculous attempt at dignity, and with wholly the look of a sneak, appeared not to know just how to act, while the hand of the "business man " trembled and his face paled, as he said hoarsely : " Take back what you said, or I'll blow daylight through you ! "

"Come away, or you'll be hurt ! " whispered Mr Bluffer's friend.

" Not much ! " blurted out the old fellow defiantly. " He daren't shoot ! He's too big a coward ! " and he looked the gambler in the face, while he bantered him to shoot.

" Give it to him—shoot ! " yelled the Texan. " Why don't you shoot ? " he howled wildly. " Give the ' pop to me ; I'll bore him ! "

" Oh, yes ! that's all very fine ! why *don't* you give it to him ? He'll shoot—oh, yes ! shoot nothing ! " snarled old Bluffer defiantly, while the taunted party looked ner vously around.

" Stop the train and call the conductor ! " shouted one frightened individual ; while Mr. Bluffer's friend stole around behind the " Chicago business man," ready to snatch the revolver on the first sign of genuine danger.

Mr. Bluffer seemed to get braver and braver. His blood was up ! He was ready for battle. His pugnacious spirit, coupled with a knowledge that the scoundrelly gang were weakening, made him bolder than a lion, and he fairly danced up and down in front of the gamblers.

" Look at the trunk of the gentleman from Chicago ! " giving the satchel a nimble kick, which sent it spinning, and disclosing an empty interior ; " nothing in it but a pack of cards ! " Don't you acknowledge ? " yelled Bluffer, advancing, " or shall we call in all the passengers ? "

" Yes, the game is up. I own up," replied the Chicago business man in a low voice of baffled rage, at the same time putting his revolver in his pocket and picking up the empty valise to follow the " senator," who still attempted to appear dignified, to the door ; while the Texan, concluding things were beginning to look warm, as he observed the now determined faces of nearly all the passengers, followed after.

" All right, my fine old snoozer ! we'll fix *you !* '

shouted the Texan to Mr. Bluffer, as the former re
treated.

The train was now nearing the suburbs, and it had
got bruited about that the demonstrative old fellow was
one of my men—"one of Pinkerton's superintendents,"
had, in fact, reached the ears of the retreating gamblers ;
and they stopped at the door to give their persistent
enemy a parting shot.

Of all the vile language ever used, the Texan, the
"business man" and the "senator" now indulged in.
They raked the sturdy old Bluffer fore and aft. Outside
of all the fine names their tongues could fling forth, they
sneered at him, jibed him, bullied him, called him a jaci-
tor, hurled at him taunts of being Pinkerton's coal-heaver,
Pinkerton's floor scrubber, Pinkerton's hostler, and altogether so hurt the old fellow's pride in his position and
badgered him on his personal appearance and infirmities,
that, had not the ancient Bluffer been restrained, he
would have thrown himself upon the three, in all the
might and power of his boundless indignation and rage,
and probably got a good, sound drubbing, if not worse.

As it was, he followed them, with trembling form,
shrieking tones, and shaking fists, to the last that he was
able, and earned another great victory, in his own estimation, in behalf of decency and justice.

The gamblers were hustled off the train at the first
stop made, breathing dire threats of revenge ; while my
triumphant and faithful employee, amid the hearty con
gratulations of the passengers, solaced himself, until the

Union depot was reached, by mighty and vigorous puff-
ings at his ancient and odorous pipe; and when the
passengers disembarked for their various destinations
might still have been seen puffing and muttering away
but wearing the dignity of a conquering hero.

———•———

CHAPTER IX.

TRAPPING A DETECTIVE.

THE "smart boy" of the period is sometimes very
smart indeed. There seems to be a period in the
life of every boy when he naturally becomes this ' smart
boy of the period," and takes to tricks of a brilliant character as naturally as a young miss takes to beaux. Philadelphia had one of these smart boys recently, and he
showed, under the pressing necessity of the occasion, an
ingenuity and shrewdness which would have much more
become the Philadelphia city detective whom he outwitted.

A Brook Street grocer lost fifty dollars from his till, and
a lad named Falvey was suspected of the theft. His
father very commendably took him to the police-station,
and put him in charge of an officer pending an investigation of the matter. After young Falvey was placed in a
cell, Detective Swan, of the city force, was ordered to
enter and "break him down," which is the detective par
lance for securing a confession from a supposed criminal

7*

The boy did finally confess to the theft with loud protestations of grief and repentance, and finally told the officer a regular "Tom Sawyer" story of having hidden it in a certain coal-yard along the docks, and promised to go with the detective and show him where he had secreted the bills.

The two sallied forth in quest of the treasure, the detective triumphant in his reflections of his ability to get at such things speedily, and the boy humble and demure as the picture of the typical good boy in the Sunday-school books. At last they reached the docks and the particular coal-yard where the stolen money had been hidden.

Now these docks, or yards, are all provided with great numbers of elevated "shutes" used in discharging coal. To one of these the guileful youth led the satisfied detective, where they found a hole just large enough for one person to crawl into. He said the money was hidden in this hole; and the officer, not suspecting the youth was playing any game upon him to escape, directed him 'o " go along in."

The boy did go in; but that same boy came out at the large instead of the small end of the horn—and that end, it is certain, was not in the immediate vicinity of the detective.

The detective soon began to think that it required a long time for the boy to get out of so small a place. He accordingly put his head into the dark orifice and shouted lustily.

The deluded "detective" being rescued.—Page—

There was no response but the sepulchral echo of his own voice, and besides, it seemed to him that he had drawn a bucketful of cinders into his lungs, while his entire features were eclipsed with the richest possible quality of coal-smut.

Again he hallooed, and threatened to shoot into the hole should the boy not make his appearance immediately at the expiration of one minute. The detective held his watch and cursed his luck; but this threat was of no avail. Finally he did shoot into the dark hole, and trembled a little at the risk he was taking; but it brought no boy and no sound to indicate his whereabouts.

While standing there cogitating what should be the next move, he suddenly heard the sound of some heavy object dropping below. He directly inferred that the keen youngster had outwitted him, and had jumped into the bins below; and he accordingly made all haste to follow, making quite a daring swinging leap over the side of the "shute," landing in the bottom of a huge bin, and where he would rather have given a ten-dollar bill than to have been.

He found to his chagrin that he and the deceitful youth had gone to very different places. The detective was in the bottom of a coal-bin, and nobody within hearing to help him out.

In this miserable position the detective remained several hours, with the sun blazing down upon him. He would yell for assistance for a time, and then he would vary this amusement by cursing, and it is thought that

some of the choicest swearing ever done in tne Quaker
City was executed on this momentous occasion.

At last some laborers came that way, and pulled up the
unfortunate officer with a rope, setting him at liberty; but
he was wholly unrecognizable, and returned to headquar
ters without his boy or money, to receive the derisive
shouts of his companions, and to be known among them
to this day as the " coal-heaver detective."

CHAPTER X.

PIPER, THE FORGER.

I THINK I can best relate the romantic history of
this remarkable criminal by extracts from his con
fession to me, in the summer of 1876, shortly after his
release from prison, and when it was hoped his profes-
sions of reform would prove all they then promised :

" I was born in Cynthiana Township, near Paris, Kentucky, on the
old Topper plantation, in 1828. My father was a gentleman in
whom courtesy and courtliness were inborn graces. My earliest recol-
lections are of this man, his wife, my mother (a brilliant French lady
he had married in Europe), flowers, happy negroes, and countless lady
and gentleman visitors. This picture passed away when I became
five years of age and my mother died. Her death brought dark
days to me, and the removal of our family to Brooklyn, where, after
a few years, my father married a wealthy lady of that city, who was
— well, what stepmothers usually are. She was not my mother, and

besides, there were two crops of children, and they cannot very well be mixed like two grades of wheat in a Chicago elevator.

" My father was wealthy for those times, worth probably two hundred thousand dollars ; and having no home in reality, I was not long in spoiling. My father was socially a favorite, and, as he took me almost everywhere with him, by the time I was fourteen years of age I was a regular pet of the lawyers, politicians, and literary men of his circle.

" Naturally precocious, and with no restraining home influences, I went to the devil at a rapid pace. My father was very desirous that I should have a fine education ; and after I had gone through the Brooklyn public schools, I was prepared for college by tutors, and intended graduating from Yale, when a little incident occurred which changed the whole tenor of my life, and led to the circumstances that forced me into being what I have been.

" My father gave me four thousand dollars, and directed me to proceed to the Wyoming Valley, to invest the same in coal, provided it could be secured at certain rates. I got as far as Philadelphia, went on a spree there, and finally went to New Orleans, where I spent every dollar before my father discovered my whereabouts.

" It almost broke his heart, as I was the man's pride. He never reprimanded me ; but I could see that it bowed him down, and, though he was always tender and considerate, had built a wall between us.

" I pursued my studies about a year after this, and then, getting hold of a few hundred dollars, went to Buffalo, not exactly as a runaway, but with a coldness that made that separation from my father a final one. I had some good letters of introduction, and several Buffalo business men knew of my family's wealth and standing, and, as I never had any bad habits, I made friends there rapidly.

" I shortly made the acquaintance of a firm named Rathburn, Pettis & Co., the senior member of which was convicted of forging grain receipts, and was sentenced to ten years at Auburn, but was pardoned out several years before the expiration of his term, and subsequently took up all the paper which had taken him down, dying a few years since worth fully a hundred thousand dollars.

" Rathburn seemed greatly interested in me, and, through the firm's influence, I became steward of the old ' Superior,' a steamer then plying between Buffalo and Chicago, ran two trips as such, and was then promoted to the assistant clerkship, which position I retained until the close of navigation. In the meantime I had become one of Rathburn's family, and they seemed to love me as a son. They lived on what was then known as Dousman Street, an aristocratic locality, with people like Dean Richmond for neighbors. Rathburn's family were very extravagant, which ruined him. He had often remarked on my wonderful penmanship—not that it was so beautiful, but on account of its being so varied and done with such fluency.

" One winter evening—it was Sunday evening, and a dreary one— he came to me in their parlor, where his two beautiful daughters and myself were sitting reading, and said : ' My son '—he always called me ' my son '—' step into the library a moment ; I want to speak with you.' I saw there was *something* wrong, but followed him in ; and he motioned me to a seat in front of his secretary, where there were writing materials, evidently just laid there. He walked the floor for a little time, and then came to where I was sitting, and began, in a rattling, gasping sort of a way, complimenting my handwriting, praising my good qualities, bemoaning his family's extravagance, and requesting me to see if I could write certain names attached to different papers as well as they were written upon them—all in a piteous, half-crazed manner, which scared me. He explained that no harm could come of it ; that he could more than meet all of his obligations if given but a chance to turn ; and concluded by reminding me that I would permit his ruin if I did not or could not do as he wished by the next morning.

"I got all worked up about it, and told him that I could not write my own name that night, but that I would go right to bed, have a good sleep. get up early in the morning, and if he would then

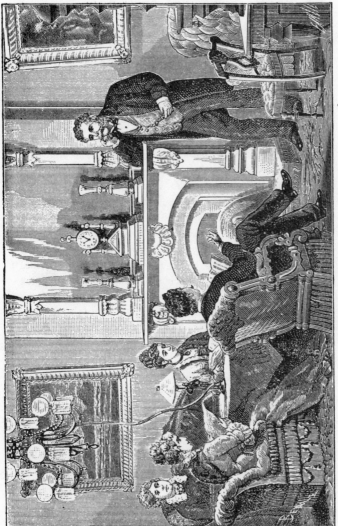

The Osborne Mansion before the forgeries.—Page—

show me what he wanted I would try and do it for him. This made the man so happy and bright, that I went to bed happy too, and got up at six o'clock, and went into the library, where I found everything ready. I worked steadily for an hour under his directions, and at the end of that time he was half wild with delight—the possessor of thirty thousand dollars' worth of grain receipts, that were good as genuine, to realize upon. He grasped me by the hand, and, with tears of joy and gratitude streaming down his face, said, hysterically, that I had saved him, and that a two thousand dollar span and carriage he owned should be my reward.

" I did not then realize the enormity of my crime, and I believe that, had I not known that man, and unconsciously fallen before that terrible temptation, I never would have been what I have; but that turn-out, the man's gratitude and manifest kindnesses, his wife's redoubled attention, his two daughters' extreme affection, everything that will whirl the head of a foolish boy and give him the first devilish taste of power, crazed me, ruined me !

" The first grain receipts thrown upon the markets were of course retired as fast as they became due and substituted by new ones, but the overplus became so great after a few months that the inevitable had to come. Rathburn was arrested, tried—ex-President Fillmore being his counsel—convicted, and sentenced to Auburn for ten years, there being a general and powerful feeling that the whole thing was a conspiracy of his partners for his ruin. When the lightning struck, his wife came to me with a thousand dollars and begged me, in heaven's name, to fly the country; which, after disposing of my turn-out, I did. But not until I had put the Atlantic Ocean between me and the United States did I realize that I was a fugitive in a strange land, and a man without a country.

" But once in Europe, and the necessity for some scheme for money goading me on, the terribly unfortunate power I held, coupled with a good education, quick wits, and a boundless self-reliance, made my subsequent career as a criminal a natural sequence.

" My next operation was in purchasing four bills of exchange for eight pounds—each the smallest bills then purchasable in England—from a Liverpool bank upon a Paris house; and I " raised" them, realizing twelve thousand dollars out of the operation. Being of a literary turn of mind and a good scholar, I then went to Heidelberg, Germany, with a view of entering the university there and becoming a thorough German scholar; but after a little time got restless, and returned to London, where I secured an attorney, who settled the Paris matter and took up the paper for me, accomplishing the whole for less than two thousand dollars.

" I was only a few months in Europe, when I returned to America; and after wandering about for a little time — though always studying banking and commercial rules and customs with the zeal of an honest capitalist, I went to Philadelphia, and purchased, at a bank there, five certificates of deposit—one for five thousand dollars and the other four for fifty dollars each. With these in my pocket, and about six thousand dollars in ready money besides, I sailed from Baltimore to Charleston, S. C., and represented myself as a wealthy Englishman traveling for his health and seeking profitable American investments, made acquaintance at the banks, where I was informed of terms of discount for cashing my five thousand dollar certificate—claiming to be in no great haste, and giving them plenty of time to ascertain by mail that my certificate of deposit was no myth. Then I raised the four fifty dollar certificates to five thousand dollar certificates, leisurely called around at the four different banks, and got them cashed, transferred the *genuine* to a wealthy friend, securing the cash for the same, and, long before my Charleston friends could secure advices from Philadelphia, I was well on my way to Cuba, with an additional fund of twenty thousand dollars. I made it an invariable rule to " settle ' these little matters up clean as I went along, and doing so in this instance only cost me four thousand dollars.

" I could do nothing in my line in Cuba. There are no enterprise

ing business men there. They want to know all about a man
They insist on knowing that a man *has* been honest, as well as that
he seems so, and has money. I soon left that country; and, while
crossing to New Orleans, developed a scheme to relieve that city of
about fifty thousand dollars, which failed. A foolish momentary
fondness for a brilliant New Orleans adventuress caused this plan
to fail, as I felt satisfied that she had learned too much of my
methods, and would levy on me heavily for silence, or expose me
outright. I left Cuba with some little Spanish paper, which I intended to expand sufficiently to enable me to purchase about sixty
thousand dollars' worth of cotton, make a *bona-fide* purchase of that
amount with the inflated paper, ship it to Liverpool, and draw
against the shipment for fifty thousand dollars, and then draw out of
the cotton trade.

"I went to Cleveland from New Orleans, and at Berea I married.
I had about twenty-five thousand dollars, and I began husbanding
it as carefully as though I had earned every cent of it by hard labor.
From Ohio I went to Rochester, New York, and there opened a
large Yankee notion and furnishing-goods store, and started ped-
dling wagons into the country. I did well; sold out well; and
went to Albion, New York, and there engaged in the stove business,
inaugurating, I believe, the system of stove-peddling, which afterward became general throughout the State, in which business I had
twelve wagons engaged.

"Everything I touched seemed to turn as if by magic into money.
About 1850 I came back into Ohio, and purchased several mills;
and in 1852 removed to Iowa, where, as I had taken fully one hundred thousand dollars, I soon became one of the leading capitalists
of the State, and in five years had come to be worth fully half a
million. I was considered worth a million, and ranked financially
next to Cook & Seargant, the well-known Davenport bankers. In
fact, I was one of *the* very few solid men of Iowa, and my paper was
as good as the gold at any bank in the State. I felt guilty and rest

less all this time, and could find no pleasure save in incessant work
I built an eighty thousand dollar residence, and one of my enterprises was building, with old Anton Marat, the City Hotel of St.
Louis, once a fine house, with the extensive sale-stables attached ·
and in Iowa I was in every enterprise that I could learn of.   I made
an immense amount of money in a very short time ; but my finan
cial ruin came from indorsing the paper of everybody who would
ask it.

" Everything was swept away in the crash of '57, save four thousand dollars, which I had deposited with Budd & Baldwin, bankers,
at Clinton.   With this I left the State, and went to Chicago, where
for a time I bought wheat on the street for a firm named Radcliffe &
Walker ; but at that time everybody was poor, scared, and running
away ; and the old fascination of the criminal's life coming over me,
I left Chicago with five hundred dollars of what remained of this four
thousand dollars, in one dollar bills, and the balance in gold, and
went to Fremont, Ohio.   Making a great show of this, I deliberately determined on swindling somebody, and soon found that a
spendthrift · Frenchman, one Falquet, who had made the wife of
the Sandusky, Ohio, postmaster his mistress, was going to the
dogs financially, and who I at once saw was the proper party for
a victim.   The result was, I went to New York, and purchased, for
one hundred dollars, ten thousand dollars' worth of the then absolutely worthless Pennsylvania Coal Company's bonds.   My next
step was to get about two hundred copies of Thompson's Stock Re-
porter, one hundred of two years previous, and one hundred then cur-
rent, transfer the covers, and slip them into their places where they
were taken.   Pennsylvania Coal Company's bonds suddenly went up
from nothing to above par, and with twenty thousand dollars' worth
of them and three hundred dollars in gold, I became the *bona-fide* pur-
chaser of Falquet's business, making a cool twenty thousand, and
sending him and his mistress on to New York in a most happy frame
of mind.   Of course I was arrested for fraud, but no fraud could be

PIPER. THE FORGER. 163

shown ; and, after honorably conducting the business for some time, I sold out, and became a desperately dangerous forger.

"In 1862 I made arrangements with the chiefs of police of a dozen large cities, by which I was to receive protection for a certain percentage of my plunder. They were not only to act as a 'fence' for the money or bonds I might secure, but act as 'go-betweens' for the purpose of effecting settlements with parties whom I had swindled. If I was too closely pressed, I was to be arrested on some trivial charge and protected in jail, or given an opportunity to get straw bail and escape. Under this protection, which for several years was absolute, my first operation was in Wisconsin, the next in Minnesota, next in Iowa, then in Illinois, next in Ohio, then in Pennsylvania, then in Indiana, next in New York, then in Rhode Island, next in Nova Scotia, then in Canada, and then in Vermont, which caused my incarceration at Rutland, in February, '69, for a term of ten years ; but, through the commutation for good behavior, I was discharged the fourth of February, 1876. From 1857 to the time of my final arrest I probably 'raised' a million dollars in checks and drafts, and made half that amount more from altering court records, forging wills, changing numbers on stolen bonds so they could be put upon the market, and in the thousands of ways in which my dangerous art could be used.

"My daring during my second career of forgery was so great, and I relied so thoroughly upon the perfect execution of my work and my complete knowledge of the French language, that I was whirled into a scheme for relieving, at one stroke, Emperor Maximilian of nearly two millions in gold stored in the treasury vaults of the Mexican capital. Preparatory to this, I went to England, provided myself with a large number of bills of exchange on different French banks, and, after proceeding to Paris, rented quiet lodgings, where I inflated these bills until they represented fabulous sums. After this work was completed, I set about forging letters, accrediting myself as a secret agent from the French government to the Mexican emperor and poor Carlotta. These forged papers gave exhaustive political and private reasons why *official* advices should not be burdened with my coming as a secret agent, and also told in writing, too familiar to be mistaken, why this secret embassador (myself) should be implicitly trusted, and even obeyed, should the condition of things in Mexico, on the agent's arrival, warrant flight.

" As in the case with the Frenchman, Falquet, at Fremont, Ohio, my scheme was to induce the self-crazed emperor to do something *from which he dare not turn back.* I would take my chances on the rest. On arriving at Brownsville, the three men who were to have assisted me in this bold and desperate scheme, learning of the alarming condition of things at the city of Mexico, refused to go any further, and I pursued my journey of adventure alone. Arriving at the capital, I at once gained an interview with the emperor, who seemed in a listless, palsied condition, as if already practically dead, and only sensible of a lingering, undesired existence, and who, while acknowledging the genuineness of my credentials and the necessity for immediate flight, desired five days in which to take counsel and give a decision, though actually ordering a count of the coin and bullion in the treasury vaults. I at once saw that I could not secure the removal of this vast weight—not knowing or daring to trust a soul in that wild country, where every hand held a dagger, and knew how to drive it home too—and felt that it was useless to waste my beautiful English paper where I might not be able to get away with the proceeds of it ; and although I held several subsequent interviews with the fated emperor, I saw that my own death was only a question of time if I remained there, and the third day after my arrival in the city of Mexico I left the place for Salt Lake, *via* Santa Fé. Two days after — completing the five days at the expiration of which Maximilian was to have given me his decision—a bullet had put the Austrian dupe beyond the need of raised bills of exchange."

There is no question but that, in his time, Piper was

one of the most skilled of forgers in any country. It is said of him that he spent the best part of eight years of his worthless life in the study of chemistry under the best professors, and at an expense, including the cost of ex-periments, of what any ordinarily honest man would consider a large fortune. His great skill secured for him among his class the title of the "invincible;" and it is undoubtedly a fact that there was no bank-note, draft, bill of exchange, certificate, or other monetary paper or legal instrument which he could not so alter, to suit himself or the parties employing him to do the work, as to absolutely defy detection.

In personal appearance he bore a striking resemblance to Professor Swing, the noted Chicago divine, and was one of the smoothest-tongued rascals it has ever been my business to know. He seemed to have a singular faculty of compelling everybody who came in contact with him to like him and even admire him, though they might be perfectly aware of his character; while the man's nature was a singular mixture of unstinted and reckless gener-osity, kind-heartedness, brilliancy, cruel recklessness, and heartless criminal daring.

On his liberation from the Vermont penitentiary, in 1876, he professed a complete reform. I believe his pro-fessions were genuine. I believe he really meant to live the life of an honest man. Neither am I ashamed to confess that I put my hand in my pocket and helped him, on condition that he would be one in everything he did. But it was too hard work for him. His luxurious habits, the ease with which he could secure money dishonestly, the fascination of the adventure and daring of his old career, all overwhelmed him, and he "broke over," and sold all the little manhood left in him for the excitement and fleeting pleasures of the adventurer's life ; and, after a short series of successes, he became ill, when of course the friends of his class forsook him, and he died in miserable poverty and disgrace—the fate of nearly every professional criminal that ever existed — on September 4, 1877, at the Robertson House, in the city of Joliet, Illinois, within a few miles of the penitentiary he had a hundred times cheated of deserved convict's service.

CHAPTER XI.

A BOGUS BARONET AND HIS VICTIMS.

THE good people of the city of Boston were greatly exercised, at a certain period during the war, over the doings of one *Sir* Henry Mercer, Bart., who came to the surface, made a ripple of excitement, and then passed from sight and thought, giving place to the next sensation, as will be the way of the world until the end of time.

The particular interest centering in Sir Henry Mercer lay in the ease with which he secured his rank, the remarkably good time he had while he held the title, and the general luxurious way in which he enjoyed the pre-

rogatives of rank and wealth—including of course sev·
eral first-class scandals while he was supposed to be their
rightful possessor.

Great men frequently spring from humble surround
ings, and Mercer was no exception to this desirable way
of getting on in the world, which used him rather shab·
bily at the start, for at the breaking out of the war him·
self and wife were found making a very ques ionable
living in a very questionable way in a then very doubtful
locality on Sudbury Street, Boston.   In fact, Mrs. Mercer
enjoyed the reputation of being one of those accommo-
dating business ladies who can conduct a cigar-store so
as to make it more profitable than the best of men,
although the actual sale of cigars would not have sup·
ported so modest a salesman as Silas Wegg, before he
met old Noddy Boffin, and became avaricious, for she
had a way of making appointments for parties, both
ladies and gentlemen, who imagined they had not their
affinities.   Added to this business basis was the employment of two slinking fellows, who were called "private
detectives," and who employed their time taking notes on
callers and parties in general who met here, following
them, learning all that was possible concerning them,
and then, after a little time, taking occasion to call on
them at their offices, if they had any, remind them of
their "little indiscretion," and secure whatever might be
got, which usually was and usually is in proportion to
the cowardice of the victim.

This was the business of Mrs. Mercer, while her hus

band had rather precarious employment as a city "drum mer" for the drygoods house of Laught & Co. and was in every way qualified for adventure, possessing a fine appearance, a large amount of self-assurance, and had several languages at his tongue's end, so that after a time he was not only able to bring a large amount of business to his employers, but considerable custom to the Sudbury Street cigar-store, where he had no trouble in inducing country merchants to go wild in their laudable endeavors to study the zoological department of society usually described by that generic phrase, "seeing the elephant."

While matters were progressing in this manner with the Mercers, Laught & Co., in their haste to become rich, in 1864 began shipping largely to Nassau, for Florida, goods that would suit the Southern market. They did not run the blockade, but they forwarded the material that was to run it. The shrewd Mercer shortly discovered this se-cret, and he was not long in using it to advantage; and while acting as agent for the firm, he informed the gov-ernment of the acts of his employers, and finally obtained the double position of drummer and government detective.

His first disclosures led to the arrest of Laught, who was lodged in jail. While lying there, by some treacher-ous arrangement Mercer so imposed on his employer that he obtained a power-of-attorney to collect all the debts of Laught & Co. at Nassau; and there, as well as in Boston, after this brilliant move, he was recognized as a partner in the firm.

On his arrival at Nassau, Mercer, who now blossomed out as a genuine English Sir Henry Mercer, a partner in the firm of Laught & Co., was received by Mr. Henry Adler, the great blockade-runner and agent for the Confederate States, with the most distinguished marks of esteem. After he had concluded his business, and just before leaving for Boston, Mr. Adler introduced him to a very attractive young widow, a Northern lady, who had lost her husband, a Southerner, running the blockade. He was of course introduced as a live baronet, and the widow naturally felt proud of such noble society ; the result of which was that on the voyage from Nassau to Boston Sir Henry wooed and won her, which wooing and winning was continued after the couple had arrived in Boston, notwithstanding the trifling obstacle remaining in the way behind the cigar-stand on Sudbury Street.

When this shadow presented itself, Sir Henry urged that a little matter like that was hardly to be considered. All English noblemen were accustomed to such incumbrances. A trifling annuity would take the cigar-stand party back to England ; and it is a fact worthy of record that she did go there, whatever the inducement offered.

It appears that the widow was worth nearly half a million dollars in her own right ; and as this was too tempting a capture to permit escaping, Sir Henry pressed his suit with greater vigor than ever, and the day for the proposed marriage was finally set, while the happy baronet succeeded in quartering himself at the widow's elegant mansion.

8

The lady's friends made a bitter fight against the man, but she seemed completely infatuated, and not until the most powerful efforts were made would she consent to even seem to doubt him by a visit to his "bankers," which was proposed as a test of the man's being all he professed. When the baronet heard of this proposition, he acceded to it in the blandest terms, giving his lovely bride-to-be a letter, over which was beautifully printed an embossed coat-of-arms in bronze and gilt, to his "bankers" in New York.

Armed with this reassuring document, the lady proceeded to New York, to find Sir Henry unknown there; and, thoroughly alarmed, swiftly returned to Boston, only to find that the bogus baronet had left on the very next train, taking with him twelve thousand dollars of her money, together with all the silver plate, and that he had started for England, *via* Quebec, in which city he was arrested. But the fair widow, afraid of the scandal and exposure it would bring about, let the scamp go with her money, plate, and honor; and Sir Henry Mercer, as a sensation, soon passed from public attention, and eventually from sight, but came back again, like a bad penny, in a way which, through my efforts, shut the doors of a prison upon him.

Just four years later, Mr. J. M. Ballard, then division superintendent of one of the express companies running in and out of Chicago, called upon me at my chief office in that city, and in a very excited manner told me that only an hour or two previous he had become convinced

"Sir Henry's wooing." —*Page* —

that an embezzlement, amounting to two or three thou sand dollars, had occurred on their route between Chicago and a large city further west.

With what slight information I could secure, I immediately detailed several of my best operatives, and within a short time had secured a happy result to my work, which brought out the following facts :

About six weeks before, J. R. Wilson, a pleasant-faced, boyish fellow of about twenty, and a messenger of the express company between Chicago and the city referred to, one of the most important express routes in the country, was introduced by another messenger to one W. S. G. Mercer, proprietor of a Randolph Street saloon and restaurant. Mercer cultivated Wilson's acquaintance assiduously—so much so, in fact, that the two were firm friends within a week or two, and, when Wilson was in Chicago, were constantly in each other's society.

About two weeks previous to the call upon me by Mr. Ballard, Mercer, who was none other than the bogus Sir Henry, and who had degenerated from a live baronet to a Chicago saloon-keeper, gambler, and ward politician— about as low as it is possible for one to get—took a trip to the western city with his young friend, and the two had a very gay time of it, during which the crafty Mercer praised Wilson's good qualities, fine appearance, and splendid business abilities, cunningly coming around to delicate insinuations that the boy was having too hard a time of it for one of his good parts, and finally, with dev ilish ingenuity, hinting at the ease with which a good haul could be made from the company.

This subject was hinted at over wine and cigars, at the theater and at places where the very devil in men is most easily awakened, until, before leaving on their return, the two had agreed upon a plan by which Wilson should secure all that was possible, without awakening suspicion, on two "runs," or trips to Chicago, when the money should be divided and the two should fly to Canada, and from there proceed to Europe on a tour of pleasure.

According to arrangements, on Monday morning, March 30, 1868, Wilson returned from his trip, and, while getting his money-box and books into the express wagon, a business-like looking gentleman stepped up to the car and inquired :

" Is there a valise for me, from J. A. Walters ? "

" Yes," replied Wilson. " You can get it over to the office in a few minutes."

" Can't you let me have it now ?   Here's the receipt."

" All right, then.   Fifty cents charges."

The stranger signed the messenger's book, paid him fifty cents, and walked away.

That valise contained three thousand dollars taken by Wilson, and the party who carried it away so nonchalantly was the ex-Sir Henry.

It was on the next day that Mr. Ballard called, and all that I could learn then was that inquiries had been made for amounts by business men which had not come to hand, and for a total sum so large that its non-arrival alarmed him ; so that my men were on hand at once to follow and observe every movement of each messenger that might by any possibility have been the guilty party.

Consequent upon this arrangement, I discovered that on Wednesday morning, as the train bearing Wilson on his " out-trip " was about leaving, a certain gentleman brought a well-filled valise to the express car, gave it to the messenger, who consigned it on his way-bill to " J. A. Walters," a mythical personage of course, and on paying the charges, and taking a receipt in a most business-like manner, walked off whistling ;—but not alone, for wherever the man, whom I soon found to be Mercer, went, there was an invisible though remorseless attendant beside him.

A certain Chicago gentleman also took a trip on the same train with Wilson, who at every station where the train halted saw that the messenger did not leave it, and after he had arrived at his destination, that he never made an unobserved move.

The reports of the two operatives, condensed, were .
" Wilson : restless ; excited ; has something on his mind worrying him. Sports a brand-new suit of clothes, a handsome gold watch, and a diamond pin."

" Mercer : neglecting business ; pretty full of liquor ; constantly borrowing money right and left."

This settled the matter in my mind.

Wilson, closely watched by my operative, left on his return Thursday night, arriving in Chicago Friday morning.

After the rush of the departing passengers was a little

over, Mercer, who had been waiting between some cars in front of the train so as not to attract attention, walked rapidly down the track, stepped up to the express-car, re peated the same inquiries as on the former occasion, was met by the same answers from Wilson, paid the charges on the valise, and, just as he turned to depart, one of my operatives, who *happened* to be passing, heard him re- mark in a low tone of voice :

"Meet me at the Sherman House just as soon as you get through. Room 86."

Two men accompanied Mercer to that hotel without his knowledge, with orders to arrest him instantly on his making the slightest sign of an intention to not keep his appointment with Wilson ; while two more detectives fol- lowed the company's wagon, in a private conveyance, to the express office, with instructions to never permit the guilty messenger to escape them, but in no manner to disturb him if he proceeded to the hotel according to ap- pointment ; while I at once dispatched a special messen- ger requesting Superintendent Ballard to meet me im- mediately in the office of the Sherman House.

By this means in less than an hour all the parties had been brought together, and helped materially to swell the crowd in the rotunda.

I kept Mr. Ballard out of sight, as I was apprehensive lest Wilson might suspect his mission, and found that this was the wisest plan, for shortly he came hurriedly into the hotel, and, after standing a moment as if irresolute, walked through and through the office, hastily scanning the face of every man in it, not excepting myself. Then, after going out and looking up and down the street in either direction, as if to be doubly assured that he was not suspected and followed, he returned and hurriedly proceeded to the room designated as No. 86.

Telling Mr. Ballard to follow in a few moments, I hastened after the retreating messenger, and arrived at the landing of the floor on which No. 86 was situated just in time to observe Wilson, a few yards in advance, pause before a door, give two quick raps, and enter immediately after.

There were two or three gentlemen in the hall, carelessly conversing together. A stranger to them would merely have regarded them as pleasant, chatty guests, who had met by chance and were enjoying the meeting. They were my operatives ; but they paid no attention to me, nor I to them.

Scarcely had the door to 86 closed, when I silently stood beside it, and could easily catch the low, earnest conversation within.

" My dear boy," said Mercer enthusiastically, " you did splendidly ! "

" I feel like death about it ! " said the messenger with such a touch of genuine remorse in his tones, that I pitied the deluded fellow from the bottom of my heart.

" O pshaw ! d—n them ! it's nothing to them, and in two days we will be out of harm's way. But we must get out of this lively. My plan is to get a livery team and drive out into Indiana, and there take the Michigan

Central train for Canada. They'll probably have a lot of Pinkerton's men watching the depots, and we will just learn these smart detectives a new trick," replied Mercer with a triumphant laugh.

By this time Mr. Ballard was beside me, and, with a slight signal, I had two of the parties in the hall, whom a stranger would have taken for chatting guests, at the door, one stationed silently at either side.

Then I rapped loudly upon the door.

A smothered oath from Mercer, a cry of remorseful surprise from the poor messenger, and a rustle and hurry inside, were the only response.

I rapped again, louder than before, and then finally told the parties that if the door was not instantly opened, it would be forced.

After another rustle and scuffle, Mercer opened the door, and Mr. Ballard and myself quickly entered, I locking the door, putting the key in my pocket.

Mercer looked me full in the face for a moment, and with the one gasping ejaculation, "My God!—Allan Pinkerton!" sank into a chair; while Wilson, white as a ghost, reeled against the wall, looking from me to Mr. Ballard, his superintendent, for a moment, and then, burying his face in his hands, threw himself upon the bed, and moaned in utter agony.

They were at once arrested; and while Mercer was consigned to the county jail to await examination, I had Wilson taken to my office, where a full confession was secured. All the money was recovered, save the few hun dred dollars expended by Mercer for the clothing and jewelry with which his dupe was led on to the commission of the second and greater crime.

At the trial which was shortly had, the judge, at my earnest solicitation, mercifully took into consideration the facts of the case, and the messenger, Wilson, was given the least punishment possible ; while ex-Sir Henry, whose crime was aggravated ten-fold by his cruel and heartless ruin of a previously honored and respected boy, was con signed to his rightful sphere of action, where, for ten years at least, he remained an honest and law-abiding citizen of the State of Illinois within its penitentiary at Joliet.

CHAPTER XII.

CANADA BILL.

THERE are some men who naturally choose, or, through a series of unfortunate blunders, drift into the life of social outlaws, who possess so many remarkably original traits of character that they become rather subjects for admiration than condemnation when we review their life and career.

On first thought it could hardly be imagined that one who has been all his life, so far as is known, a gambler and a confidence man, whose associates were always of the same or worse class than himself, who had no more

8*

regard for law than a wild Indian, and who never in his entire career seemed to have an aspiration above being the vagabond, par excellence, could move us to anything beyond a passing interest, the same as we would have for a wild animal or any unusual character among men and women.

But here is a man who, from his daring, his genuine simplicity, his great aptitude for his nefarious work, his simple, almost childish ways, his unequaled success, and a hundred other marked and remarkable qualities, cannot but cause something more than a common interest, and must always remain as an extraordinarily brilliant type of a very dangerous and unworthy class.

Such was " Canada Bill," whose real name was William Jones. He was born in a little tent under the trees of Yorkshire, in old England. His people were genuine Gypsies, who lived, as all other Gypsies do, by tinkering, dickering, or fortune-telling, and horse-trading. Bill, as he was always called, grew up among the *Romany* like any other Gypsy lad, becoming proficient in the nameless and numberless tricks of the Gypsy life, and particularly adept at handling cards. In fact, this proficiency caused him finally to leave his tribe, as, wherever he went among them, he never failed to beat the shrewdest of his shrewd people on every occasion where it was possible for him to secure an opponent willing to risk any money upon his supposed superiority in that direction.

Having become altogether too keen for his Gypsy friends, he began appearing at fairs and traveling with

provincial catchpenny shows in England. Tiring of successes in that field, he eventually came to America, and
wandered about Canada for some time in the genuine
Gypsy fashion. This was about twenty-five years ago,
when Bill was twenty-two or twenty-three years of age,
and when thimble-rigging was the great game at the fairs
and among travelers.

Bill soon developed a great reputation for playing short-
card games, but finally devoted his talents entirely to
three-card monte under the guise of a countryman, and
may be said to have been the genuine original of that
poor, simple personage who *had* been swindled by sharpers, and who, while bewailing his loss and showing interested people the manner in which he had been robbed,
invariably made their natural curiosity and patronizing
sympathy cost them dearly.

Himself and another well-known monte-player, named
Dick Cady, traveled through Canada for several years,
gaining a great notoriety among gamblers and sporting
men ; and it was here that this singular person secured the
sobriquet of " Canada Bill," which name clung to him
until his death, in the summer of 1877 ; and he was known
by everybody throughout the country who knew him at
all by that name, it being generally supposed that he was
of Canadian birth.

As a rule, three-card monte men are among the most
godless, worthless, unprincipled villains that infest society
anywhere ; but this strange character, from his simplicity,
which was genuine, his cunning, which was most brilliant

his acting, which was inimitable, because it was nature it-self, created a lofty niche for himself in all the honor there may be attached to a brilliant and wholly original career as a sharper of this kind; and however many imitators he may have—and he has hundreds—none can ever approach his perfection in the slightest possible degree.

Any deft person, after a certain amount of practice, can do all the trickery there is about the sleight-of-hand in three-card monte; but the game is so common a dodge among swindlers, that unless the *confidence* of the dupe is first fully secured, he seldom bites at the bait offered.

This must either be confidence, on the part of the person being operated on, that he is smarter than the dealer, if his real character is known; or, in case it is not known, a conviction that he is a genuine greenhorn who can easily be beaten the second time.

It was here that Canada Bill's peculiar genius never failed to give him victory; and it is said of him that he never made a mistake and never failed to win money whenever he attempted it.

His personal appearance, which was most ludicrous, undeniably had much to do with his success. He was the veritable country gawky, the ridiculous, ignorant, absurd creature that has been so imperfectly imitated on and off the stage for years, and whose true description can scarcely be written. He was fully six feet high, with dark eyes and hair, and always had a smooth-shaven face, full of seams and wrinkles, that were put to all manner of difficult expressions with a marvelous facility and ease.

All this—coupled with long, loose-jointed arms, long, thin, and apparently a trifle unsteady legs, a shambling, shuffling, awkward gait, and this remarkable face and head bent forward and turned a little to one side, like an inquiring and wise old owl, and then an outfit of Granger clothing, the entire cost of which never exceeded fifteen dollars—made a combination that never failed to call a smile to a stranger's face, or awaken a feeling of curiosity and interest wherever he might be seen.

One striking difference between Canada Bill and all the other sharpers of his ilk lay in the fact that he *was* the thing he seemed to be. Old gamblers and sporting-men could never fathom him. He was an enigma to his clos-est friends. A short study of the awkward, ambling fellow would give one the impression that he was simply su-premely clever in his manner and make up ; that he was merely one of the most accomplished actors in his pro-fession ever known; and that he only kept up this *ap-pearance* of guilelessness for the purpose of acquiring greater reputation among his fellows. But those who knew him, as far as it was possible to know the wander-ing vagabond that he was, assert that he was the most unaffected, innocent, and really simple-hearted of human beings, and never had been anything, and never could have been anything, save just what he was.

This would hardly seem possible of even an exceptional person among ordinary people , and I can only reconcile this singular case with consistency when I call to mind many of the interesting old Gypsy tinkers I have myself known, who, with all their wise lore and cunning tricks were the merriest, kindest-hearted, jolliest, and most child like simple dogs on earth.

It seems almost impossible that any living person waging such a relentless war against society as Canada Bill did, until the day of his death, could have anything generous and simple about him ; but he certainly had those two qualities to a remarkable degree. They were uppermost in everything that he did. It almost seemed that this man had no thought but that his vocation in life was of the highest respectability ; that skinning a man out of a thousand dollars as neatly as he could do it was an admirable stroke of business, even if it led to that man's ruin ; and that every act of his criminal life was one of the most honorable accomplishments; so that this sunny temper and honest face was an outgrowth of a satisfaction in upright living.

He was certainly different from all other men whom I have been called upon to study. He always had a mellow and old look about him that at once won the looker-on and caused a real touch of warmth and kindliness toward him. His face was always beaming with a rough good-fellowship and a sturdy friendliness that seemed almost something to cling to and bet on, while every movement of his slouchy, unkempt body was only a new indication of his rustic ingenuousness.

One November night, several years since, I started on a hurried trip over the Pittsburg and Fort Wayne road from Chicago to the East, for the transaction of some im-

portant business of such a nature that I did not desire the
fact of my presence known there ; and, noticing several
eastern and western people of my acquaintance in the
sleeper and throughout the cars, before the train started,
I quietly entered the smoking-car, and took a cigar and a
seat in a quiet corner, with the object of avoiding my
friends as much as possible, and remaining where I was
until everything had got quiet in the sleeper for the
night, so that I could safely retire without observation.

Being very tired, after a casual glance at several other
persons in front of me in the car, I settled myself snugly
in my seat, hoping to be able to get a little nap ; but I had
scarcely got myself comfortably arranged, when the train
halted at Twenty-second Street, and my attention was attracted by the entrance into our car of a tall, stumbling
fellow, dressed in some cheap, woolen, home-spun stuff,
that hung about his attenuated frame like a dirty camp-
meeting tent around a straggling set of poles.

Pausing just inside the door for a moment, he deposited
on the floor a valise whose size and cavernous appearance
would have won the heart of an audience at a minstrel
show, and then, giving his big hand a great ungainly wave
as if to clear away the smoke immediately in front of him,
peered into the murky distance, and ejaculated, " Gaul-
darned thick ! "

He probably referred to both the smoke and the passengers. In any event, he sat clumsily down upon the
stove, from which he suddenly bounded like a rubber
ball, although there was no fire within it. It appeared as

though it had crept into his bucolic mind that he *was* sitting on a stove, and that there *must*, of course, be a fire within it, and, consequently, he *must* be burned.   Whatever impelled him, he and his cavernous valise went *ricocheting* along the aisle, finally coming up short, like a "bucking" mule, at about the center of the car, and there, tumbling noisily into a seat, which, taking into consideration the crowded condition of the coach, singularly enough was vacant.

By this time there was a broad smile on the faces of all the passengers, and many mirthful references were made in an undertone to the wild "Hoosier," some of which he evidently overheard, but which were received in the best of humor, the subject of such witticism turning a benign and smiling farmer face upon all, but holding on to his big, though evidently nearly empty valise with both hands, as if indicating that he was quite ready for any good-natured joke with "the boys," so long as none of them attempted any sharp city tricks upon him, which, it could be easily seen from his manner, he had already experienced, as he thought, and was quite ready to have it generally known that quite a mistake would be made when anybody took him for a "young man from the country."

After the Twenty-second Street crossing was passed, we sped along rapidly, almost the majority of the car seeming to be of that very common class of travelers that are usually considered "good fellows," who were ready for jest, whether it were ordinary or of the first class,

We had been bowling along for but a short time, however, before the conductor made his appearance.

His was mere business—to collect fares ; that was all He came through the car like an " old campaigner," with no favors to ask and none to give.

He got along to where our bucolic friend was sitting without trouble, when that lively individual seemed ready for an argument.

" You're the conductor ? " he remarked dryly.

" Yes."

" You takes the money for ridin' on this machine ? "

" Yes ; where ye goin' ? "

" Fort Wayne, God willin'."

The countryman clumsily produced a bill from out a huge roll, and then remarked :

" Lots of good boys on the train ? "

" Dunno ; guess so," replied the conductor. The conductor gave the innocent party his change, when that ubiquitous individual remarked :

" Lots of funny fellows on this train ? "

The conductor had passed, but he took the time to turn and say :

" Don't trust 'em, my Granger friend."

" D——d if I will," said he, as he took a stronger and firmer hold of his priceless "grip-sack." " D——d if I will, fur I ve been thar ! I've been thar ! "

A roar of laughter followed this sally from the " In jeanny Granger," and I noticed at the time, without giving it any particular attention so far as this countryman

and his immediate remarks were concerned, that, at
various intervals throughout the car, the laughing which
followed his remark was extremely well distributed; but
being tired, I received all this merriment as a common
occurrence, and, after the conductor passed, fell into a
heavy drowse, in which tall Indiana Grangers, brusque
conductors, commercial travelers, and the ordinary railroad riffraff danced back and forth through my disturbed
dreams.

I was of course unconscious of what passed for a little
time, but was eventually disturbed by renewed laughter
through the car, and noticed that quite a group had gathered around the Granger, whose members were evidently
greatly interested in whatever he was doing and saying;
while his great, honest face, all alive with enthusiasm, was
wreathed with smiles at being such an object of general
interest.

As before stated, up to this time I had given the matter no thought; but when I now heard one of a couple ir
front of me remark: "Very quaint character; very quaint
character. I believe some of those Chicago rascals have
victimized him, and he is telling the passengers about it,'
which was followed by a request to his companion to
"come along and see the fun," I immediately understood that we were to be given ar exhibition of three-
card monte of a very interesting character, and that many
of the persons in the car were "cappers," or those members of the gang who are used to persuade fools to bet
upon the game.

My first impulse was to put a stop to the villainy at any personal risk ; but I recollected that the very reason which had forced me to take up with the discomforts of the smoking-car—an absolute necessity for remaining unknown—prevented this, and though my blood boiled with a desire to frustrate the already ripened and charmingly-working plans of the keen scamps, I was forced to swallow my indignation and content myself with taking up a position where I could get a comprehensive idea of what might follow.

By this time so much interest was being exhibited in the uncouth fellow's manipulations, that two seats had been given him ; and there he sat in one corner of the space thus made, with his legs crossed under him like a tailor's, his huge valise lying across this framework in such a manner that a most neat, level, and glossy surface was made, and all this with a nicety of calculation really remarkable, while his whole form, manner, and action showed him to be the simplest, most honest of men, who, out of the pure goodness of his heart, — rough, ignorant, and unkempt as he was,—proposed giving the crowd about him his experiences merely for what benefit it would certainly prove to them.

'Yaas," he said in an indescribably droll tone of voice, "yaas, them dogoned Chicago skinners cum nigh a ruinin' me. Now, I do 'low them fellers beat the hull tarnal kentry. But, gosh ! I found 'em out ! "

Here the Hoosier laughed with such a ridiculously childish air of triumph, that general laughter was irresis'ible.

He then reached his long, skinny fingers down into his huge valise and brought out a handful of articles of various kinds, among which were a couple of sickle-teeth, tied together with a string, a horn husking-pin, and a " snack " of chicken covered with bread-crumbs. These caused another laugh, but were suddenly returned to their resting-place and several other dives made into the greasy cavern, evidently to the great discomfiture of the gawky; but he chattered and grinned away, until finally a brand-new pack of cards had been secured.

This was bunglingly opened, the greater portion of the cards slushing out of his hands upon the floor and flying in different directions upon the seat.

To any casual observer it was more than apparent that the poor silly fellow was not more than half-witted, and the fun of it all seemed to lie in his sincerity, which the passengers took for one of the hugest of jokes.

After things had been got to rights—which took the clumsy fellow a long time, during which he enlivened his listeners with his idea of Chicago as a city, its people as sharpers of the first order, and the grandeur of his own great State, Indiana—he selected three cards from the pack, and, wrapping the balance in a dirty bit of brown paper, put them away carefully in the valise.

The three cards selected were the five of spades, the five of clubs and the queen of hearts, and the gentleman from Indiana now began his exposition in real earnest.

" Wy, d'ye know, the durn skunks said they knowed me, 'n' 'fore I knowed what I was a doin' these old friends, as they said they wus, had me bettin' that *I* could jerk up the joker. Now, yer see, fellers," remarked the dealer, as he held up the queen, " they called this keerd the joker, fur why I can't tell yer, lest it's a joke on the dealer if yer picks it up."

" Of course *you* picked it up . Remarked a flashy gentleman, who had the appearance of a successful commercial traveler on a good salary.

Such a look as the dealer gave the man.

"Picked it up !—picked it up ? My friend, mebby you think you're smart enough to pick it up ! Don't you ever squander yer money like I did a-tryin' ! Pick her up ! Pick up hell ! 'Tain't in her to git picked up. She can't be got. Them cussed coons has worked some allfired charm on that durned keerd, so that no man can raise her. Mebby you kin lift the keerd ? She allers wins, she does ; but don't bet nuthin'."

Here the dealer bunglingly shuffled the cards, and made such a mess of it that the effort only brought forth more peals of derisive laughter.

" Now, ye see, fellers," pursued the imperturbable dealer, " this is the five uv spades, hy'r is the five uv clubs, and thar is the rip-roarin' female that wins every time she kin be got. I'm jest a-goin' to skin the boys down hum in Kos-cus-ky County ; fur it's the beautifullest and deceivenst game out ; but," he added, with the solemnity of a parson at a funeral, " fellers, d'ye know I wouldn't hev a friend o' mine bet on this yer game fur anything—not fur a good hoss ! "

He closed this admonitory remark with such a droll wave of his long arm and hand, that a palpable snicker greeted the performance; and the flashy gentleman who had suggested that the greeny must have been able to pick up the card when being entertained by his Chicago friends, bent forward, and after a moment's hesitation over the three cards, which were lying face downward upon the valise, picked up one, which, with an air of triumph, he held aloft for a moment and then slapped down with a great flourish.

This was the "rip-roarin' female that wins every time!" and his honor, the gentleman from Kosciusco County, Indiana, turned white as he observed how neatly her ladyship could be brought to the surface by one of a miscellaneous crowd.

"Jehosiphat!" he exclaimed, as he grabbed the cards and began another bungling shuffle of them—"Jehosiphat! Stranger, d'yer know I've got pea-green scrip in my pocket as says as yer can't do that agin?"

"Oh, I wouldn't take your money!" the flashy man replied, as he nudged a man near him. "'Twouldn't be fair, you know."

"Now—now, see hy'r, stranger," answered the Indianian, "I've told ye already that ye hadn't ought to bet on this deceitful game; but yer is too sassy and bold. Yer thinks yer knows it all, 'n' yer doesn't. Jist wait till I fix the keerds. Thar now! Old Injeanny agin the field!"

The dealer had rearranged the cards in a reckless wild fashion; but there they lay, and the passengers crowded closer and closer about the group to see all the fun that might happen.

Slowly and ungainly enough the dealer reached down into the outside pockets of his homespun suit with both hands. Finding nothing there, he tremulously went into his pantaloons pockets; but he found nothing there.

" Oh, he's a fraud!" suggested a big-bellied man near me, turning to a rural-looking fellow at his side. "Do you know," he continued warmly, "you and I could go in together, and clean that 'old Jasey' out—if he's got any money. But," he added, confidentially, to his companion, "I don't believe he's got a copper; and I wouldn't be surprised if he passed around his hat, begging for car-fare, or lodging, or for his supper-bill, or something of that sort, before he leaves the train. Oh, I've seen too much of that sort of thing, *I* have!"

His companion, whom I had already taken for a country merchant, or something of that kind, as he afterward proved to be, looked nervous, and only replied:

"Wait a bit; let's see what he can find in his clothes. Perhaps these gentlemen wouldn't let us win anything anyhow."

I did not catch the answer, only observing that a pretty good understanding had been arrived at between the two. The party from Indiana by this time, after going through nearly every pocket in his clothing, had brought out from an inside vest-pocket a great, rough, dirty-looking wallet that contained, as could be seen at a glance, a very large though loosely arranged package of green

backs, which he had denominated "pea-green scrip,' and
which he shook out into his broad-rimmed hat at his side
in an alarmingly careless way.

"Thar's what I got left, after comin' outn' that d——d
Gomorer, Chicager!" the dealer said feelingly. "Stock's
down, 'n' grass is dry, but I'll be gol-walloped ef I don't
believe for a hundred-dollar pictur the female boss can't
be lifted agin!"

"I'm your sweet potato—just for once, mind you, just
for once, for I ain't a betting man. But I'll risk that much
just to show you how easily you can be beat at your own
game!" remarked the flashy man, carelessly, at the same
time covering the hundred-dollar "pictur" with ten ten-
dollar bills.

"Can't I go halves on that?" eagerly asked a rough-
looking fellow, who stood on a seat peering over the heads
of the passengers, and at the same time holding up a fifty-
dollar bill.

I saw that the scheme for getting outside parties to bet,
and divide chances with those who considered themselves
"up to the game," was being given a fine impetus.

"Well, I don't mind, although I'm sure of the whole,"
said the flashy party, as he received the fifty dollars nonchalantly.

The honest Granger from Indiana looked dumbfounded
at this new evidence of a want of confidence in his ability, but spoke up cheerily: "Wall, thar's the keerds; yer
kin take yer pick!"

Upon this the flashy party pushed his way into the

The famous Canada Bill at work.

open space, sat down opposite the dealer, and, without any further ado, reached forward with one hand and turned the queen in a twinkling, and raked in the money with the other, immediately rising and handing the party who had taken half the bet the one-hundred-dollar bill, and pocketing the ten ten-dollar bills, and then immediately leaving the luckless dealer, to communicate and comment upon his good fortune to his friends throughout the car and tell them how easily the thing was done.

"Gaul darn the keerds, anyhow!" blurted out the dealer; " the hull cussed thing's gone back on me ; but I swon ef I don't keep the fun a-goin' ! "

Several small bets were made by various parties, the winnings being almost equally divided—if anything, outside parties getting the best of what was to be got.

Suddenly there was a movement near me, and I heard the country merchant remark to his friend :

"Well, I'll go in five hundred with you. Be careful now, be careful ! "

Another "capper" in the crowd, having a Jew in tow, now bet a hundred dollars, and won, dividing the winnings with that party, who received his share with rapturous delight ; and it could be easily seen he was in a fine condition to be "worked."

The large man with the country merchant now stopped and turned to his friend, saying in an undertone : " No, you're a stranger to me, and I'd rather you'd bet the money. We will fix it this way: I'm certain of picking up the card, but I might be mistaken. I'll make two or

9

three small bets first, or enough, so that I can pick up the card. While I have it in my hand, I'll turn one corner under, so that the card, after it is dealt, won't lay down flat. You'll see it plainly, and you can't make a mistake. Now, watch things!"

With this fine piece of bait, the corpulent fellow, who was none other than a "capper," sat down opposite the dealer and made a few small bets. He lost three in quick succession, but on the fourth trial he turned up the queen, and won.

I watched him closely, for I had overheard him state to his dupe that he would mark the card by turning one corner of the same under toward the face. Surely enough, he did so very deftly, and I noticed that the country merchant had also seen the action, for he immediately stepped forward and took the place made vacant for him.

·"Careful now!" said the stout man, as they passed each other.

An answering look from the merchant showed that he considered himself up to a thing or two ; and, as he seated himself, he inquired of the ignorant dealer if he limited his bets

"Ye kin jist bet yer hull pile, or a ten-cent pictur, stranger!" replied that worthy, with a silly, childish chuckle, as he tossed the cards back and forth in a seemingly foolishly-reckless way.

The crowd now pressed forward, all interest and attention. There is always an inexpressible fascination about either winning or losing money. The flush of winning communicates itself to every looker-on, while the wild hunger to get back what one has lost has just as firm a hold upon the bystander as the victim; and one feels almost impelled to try his luck, when he sees that the very fates are all against him.

"Two hundred dollars on the queen!" said the country merchant. laying that amount on the old valise. I noticed that a quick look of intelligence passed between the stout man and the Hoosier dealer. The stout fellow was mistaken in his man. He was betting too low. I made up my mind that his look to the dealer expressed all this with the additional advice: "Let him win a little!"

The money was covered, and the merchant's hands fluttered tremulously over the cards for a moment. But he picked up the queen and won. A buzz of excited comments followed.

"Be ye one o' them Chicager skinners?" asked the dealer. "Confound it! I'm a-gittin' beat right an' left!"

The merchant was flushed with his winnings. He was evidently flattered by being considered so shrewd as a "Chicago skinner." Over behind the front ranks of the lookers-on came a pantomime order from his stout friend, which seemed to me to mean: "Bet heavy while you are in luck."

"You don't limit bets?" asked the merchant eagerly.

"Nary time, nary time. Hyr's a hatful of picturs as backs the winnin' keerd, which is always the queen."

"Well, then," said the dupe with painful slowness, while

the corners of his mouth drew down and his lips became colorless, " I'll bet fifteen hundred dollars I can pick up the queen ! "

There laid one of the cards, showing it had been doubled enough to prevent its resting flatly upon the old valise. The merchant counted out the money in a husky voice, making several errors, and being corrected by some of the passengers. The dealer, who might have had just a trace of a glitter in his black, fishy eyes, groped around among his " picturs " and provided an equal amount. Every person in the car bent forward, and in a painful, breathless silence awaited the result.

" Yer pays yer money, 'n' yer takes yer choice ! " remarked the dealer, leaning back in his seat, and whistling as unconcernedly as if at a town-meeting.

The merchant leaned forward. He looked at the cards as though his very soul had leaped into his eyes. He suddenly grasped the card that refused to lie flatly upon the valise, and turned it over.

He had picked up the five of clubs, and had lost !

Something like a moan escaped the poor victim's lips. My own blood boiled to rescue him from this villainous robbery. I could not do it without jeopardizing far greater interests, but my heart bled for him in his misery.

" I'm a ruined man ! " he gasped, and then staggered through the crowd to sink into a vacant seat.

Even then he could not be left alone. His stout friend, the " capper," sought him out and upbraided him for his foolishness in picking up the wrong card and losing *his* five hundred dollars with his own. He even begged him to try again, and, finding that he had a few hundred dollars left out of what he was going to New York to buy goods with, cursed him because he would not risk that in order to retrieve himself and pay him back his money, which the reader will readily understand already belonged to the honest, simple-hearted Hoosier who was manipulating the cards.

But the game went on. The loss of so great a sum of money put rather a dampener upon it; but the " cappers " came to the rescue with twenty, fifty, and one hundred dollar bets, which were so rapidly won that the Jew was at last " worked " out of six hundred dollars in two quick bets of three hundred each; and amid a great row and racket which he made over his loss, the voice of the brakeman could be heard, crying out :

" Valparaiso ! Twenty minutes for supper ! "

Not a minute more had passed, and the train had not even come to a halt, when every one of the nefarious gang had disappeared.

The flashy man, with the look of a successful commercial traveler, was gone ; the stout man, who had " stood in " with the country merchant, had gone ; the party who had entertained the Jew was gone ; and the honest, simple, cheery countryman from Kosciusko County, Indiana, with his cavernous valise half full of loose bills, which he had not even taken time to arrange in the old book for carrying in his side-pocket—and who was none other than the notorious " Canada Bill "—was gone. They were all gone, and they had taken from their dupes from eighteen hundred to two thousand dollars.

I could not but pity the poor victims, who were left on the train to brood over their foolishness; but at the same time a sense of justice stole in upon my sympathy. Every one of these dupes had got beaten at his own game. They were just as dishonest as the men who fleeced them. They would not have risked a dollar had they not, one and all, believed that they had the advantage of a poor, foolish fellow. If he *had* been what they believed, and they had won his money, it would have been robbery just as much as it was robbery to take their money as neatly and easily as it was taken.

Just after the close of the war Canada Bill, in company with a river gambler, named George Devol, or "Uncle George," as he had a fondness for being called, started for the South, and began operating in and about New Orleans. This George Devol was himself a character, as he had once been a station-agent of some railroad in Minnesota, and on being "braced" and beaten out of his own and considerable of the company's funds, had such an admiration for the manner in which he had been beaten, that he turned out a gambler himself, and became quite well known along the lower Mississippi.

The two men, in company with one Jerry Kendricks, did an immense business in New Orleans, in the city, upon the boats, and on the different railroad lines running out of that place. Here, in New Orleans, Bill was the green, rollicking, back-country planter, and nearly always made his appearance upon a boat or a train as though he had had a narrow escape from a gang of cut-throats, but was in high glee over the fact that they had not stolen quite all of his money, and had left him a fine package of tin-ware, two or three packages of cow-hide shoes, large enough for a Louisiana negro, and a side or two of bacon. Old "Ben" Burnish, a character well known among sporting men in the North, was one of his most accomplished "cappers" during these days, and the gang made vast sums of money.

But finally "Uncle George" Devol hoped to get the best of Bill, he was so careless and really ingenuous among his friends ; and, knowing that he carried a twenty-five hundred dollar roll, got a man and arranged things to beat him. Through his wonderful faculty for reading people and character, Bill permitted the play, and when his opponent won, remarked quietly : " George, you sized my pile pretty well, and got things fixed nice. Your friend will find that roll the smallest twenty-five hundred dollar pot he ever grabbed. Good-by, Uncle George ! "

Bill having arranged a " road-roll," or a showy pile of bills of small denomination, was willing to expend that much to ascertain definitely that Devol had played him false, and immediately took leave of him forever.

When the Union and Central Pacific Railroads were in process of construction, this field proved a grand harvest for Canada Bill ; and, on leaving the South, where he at one time owned nearly half of a town at the mouth of the

Red River, he proceeded to Kansas City, where, with " Dutch Charlie " as principal "pal," he certainly must have won from a hundred and fifty to two hundred thou- sand dollars.

From Kansas City he went to Omaha, and drifted back and forth between these points for some time, never failing to win money where he attempted, becoming a perfect scourge to the railroad companies and travelers, but, strangely enough, establishing the highest regard among all business men with whom he came in contact, hardly one of whom would not have taken his word for almost any amount of money.

The man did not seem to realize what money was worth, and gave it to anybody that might ask it. It has been related by those who should be capable of judging, that Bill gave away, gambled, or foolishly expended, fully a quarter of a million dollars.

On one occasion, in Omaha, some policemen, having a spite against Bill, arrested him and brought him before a police magistrate. He was fined fifty dollars.

Bill, rising in the box, with one of his most droll and happy expressions of voice and face, asked :

" Jedge, who does the money go to ? "

" This class of fines goes to the school fund. Why ? " replied the justice.

" Wall, I reckon ef it goes to so good a cause as that, you can chalk her up to a hundred and fifty, jedge ! " and Bill put down the money and left the court.

But finally his prowess became so great and the win

nings of his crowd so large upon the Union Pacific Railroad, that a general order of the strictest terms was
issued forbidding any monte-players riding or playing on
the trains of the road, and instructing conductors, on peril
of dismissal, to eject them from the cars at all risks and
with whatever force might be required. It was upon the
appearance of this order that Bill wrote—or caused to be
written, as he could not write his own name—his noted
impudent proposition to the general superintendent of
that road, in which he offered the company ten thousand
dollars per annum, if he were given the sole right to throw
three-card monte on the Union Pacific trains, and
making his offer more attractive by pledging his word
that he would confine his professional attentions ex-
clusively to Chicago commercial travelers and Methodist
preachers.

It is unnecessary to add that Bill's proposition did
not receive the attention which he imagined it deserved.

After this, in 1874, in company with "Jim" Porter
and the veteran gambler, "Colonel" Charlie Starr,
Canada Bill proceeded to Chicago, where, by means
best known to this class, he secured an understanding
with the police, and at once opened four "joints," or
playing-places, and soon had half the "bunko" men in
Chicago "steering" for him. The following lines, from
the Chicago *Tribune*, of August 7, 1874, were in his
honor, although his name was not mentioned. They are
entitled :

9*

JONES OF KALAMAZOO.

It was an ancient Farmer Man
  Who was stopped by one of three.
" By thy black moustache and oroide ring,
  Now wherefore stopp'st thou me ? "
" Hail, Mr. Smith ; hail, Mr. Smith !
  What news from Kankakee ? "

Then up and spake the Farmer Man :
  " Mistaken ye mote be,
I am not Smith, nor have I kith
  Nor kin in Kankakee ;
But I till the soil in Kalamazoo
  And my name is Jones—John P."

The Stranger Man apologized :
  " I'm sorry that I did
Mistake you, sir, for my friend Smith ;
  Excuse me ! " and he slid.

It was that ancient Farmer Man
  Was stopped by the second of three ;
" By thy blonde moustache and Alaska pie,
  Now wherefore stopp'st thou me ? "
" Why, welcome Jones, of Kalamazoo,
  Dost thou remember me ?

" Thou dost not ?—not remember Brown ?
  Strange, strange ! but I do thee ;
Nor shalt thou quit me till thou drain
  A friendly cup with me.
Some news would I of Kalamazoo,
  And friends that thereat be !

" The bar-room doors are open wide,
    And we must go therein;
A health I claim ! come, give it name ;
    Or whisky, beer, or gin ? "
And the Farmer hoar his fingers four
    He loyally hoisted in.

·Twas then the ancient Farmer Man
    Beheld a carl * full drunk,
Who at a table in the room,
    Had negligently sunk.

His hair was grizzled, beard unshorn,
    His eyes were red and blear,
His whole appearance spoke him one
    That drives the Texan steer,
And full well grips the blacksnake whips
    A merry bull-whackeer.

And still he hiccupped, still he reeled,
    And muttered, " Woe is me !
For I have lost of dollars a host
    A-bucking the paste-boards three;
Yea, *this* is the way them thieves did play
    The sinful three-card monte."

And still he shuffled and chuckled eke:
    "There's a Jack, a Seven, a Three,
And spotting the Three, the Seven, the Jack,
    Them gamblers they plundered me; "
While under, and over, and under again,
    He threw the three-card monte.

* " Carl "—Countryman, greeny.

And youths and men who sat around
 Did wagers with him lay ;
And which was the Jack, the Seven, the Three,
 Infallibly did say,
While he lost his pile with maudlin smile
 And muttered, " Thazzer way ! "

Who was it then but pseudo Brown
 To the Farmer whispered, " See !
Drunk as a loon this herder of mules
 And possessed of much monie.
Others already are in the field,
 Why here stand idle we ? "

And who was it but the pseudo Brown
 That betting did begin,
And laid a C with the Texan clown
 And eke the same did win,
While nudging Sir Jones of Kalamazoo,
 And bidding him "go in ! "

But the gentle heart of the guileless Jones
 Rebelled against the game ;
Quoth he, with a smile, " I'll win his pile,
 But will not keep the same,
But will it return with a lecture stern,
 And put him thus to shame ! "

And lo, the merry bull-whacker
 A card did careless spill,
And his nerveless fingers could not grasp
 The Seven and Jack until
The pseudo Brown had marked the Three
 Plain with his lead-pencil.

Then up and spake the gallant Jones,
  " These bills I wager thee,
That I can pick the Trey from out
  The shuffled paste-boards three."
And the Texan clown put his money down
  And said, " Thou art meat for me ! "

Over and under he threw the cards,
  Under and over and back ;
Jones laid his finger on that one
  Scored with a cross so black ;
"'Tis the Three ! " he cried, with honest pride.
  But lo ! it was the Jack !

. . . . . .

At Kalamazoo, a Farmer Man
  May at this day be seen,
Who talks of Sodom and Babylon
  As one who has therein been,
And frowns at the sight of his lambkins white
  When they gambol on the green.

It is estimated that he made fully one hundred and
fifty thousand dollars in Chicago ; but as he was an invet-
erate gambler himself, and played into faro banks nearly
all he took at monte, he left that city comparatively
" broke," and, in company with " Jim " and Alick Porter,
went to Cleveland, where his last active work was done.

Countless instances are related of the shrewdness and
success of this strange man.   Among his kind he was king
and I have only given this sketch of him as illustrative of
a striking type of a dangerous class, still powerful and

cunning, which the public would do well to avoid in whatever guise they may appear.

Canada Bill, after an unprecedently successful career of over twenty years in America, died a pauper—as nearly every one of all the criminal classes do—at the Charity Hospital, in Reading, Pennsylvania, in the summer of 1877.

———•———

CHAPTER XIII.

REMARKABLE PRISON ESCAPES.

I AM certain that my readers will be interested in the recital of a few instances within my recollection where criminals, either convicts or prisoners awaiting trial for general offenses, have escaped their prison confines in a most ingenious and dramatic manner.

On July 8, 1878, the city of Columbus, Ohio, was startled by a report that some forty prisoners, confined at the State penitentiary there, had escaped, and were "making a lively trial for tall timber" in all directions. A visit to the penitentiary proved that the reports were greatly magnified. Only three prisoners had escaped, but these had shown an amount of enterprise in getting outside of the walls that was truly remarkable.

It was found, too, that even the three did not make their escape together, but that one had got out the previous night. He had been recaptured, and was once more a prisoner, although the other two were still at lib

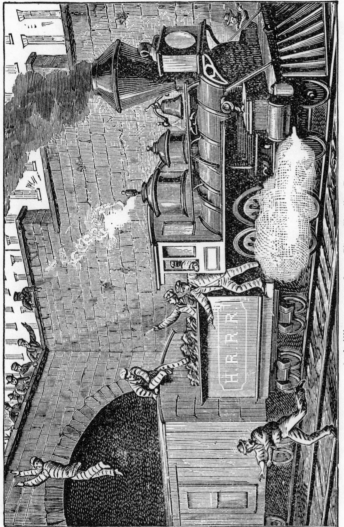

"A thrilling escape from Sing Sing." —Page.—

erty   The one that had been recaptured had occupied a
cell in one of the tiers of cell-houses on which the State
was then placing a new roof.   He managed, in some way,
to dig out of his cell and gain access to the roof.   A
large derrick for elevating stone, used in the walls during
the day, stood against the prison, but at night was pulled
back quite a distance from it.   The prisoner stood on top
of the wall, and, calculating the distance in the darkness,
made a leap, the like of which has never been attempted
by any acrobat on earth, and, after descending at least
thirty feet through the air, caught the derrick-rope and
slid down the remaining distance, making his escape
unobserved.

What nerve and actual bravery were required for this !
The convict risked his life more surely than if taking his
chances in battle.   The slightest miscalculation, the
merest mischance, the least failure in estimating his
power for leaping, would have caused him to have fallen
a mangled corpse upon the stones below.

But all this daring brought no reward to the poor
fellow, for he was captured on the Pan Handle Road,
near Summit Station, not ten hours subsequent to his
marvelous escape.

The other men did not show as much daring in their
escape, but even more shrewdness and ingenuity.   They
were engaged cutting stone just north of the penitentiary
Through the aid of friends they supplied themselves with
citizens' clothing, which they secreted in a closet near
where they were working, and leaped from this into a sewer

leading into the Scioto River. As soon as they reached the bank, they stripped off their prison garb, and, donning their citizens' clothing, strolled leisurely away. For all that is known, they are still leisurely strolling, as they have never been recaptured.

Cne of the most desperate prison escapes ever known was made from Sing Sing prison on the morning of May 14, 1875, and would have ended disastrously to more than a score of lives had it not been for the presence of mind of Dennis Cassin, a Hudson River Railroad engineer.

Just north of Sing Sing prison, between the extreme northern guard-house and the arched railway bridge, as you go south, is located the prison quarry, on the east side of the railroad track. From it, over the railroad track, on the west side, extends a bridge over which stone from the quarry is trundled in wheelbarrows by the convicts.

At about eight o'clock, on the morning mentioned, an extra freight train, bound south, slowly approached the prison bridge. The train was drawn by " No. 89," Dennis Cassin, engineer. They were slowly following the regular passenger train from Sing Sing to New York, which had left a few moments before. As the engine reached the trestle, or prison bridge, five convicts suddenly dropped upon it, from the bridge above ; they were led by the notorious "Steve" Boyle and Charles Woods.

Four of them ran into the engineer's cab, while the other hastened to the coupling which attached the train to the engine. The convicts on the cab, with drawr revolvers, ordered the engineer and fireman to jump off, which they did, when the convicts put on steam, and the engine started down the road at lightning speed.

Their escape was detected almost immediately, and several shots were fired after them by the prison-guard, but without effect. Then began the pursuit. The superintendent of the raiload was notified quickly, when a telegraph alarm was sounded at all points south of Sing Sing. A dispatch was sent to the Tarrytown agent directing him to turn the switch at that station on the river side, so as to let the engine, with the convicts on board, jump the bank and plunge into the river. Danger signals were also ordered to be set on the down track, and prompt measures of every kind were taken to prevent danger from collision with the stolen locomotive. The trackmen in the vicinity of Scarborough saw the engine coming like lightning, or rather saw a vast cloud of smoke and steam and water, whirl by with a deafening roar, and gazed with terror at the frightful speed the engine had attained. At Tarrytown crowds of people were gathered, expecting to see the engine dash into the station, and off the switch into the river; but it did not arrive.

After waiting a short time, the Tarrytown agent sent an engine cautiously up the road to look for the stolen property; and "No. 89" was finally found, with both cylinder-heads broken, three miles north and opposite the "Aspinwall Place." The boiler was full of water and the steam down. The convicts had left the disabled engine a half mile further north, and had disappeared into the dense Aspinwall woods, having first stolen all the clothing which could be found in the engineer's and fire man's boxes in the tender.

Engineer Cassin's wonderful presence of mind undoubtedly prevented a large destruction of property and human life. He was surrounded by the four convicts before being conscious of it, and could feel the cold muzzles of their revolvers against his head. Instantly after he realized what had occurred.

"Get off! get off!" the desperate men shouted. They did get off, and that right lively; but Cassin did not turn from his place until he had prevented disaster. Just before the convicts jumped into the cab, he had three gauges of water in the boiler, and had shut off the pumps; but, as he turned to go when ordered, he shoved the pumps full on, the convicts not noticing the movement. The desperadoes undoubtedly pulled the throttle-valve wide open when they started, and for a little time the engine attained a terrific speed; but finally the cylinders got so full that both heads were blown out, or broken, and that necessarily ended the trip.

None of the daring fellows were immediately recaptured, but the eventual return of the leader of the escapade was effected through my office; and how it all came about necessitates a short sketch of "Steve" Boyle, the leading and most desperate spirit in the escape just narrated.

Boyle is a noted "houseworker," or house-burglar, and general thief, and has nearly always been brilliant and successful in whatever he has undertaken. His work was principally done in the East, until 1867, when that part of the country became too warm for him, and, in company with his "gang," consisting of "Bob" Taylor, "Tom" Fitzgerald, *alias* "Big Fitz," and William ———, *alias* "Black Bill," he removed to Chicago.

Their first operation in that city was very unfortunate for Boyle. They were "working" a residence in the West Division, and Boyle was "doing" the rooms and passing the plunder out to his confederates, when, being very weak from a severe attack of the asthma, he made a misstep, stumbled, dropped his revolver, and caused such a noise that in an instant the gentleman of the house was upon him with a cocked revolver in his hand, and effected his capture easily.

As he was then comparatively unknown in the West, on the plea of ill-health, first offense, respectable parents, and the like, he succeeded in escaping with a sentence of but one year's imprisonment at Joliet, Illinois.

His comrades now employed every effort in their power to secure a pardon for Boyle, using large sums of money for this purpose; but this failing, they eventually found a way of conveying money to him within the penitentiary. Whether or not this was more powerful than whatever instruments to effect his escape Boyle may have secured, I cannot say; but, at all events, a plan of escape was determined on, which proved successful; and, on a certain night, Boyle, at the head of eleven other convicts, made their way from the cells up into one of the guard

towers used for the sentry, and thence, in some mysterious manner, which has never since been fully explained,
not only made good their escape, but carried away all
the arms—quite a number—which were stored in the
tower.

Boyle's hard luck seemed about equal to his good for
tune and ability to conquer difficulties.

The second day after escaping from the Illinois peni
tentiary, as he needed money, himself and another of the
escaped prisoners were arrested in Chicago while in the
act of "tapping" the till of a North Side German gro-
cery. They were locked up for the night together at one
of the North Side stations. Boyle's companion was possessed of a terrible fear that he would be recognized and
returned to Joliet.

"Oh, I'll fix all that!" said Boyle jauntily; and forth-
with he set to work and gave his ex-convict comrade
such a pummeling, disfiguring his face and blacking his
eyes, that his own mother would not have recognized
him.

The next morning they were put in charge of separate
policemen, who started with their prisoners for the police
court on the South Side. The officer in charge of Boyle
was a huge German, weighing fully two hundred and
twenty-five pounds. When the two had arrived at a
point on North Wells Street, near the river, Boyle's keen
eyes discovered a house of disreputable character, which
he had formerly frequented. A negress, a servant at the
establishment, was scrubbing the steps in the early morn-

ing before the inmates had arisen, and the basement-door stood wide open. As quick as thought, Boyle planted a terrific blow squarely in the big Dutch policeman's belly, doubling him up like a stage harlequin going backward through a trap, and then, leaping over and beyond the horrified black woman at one bound, darted into the house, and shut and bolted the door behind him. Then he sped through the basement to the rear of the house and escaped. His companion, who had been herded in the "bull-pen" along with the regular daily collection of petty offenders, was finally brought before the police justice, and the grocery-man whose till had been robbed failing to identify him, he was fined five dollars, as a simple case of "drunk," on general principles. The fine was paid by some of his friends, who had learned of his predicament, and thus he too escaped.

About this time the other portion of Boyle's gang had endeavored to rob a bank at Schoolcraft, Michigan. They had succeeded in getting into the vault, and had already got open the outer door to a large safe standing within it, when a sleigh-riding party, out on a lark, came dashing up to a point near the bank, shouting and hallooing in a boisterous and roystering fashion. The thieves, thinking they had been discovered, fled from the place, leaving their tools and their nearly secured booty behind them.

From here they went to Kalamazoo, Michigan, and, securing new tools from Chicago, made an attempt to rob a bank there, but were all arrested, and, being recognized as the parties engaged in the unsuccessful Schoolcraft job, were held without bail.

Through a friend in Kalamazoo who was then closely allied with rogues of this class, but who is now a respected citizen of that city, word of their misfortune was conveyed to Boyle in Chicago, who, with a New York thief named Harry Darrah, returned the cheering intelligence that they would be over to Kalamazoo on a certain night, and give them "a break," that is, liberate them.

On the night in question, true to their word, Boyle and Darrah got so far toward the liberation of their friends as to have passed pistols and small steel saws in to them in the jail, when Colonel Orcutt, the sheriff, whose apartments were in the jail building, discovered the efforts being made, and, coming upon the scene *en dishabille*, with cocked revolver in hand, endeavored to arrest the jail breakers.

The men instantly fled, Colonel Orcutt pursuing. He ordered them to halt, but they did not comply; and he began firing upon them, succeeding in shooting Darrah's hat from his head. This only had the effect to increase his efforts to escape. Boyle, whose chronic asthma made it impossible for him to run any distance, suddenly dodged behind a tree, unperceived by the sheriff, and, when the latter passed him in hot pursuit of Darrah, the cowardly ruffian Boyle fired upon him, shooting him through the spine, and effecting a wound from which Colonel Orcutt died twelve hours after. Darrah skulked about the place for a few days, and finally disappeared, while Boyle, on the same night, secreted himself upon an eastern-bound freight-train, went to Detroit, and from thence into Canada, where, after remaining under cover for a few weeks, he proceeded to New York, being soon after rejoined by Darrah, who was subsequently arrested for pocket-picking, and, being identified, was returned to Kalamazoo, where he made a full confession, implicating Boyle in the murder of Colonel Orcutt.

He eluded arrest, however, for nearly a year, when, his bad fortune following him, he was captured in New York while attempting to do what is known as the "butcher-cart job." This is effected in the following manner :

At a time of the year when street doors of jeweler shops are usually closed throughout the day as well as the evening, a common grocer's, or delivery wagon of any sort, but always selected for its easy-running qualities, and to which is always attached a fast horse, will be driven up to the vicinity of some jewelry-store, which has already been fixed upon, and which always has a fine display in the window This wagon will invariably contain one, and sometimes two persons, aside from the driver. In the meantime a confederate of this "butcher-cart gang" slips up to the door of the shop in question, and deftly inserts a wooden peg or wedge beneath the door, between that and the sill, driving it home with his heel or in any other manner possible. The moment this is done another of the gang at one stroke smashes in the entire window, and the two then grab whatever they can lay their hands upon, always of course selecting that which is the most valuable, and rush to the covered wagon in waiting, when, with their booty, they are driven rapidly away, nine times out of ten getting wholly beyond pursuit before the astonished and shut-in shopmen are able to get their own door open.

It was while Boyle was conducting an operation of this kind that he was captured, and, rather than be conveyed to Michigan, to answer the charge of murder, he made no defense, but pleaded guilty to everything brought against him, and was finally sentenced to twenty years' imprisonment at Sing Sing.

It was the boast of himself and his friends that no prison had been built strong enough to hold him, and a special guard was for a time placed over him.

Illustrative of the man's cunning is the fact that, one day, while being so watched, he slipped his jacket and hat upon a broom standing near, and then, noiselessly placing it where he had sat, stole away from his guard entirely. It was some minutes before the watchful guard discovered the trick which had been played upon him, and Boyle had made so good a use of his time that eight hours had elapsed before he was found. He had secreted himself in the prison, with the hope of escaping the same night.

The next instance in Boyle's career worthy of note was the planning and execution of the desperate escape from Sing Sing upon the engine " No. 89," as has been related.

In company with Charles Woods, one of the convicts escaping with him on that occasion, Boyle then secured a " kit " of burglar's tools, and the two proceeded to St Louis, where they began operating upon small safes in real estate and brokers' offices. They deposited their tools in what they believed to be a deserted carpenter's shop. The proprietors, returning unexpectedly, discovered the tools, and, informing the police, a detail of officers was at once made to lie in wait for the owners of the suspicious goods, who returned, and, before being given time to explain any-thing, were unmercifully clubbed and taken into custody.

The men being utter strangers to the St. Louis author-ities, were only given six months in the workhouse. Their pictures were taken, however, and, a set coming into my office, that of Boyle was recognized, when, on his being fully identified by my son, William A. Pinkerton, he was returned to Sing Sing, where, fortunately for society in general, he is now serving his unexpired term of twenty years' imprisonment.

In 1870 George White, *alias* George Miles, *alias* George Bliss, made one of the most remarkably brilliant prison escapes on record.

He had, in company with one Joe Howard, another bank burglar, robbed the bank of an interior New York town, and, securing a noted race-horse of the locality in escaping from the place, ran the animal nearly thirty miles at its fullest speed, until it fell to the earth from sheer exhaustion. The men then brutally cut the throat of the horse, leaving it dying. The men were subse-quently captured, convicted, and incarcerated in Sing Sing. While here, White made the acquaintance and friendship of a noted character, named Cramer, familiarly called Doctor Dyonissius Cramer, or "the Long Doctor,"

10

now a reformed thief, but in his day one of the cleverest known " stalls " of the " bank-sneak gangs." This " Long Doctor" had a peculiarly inventive genius, and I am happy to say that now, as he has become an honest man, it is securing for him considerable wealth.

His familiarity with White resulted in his inventing— more as a curious experiment than anything else—a hollow rubber apparatus, which, when completed, had the exact appearance of a very large decoy duck. This was also provided with rubber tubes for breathing through ; and one morning, when a party of convicts were working along the docks by the side of the river, White, who had secreted the contrivance in his clothing, at an opportune moment adjusted it, and, slipping into the water, calmly floated down the Hudson, passing within twenty feet of the guards, thus making his escape.

His recapture would have been certain, but Colonel Whitley, then Chief of the Secret Service, made such strong representations to the Government authorities that his use by the Government in ferreting out several important counterfeiting cases would be valuable, that he eventually secured for him from the Governor of New York a free pardon. The value of his subsequent services may be inferred when it is stated that Colonel Whitley used him as one of the chief actors in the infamous sham robbery of the safe of the district attorney's office in Washington, when it was sought to ruin the Hon. Columbus Alexander, who was nobly fighting the Washington ring and its corruptions.

CHAPTER XIV.

AN INSURANCE CONSPIRACY FOILED.

OF al. species of business there is none so liable to the machinations of dishonest persons as the insurance. The large sums which are often secured from death or loss, with the undeniable obligations which the companies labor under to cancel their indebtedness, upon the showing of good and sufficient causes for the same, are incentives that have often urged men to employ their ingenuity and villainy in endeavors to defraud insurance companies. There may be something like a law of compensation about this kind of swindling, as the insurance business itself has harbored most accomplished scamps, and presented to the world about as brilliant schemes of commercial piracy as have come to light in any other kind of business. Of these instances Dickens has given us the type in " Martin Chuzzlewit," in the operations of Montague Tiggs, Anglo-Bengalee Disinterested Loan and Life Insurance Company ; and, as an illustration of the consummate plans for defrauding honestly-conducted insurance companies, the following case, where I was fortu nately able to defeat an exceedingly clever scheme of fraud, will stand as an interesting illustration cf conspiracies against such corporations.

In the month of June, 1866, one Monroe Rigger, a sailor, at that time a resident of Chicago, called at the office of a certain life insurance company, and effected an insurance upon his life for the sum of five thousand dollars. For this policy he paid the sum of thirty dollars. This was an ordinary case of insurance, and comprehended only such accidents and disasters as one is ordinarily exposed to on shore.

A few days afterward he returned to the insurance office, and expressed a desire to have the terms of the policy altered, as he wished to sail upon the lakes during the months of September and October. This permission was granted upon the payment of an extra ten dollars, and a new policy, covering accidents on the lake during those two months, was issued. On the very next day he returned to the office, and informed the officers that he had concluded to sail during the entire season, having secured a position on a vessel, and that he wished the policy changed from a special to an extra-hazardous one, in order to guard against his increased liability to accidents and dangers. Upon the payment of twenty dollars additional, the extra guarantee was granted, and Rigger took his departure. This was the last the company ever saw of him.

On August 8th following, Mrs. Susan Rigger, the wife of Monroe Rigger, called at the office of the insurance company, and informed the officers that her husband, who held a policy in their company, had been drowned. This lady was dressed in mourning, and told a straightforward story.

She stated that her husband had been drowned in Lake

Erie on the night of July 20th, about fifteen miles north west of Cleveland, while sailing on the brig " Mechanic,' James Todd, master. There was no constraint or indica- tions of dishonesty in her statement. She further said that on the evening in question her husband, acting under instructions from his superior officer, had gone out on the bowsprit of the ship to adjust the rigging ; that his foot suddenly slipped, precipitating him into the lake ; and that efforts were made to save him, but all in vain.

To substantiate her story, she furnished several affi- davits, duly attested and authenticated, corroborating the details of her husband's death. These affidavits were fur- nished by persons who professed to have seen Rigger fall into the lake, and were signed by the owner of the brig— an old and respectable citizen of Chicago, largely identi- fied with shipping interests—the captain, the mate, the helmsman, and several others, all evidently trustworthy and reliable persons. Their affidavits certainly were de- serving of consideration ; but, in accordance with their usual custom, the officers desired time to look into the matter, and they dismissed the lady, requesting her to call again.

This was all the information that came to me about the matter, with a request from the company that I should make a speedy and most rigid investigation ; and I confess that, when I first gave the subject a cursory examination, I saw nothing about it which did not have a clean and straight appearance. But upon perusing the affidavits, certain little discrepancies therein began to excite my curiosity. I began to see that the name of a certain Joseph Wagner, mate of the brig " Mechanic,' from which it was alleged that Rigger had been lost, appeared with a frequency, which, to say the least, was noticeable.

The affidavits were taken before a magistrate in Buffalo ; and I at once dispatched a keen, careful man to that city, who soon returned with the information that this Joseph Wagner, mate of the brig, who had become fixed in my mind as in some way mixed up with the matter, if it should be found that it was tainted with fraud, had been chiefly instrumental in procuring the affidavits. He had been present when they were made, had signed one of them himself, had defrayed the expenses of executing them, and had finally brought them to Chicago to Mrs. Rigger. Here was a circumstance, trivial enough in itself, easily accounted for on the ground of solicitude for the widow of a deceased comrade, and might seem to have no special relation to the case ; but it continued to strongly impress me. I *felt* that this man had exhibited too great an officiousness. He had been at too much trouble ; he had expended too much money for a wholly disinterested party.

Besides all this, the haste which had been exercised in securing the affidavits was worthy of notice. It occurred to me that sailors, as a rule, are easy-going fellows, and they seldom do things in a hurry. The " Mechanic " had hardly reached Buffalo before Wagner had set about securing evidence of Rigger's death. These papers had been immediately forwarded to Mrs. Rigger, so that she had been able to call at the insurance office within a very few days after the alleged drowning of Rigger and some time before the "Mechanic" returned to Chicago. In my mind this was another noticeable feature of the case. It might be, I even reasoned, that there had been murder done; that Mrs. Rigger had conceived an unlawfu' affection for this mate, Joseph Wagner; that the two had not conspired against the insurance company so much as against the life of the husband whom the woman had urged to become insured, so that should he *happen* to fall overboard while in Wagner's company, there would be a snug little sum coming to the two; and that the whole thing, from beginning to end, was a terrible plan to both get rid of an obnoxious person and secure a small fortune.

In any event, I could not but couple the mate of the "Mechanic" and Mrs. Rigger in a conspiracy, either against the company, in which case Rigger himself had joined in a conspiracy against the life of the latter; or, indeed, in a conspiracy against the company, in which Rigger had readily joined, but which might not have been wholly understood by him, and which was wedded to the darker crime that had been privately planned by his wife and friend, and too well executed by the friend.

In casting about for a starting-point in detective operations, wherever a crime is to be unraveled, one of the most essential things to be done is to determine what motives probably caused the commission of the crime.

When the causes leading to a crime are fully known **half** your work is done, for you then at once know *how to go to work.*

I determined to ascertain what relations existed between Mrs. Rigger and the mate Wagner. I found that Mrs. Rigger lived in a quiet, respectable manner, as befitted the wife of a sailor, and no suspicious circumstance could be developed against her, although I felt that the facts justified keeping a strict surveillance upon her.

The reader will recollect that, on account of Wagner's great haste in securing proof of the sailor's death, there had been both time for Mrs. Rigger to make her application at the insurance office for her five thousand dollars, and for me to get a man to Buffalo and return with the information referred to.

I had also taken means to ascertain that Wagner had left Buffalo on the return trip in the "Mechanic," and of the date of her probable arrival in Chicago. So, finding the owner of the brig, I easily made arrangements to be informed of her arrival in port, as well as to ship a man as a common sailor upon her, on her second trip to Buffalo, should I so desire.

When the "Mechanic" arrived, Wagner, as soon as his duties would permit, went straight to Mrs. Rigger's house. He remained inside but a few hours, and made his exit upon the street with a thoughtful, anxious face. In the little time he had been in the house I had taken measures which conclusively proved to me that no criminal intimacy existed between the mate and the alleged

widow Rigger, and this clearly demonstrated that no conspiracy by the two against the life of the missing sailor
had been entered into.

If there had been a conspiracy, I concluded that it had
been between the entire three against the company ; and
as a persistent watching of the house had failed to discover the arrival of Rigger, who, I hoped, might secretly
reappear, I knew that the only way to get a hold upon
the shrewd trio was to fall back upon my old and successful plan of placing some person, capable of winning
and holding Wagner's confidence, with him, which I had
already provided ; for, as will presently be seen, in the
person of an operative named Dick Hamilton—since lost
at sea, poor fellow !—who seemed to possess a combination of every known interesting trait of the Irish character.

Generous, brave, faithful, cunning ; full of unconquer-
able antics and irrepressible humor ; quick as lightning at
repartee or jest ; but possessing good judgment ; a great
traveler and salt-water sailor ; and withal the biggest liar
on earth when it came to a cock-and-bull story, or to a
match at story-telling : this was the man I had detailed
to operate upon Wagner, and that individual, with a worried look upon his face, had not been absent from Mrs.
Rigger's humble dwelling half an hour when the two had
become firm friends.

Wagner, with his worry upon him, had stepped into one
of those saloons along the wharves of great cities where
sailors and their friends congregate, to get a glass of grog,

10*

and, being in a rather ugly frame of mind from receiving the ill-tidings from Mrs. Rigger that there was a suspicious delay in the payment of the insurance money, was in no mood for joking. As the place was full of carous ing sailors, some silly drunken remark was made to him, which he resented. In a moment the place was in an uproar; Wagner was violently assaulted, and only rescued from a hard drubbing by Hamilton, who laid out the assailing parties right and left, and finally got Wagner away in safety.

He was very grateful of course, and finding, according to Hamilton's story, that he was a salt-water sailor and a great fellow altogether, and had come to Chicago with a little money ahead, not caring where his fortunes took him, a great friendship immediately sprang up between the two; and it was arranged, over many and copious glasses, that Hamilton and Wagner should pass the time together while in port, and that my operative should then ship with Wagner on the brig "Mechanic" for the trip to Buffalo and return; when, if everything still went well between them, they would join fortunes and sail regularly together.

The "Mechanic" and its crew remained in port but three days; but during that time enough came to the surface to show me conclusively that I was upon the right track, and that it was but a question of time when my shrewd Irish operative would unearth the mystery en-shrouding the sailor's supposed death.

Hamilton became a welcome visitor at Mrs. Rigger's

cottage the next day after making Wagner's acquaintance. Not a single thing could be seen to warrant a suspicion of wrong between the woman and the mate, with the exception of several private and earnest interviews between the two, during which an occasional unguarded word was let fall which showed that some new move was on hand. This was made plain on the third day, just before the vessel left, when Wagner and Mrs. Rigger visited a lawyer's office and began suit against the company for the payment of the policy. They felt so certain of the strength of their plans that they were either willing that the whole matter should be raked up, or they hoped to force the payment of the money by a show of fight.

In the meantime Wagner and Hamilton got along famously.

Dick, who had become acquainted with the entire brig's crew, from captain to cook, made things lively for them all. A book would not have held the infernal lies that he told, and not all of the sparkling " Irish Dragoon" contains such irresistible wit and droll humor as he was capable of, on the least pretext, so that before the " Mechanic" sailed every man on board was in love with Dick and congratulating Wagner on finding such a capital fellow for the voyage. Of course Wagner felt flattered and glad at the turn matters had taken, and seemed to begin to place great confidence in his new found friend. When drinking, as is quite common with sailors when ashore, he made great promises for himself and friend, and hinted in various ways that before the season was over he would command a first-class vessel himself, and would make Hamilton no less than mate.

One trip was made to Buffalo without result, so far as the operation was concerned, save that Wagner seemed drawn closer and closer to his companion. They became greater friends than ever; but Wagner had not got wholly ready to trust him. In a hundred ways he endeavored to test him as to his being one he could trust and *use*, and during the trip gradually unfolded a scheme to rob a brother-in-law of Mrs. Rigger's, an honest and hard-working mechanic in Milwaukee.

The wife of this man frequently visited her sister, Mrs. Rigger, in Chicago, and Wagner had in some way learned that the couple, by years of hard labor, had saved several hundred dollars, and kept the same in a certain bureau drawer. As the husband was compelled to leave the house at an unusually early hour in the morning to reach his work, and was so kind and considerate to his wife that he never awakened her, it would be an easy matter to leave Chicago on the late train for that city, watch the party's house until he had left for his daily toil, and then, easily gaining access to the house, secure the money, and return to Chicago on the next train. The whole thing could be done inside of twelve hours, and there was certainly four or five hundred dollars apiece for them.

Hamilton entered into the scheme with all his heart, and suggested so many capital ideas concerning carrying out the robbery, that Wagner was more in love with him than ever ; and he hinted at many other schemes which they would mutually profit by.

On the arrival of the brig in Chicago, the plan of this projected robbery was immediately laid before me. I indorsed what Hamilton had done, as a means of winning Wagner's thorough confidence, and also as a measure of establishing the character of the man; while I at once arranged matters in Milwaukee, so that when the robbery was attempted, a sham policeman would be on hand to prevent the *actual* robbery. I believed it necessary to permit this to *seem* to go on, as I knew that, should the two attempt anything criminal together, this would prove the last bond of confidence. required to enable my operative to compel a revelation of his connection with the conspiracy against the insurance company.

As luck would have it, however, the " Mechanic" only remained in Chicago one night and a day, and the robbery of the honest Milwaukee workingman was necessarily postponed. But Wagner was now certain of his man.

There had been two or three interviews between Mrs. Rigger and Wagner, which Hamilton could not secure the gist of, and, just as the boat was leaving her slip, a small lad brought a large package, evidently containing clothing, which Wagner quickly received and stored snugly away under his bunk.

Hamilton had also laid in a package for this particular trip, but it contained something more to the liking of sailors than clothing. It was two gallons of the best of liquor and, as himself and Wagner were sampling the article while a grimy little tug was pulling the ' Mechanic " swiftly out past the Chicago lighthouse to the broad expanse of the lake, where the regular evening breeze from the land should speed the brig on its trackless way, Wagner, after filling a glass unusually full, touched it against the rim of Hamilton's glass in a most friendly way, and remarked :

" Dick, old boy, you've been the great story-teller of this craft ever since you came aboard her. Before we get to Buffalo I'll tell you a better story than you ever heard."

" Give it to us now, while the brig is gettin' her wind," replied Hamilton, with a knowing wink.

" No, no ; not yet—not before we get almost to Buffalo. And, Dick, if you're the man I take you for, and the friend I believe you to be, before the last chapter of the story's done—it'll be only two or three chapters, I'll tell you then—there may be a little 'spec' in it for you. This is no gammon story. There's a *live* corpse in it, and a *stiff one* to be got ! "

" All right, then, me hearty," responded Hamilton, clinking the glasses again ; " I'm your boy for any lively game, and here's luck to ourselves and both corpses, God rest 'em ! "

The liquor was drunk, and the two shook hands heartily, and went on deck.

There never was a finer trip than that from Chicago to Buffalo, " around the lakes ; " and this one proved a lovely one to the " Mechanic" and all on board.

Dick was in his happiest vein, and kept everybody on board roaring with laughter with his mad pranks and ri diculous yarns. Through the long sunny days it was story and joke and trick, and yet always so harmless and jolly as to cause no feeling of antagonism or offense, and, through the moonlit evenings, the same round of pleasures, so that the slight labor involved in handling the vessel amounted to nothing but a desirable change from what would otherwise have been a surfeit of enjoyment.

At last, one night, when within a few miles of Buffalo, Wagner came on watch and Hamilton with him. After everything had become quiet for the night, Wagner, after a liberal supply of liquor, in a low, careful tone, told Hamilton the following story :

"You know about the Rigger case, of course ; you have heard the men talk about it, and know that Mrs. Rigger has begun suit against the insurance company for five thousand dollars.

" Well, Dick, *we three put that up !* "

" Faith, is that where the corpses come in ? " asked Hamilton, with a well-assumed look of cunning praise.

" That's it, Dick. I'll come to that shortly."

" We were just about this distance from Buffalo, about thirty miles, and Rigger and I were on watch. The night was fearfully foggy, and I run her (the boat) into within half a mile off shore. Then I had Rigger go forward and fix a line on the bowsprit, taking pains to have one or two of the crew on deck. He kinder weaved when he got to the timber, and I yelled out : 'Take care, Rigger, mind your footing ! ' I hadn't more than said that, when up he slips and pitches headlong into the lake !

" It was all in the game, you know, and he had two big life-preservers, a couple of biscuits, and a little compass, fast on him. But I raised a fearful rumpus, got the boats out, and for an hour we tried awful hard to find him, I sending the boats in the opposite direction from which he fell in and struck out for shore. After a time we give it up, and by the time I took hold of the brig again, and set her out into deep water, Rigger was ashore ! "

" Tare an' ages ! but you're a slick one ! " ejaculated Hamilton ; " an' won't the haythen insurance company pay up like men ? "

" No ; that's just what's the matter. Mrs. Rigger has begun suit against them ; and now, Dick, I want you to help us out ! "

" I'm your buck ! What's the game ? "

" You remember that big bag I've got under my bunk ? "

" Faith, I do ! "

" Well, that's the very suit of clothes Rigger wore when he went over. He skipped back to Chicago, changed his togs, and left for California on the next train. We're all going out there after we beat the d——d company out of the money."

" Yes ; splendid ! "

" Now, when we get down to Buffalo I want you to help me look up a convenient cemetery, and then we'll dig up some fellow that's been under the sod a month or so, take the body out along the shore, and, after mashing it up so the very devil wouldn't recognize it save by the clothes, chuck it in the lake, let it wash ashore, and be found—his letters and papers, and all that are in the clothes. And then, by the Eternal ! we've got 'em fixed : Are ye in, Dick ? "

"In !—in ! Bedad I'm in for *any* fun of that kind, and we'll have the corpse in the water, 'n' out of it, upon the shore and discovered, before even a fish can get a smell of 'em ! "

With a hearty hand-shake and a parting glass of grog, the two turned in as the next watch came on ; and I had won the case.

The next morning the " Mechanic " arrived at Buffalo, and Hamilton had not been on shore thirty minutes before Wagner's confession and plans came spinning over the wires to me at Chicago.

I at once laid the information before the company, and requested that its officers permit me to arrest both parties, and that they would prosecute them to the fullest extent of the law, for I have always bitterly opposed any compromise with criminals. But it seemed to be their policy to keep out of the courts and the newspapers, and, with what had been got, with which they were highly elated, Mrs. Rigger was confronted ; and scared and half-crazed with the turn things had taken, she at once proceeded to the Circuit Court, and signed a waiver and release of all obligations held by her against the company.

This much done, Hamilton was recalled by telegraph. And I subsequently learned that Wagner, becoming alarmed at his co-conspirator's sudden disappearance, left the "Mechanic" at Buffalo never to reappear among his sailor friends at Chicago ; while the bogus widow evidently quickly took honest old Horace Greeley's advice, and went West to grow up with the country, for the little cottage was utterly deserted, and "For Rent" but two days after.

———•———

CHAPTER XV.

QUICK WORK.

B ANG, bang, bang ! "
There was no response to this impatient knocking upon the heavy door of the small Adams Express Company building near the end of the Columbus, Ohio, Union Depot, that night.

There stood the train with all its usual bustle about it, the engine snorting like a spirited steed impatient to be out upon the road again, but the Adams Express clerk and assistant had not made their accustomed appearance. The express messenger, John Gossman, had become greatly-alarmed, for but a few moments more elapsed before the train would pass on, and it was one of his guards who had been sent to awaken the two careless employees and hasten their regular visit to the train.

" Bang, bang, bang !" This time louder and more persistent than before upon the heavy oaken and riveted door. But there was still no answer from within.

Then the guard took hold of the door-knob, and, throwing his whole weight against the door, shook and rattled it frantically. Still no answer, and the guard rushed back to the train.

" Can't wake 'em up, John. Mebby they ain't there at all ! "

Not daring to leave his car, the messenger, now fearing that foul play of some kind had transpired, directed the guard to return to the express building and get into it if he had to break in. In a moment more he was at the door, and, turning the knob, as he ordinarily would have done, the door swung readily upon its hinges, and he walked into the room.

It was very dark inside, and striking a match, he went to the gas-light, where he found that it had been turned very low. Letting on the full light, it was seen that the papers and packages lay about the floor in the wildest confusion, while the clerk and his assistant, who were lying in bed but a few feet from the safes, seemed to be in a sort of stupor ; for, although the guard had hallooed lustily to them after entering, he was obliged to give them a pretty thorough shaking.

It was evident that the two men had been chloroformed —the sickening, deathly aroma of that drug still pervading the atmosphere of the room—and that the company had been robbed. The agent of the company at Colum bus, although it was about two o'clock in the morning, immediately informed the officers of the company of the affair, who called upon me, by telegraph, for help, and I was able to put Superintendent Warner, of my Chicago office, upon the ground during the next forenoon after the robbery, with two shrewd operatives in the background, ready for any possible emergency which might arise in the case.

But little information had been forwarded with the brief telegram, but I was familiar with the working of the express company's matters at Columbus, and I could hardly imagine how any thief or thieves could approach this building in so public a place, chloroform the inmates, and rob the safes, without attracting notice.

The main office of the company was located in the more business portion of the city, a considerable distance from the depot, and it had been for a long time necessary to keep a clerk and assistant at the depot to deliver and receive express matter, and the custom was for the clerk to leave the down-town office at about six o'clock in the evening, proceed to the depot, put everything snugly away in the safes, and then retire until the arrival of the late night trains, being awakened to attend to his duties, by the depot watchman; and I could not shake off the feelings which I impressed upon Mr. Warner before he took his departure, that this robbery could hardly have been committed without the complicity of some one of the express employees at Columbus.

A searching investigation by my superintendent developed the following facts :

On the evening before the robbery, May 16, 1871, John Barker, the depot express clerk, left the main office on Broad Street for the depot office at six o'clock, with seventy-two thousand dollars for different points, thirty-two thousand of which was in revenue stamps, and all of which was put into the safes. On the arrival of the late train at twenty-five minutes past two in the morning, the clerk did not make his appearance, although he had been called as usual by the watchman who was not certain that he had been answered, but who supposed Barker had been awakened. The guard had found the door open, as previously explained, and on gaining an entrance, and turning on the light, the keys had been found in one of the safe doors; everything seemed to be in confusion in the office; and Barker and his assistant were still in their bed, apparently stupefied from the effects of chloroform. A bottle still containing a small amount of chloroform was discovered, as also a sponge used in applying it to the faces of the sleeping employees. When they had finally been awakened, Barker was the first to speak, and he remarked : "Why, we've been robbed !" and, after noticing the package of revenue stamps, " I'm glad they left that much ! "

Both Barker and his assistant acted in an honest, straightforward manner, and readily answered all questions put to them. A casual investigation would hardly have developed anything save that the office was entered, the men chloroformed, and the safes robbed ; but a thorough examination did show, among other things, that the bolt on the door had been bent back, as if the door had been forced open. Unfortunately for this theory, how

ever, the bolt, which ran from the frame across the edge
of the door, had been bent considerably further than necessary, to permit the edge of the door to pass it, while there
was no evidence of a "jimmy" or other instrument having been used to force the door open and thus bend the
bolt.   It had been done from the inside; and the very
important query was : Who did it ?

This trifling circumstance, which an amateur detective
would be likely to wholly overlook, clinched the conviction in both my own and Mr. Warner's mind, that one of
the two employees in the little office, or possibly both,
had some criminal knowledge of the robbery, if, indeed,
they had not done the work themselves.

While the investigation was progressing the two men
were kept under constant espionage, and it was very soon
discovered and communicated to me by Mr. Warner that
John Barker, the express clerk, had a brother named
Henry Barker, who had been seen at Columbus, and in a
way to indicate that he had made every possible effort to
prevent being seen in the city.   It was also learned that
this mysterious brother was from Chicago.   These two
facts ascertained, I soon learned, in Chicago, that Henry
Barker had borne a rather unpleasant reputation, and had
been discharged from the employ of the Adams Express
Company, as also from service on the Chicago and Alton
Railroad.   This might not amount to much, but taken in
connection with other circumstances, it looked suspicious.

I was also informed by Mr. Warner that the express
clerk, when questioned about his brother, at first denied

all knowledge of him ; but after a time he confessed that
his brother had been in Columbus, but was there merely
on a little friendly visit ! He also laid great stress on the
fact that his brother was wealthy, or rather that he had
married a wealthy Chicago lady, and had no need to work.
Following this out, I found that, instead of the wife of
Henry Barker being a respectable and wealthy Chicago
lady, she was neither. She proved to be merely the
daughter of a noted proprietress of a Chicago house of
ill-fame, who had given her the choice of marrying Barker, or being sent to the Reform School in that city ; and
that she was then living a disreputable life in mean apartments, and without a dollar of honestly acquired money
on earth.

I judged that all these facts warranted the conclusion
that the brothers were guilty of the robbery, or at least,
had planned it, and had largely participated in the proceeds of the same. I accordingly intrusted Mr. Warner
to at once cause the arrest of the express clerk, and use
every effort to wring from him a confession, while his
assistant and brother should be remorselessly watched
and followed, hoping that they might in this way betray
some evidence of guilt which would give me the truth of
the whole matter.

It is a principle in criminal matters, which almost invariably holds true, that successful detection of crime is in
nearly every instance defeated when all suspected parties
are at once incarcerated. Let one or two, as the case
may be, be held so closely that they cannot be approached

or communicated with, and their accomplices will then, if they are watched by keen detectives, always make some move which will betray them. But, if all parties are arrested, all mouths and sources of information are instantly closed, and, in nine cases out of ten, though the authorities may be morally certain that they have the right parties, their discharge or acquittal will be the result, simply because no evidence of their guilt can be secured.

So, applying the result of my experience to this particular case, I reasoned that if the express clerk was arrested, and put where he could secure no assistance and sympathy, his accomplices would at once exhibit a nervousness and alarm which would definitely betray them.

According to this programme, Mr. Warner caused John Barker's arrest, formally charging him with the robbery, and intimating that the whole plan of his operations was known, and in every possible way endeavoring to secure from him a statement which would implicate others. But the young man was obdurate, and nothing save that which might be learned from an utterly innocent person could be got from him. He very *naïvely* admitted that he could readily see how he might be reasonably suspected; how the bending of the bolt apparently from the inside might be attributed to him, but he argued in the same breath that it might have been done by the party who did the work for the purpose of casting suspicion upon him.

The closest of watching could develop nothing of a

suspicious nature against the assistant. He was a simple, hard-working fellow, who seemed to be merely dazed and stunned by the robbery, and it seemingly had not once entered his head that he could be suspected of any manner of complicity in the matter.

But the results from watching Henry Barker, who had married the " wealthy Chicago lady," were far different.

He endeavored to keep quietly at home in Columbus, and it was observed that he never left his mother's house for any purpose until after night had wrapped its protecting folds around the city. Neither did he, after his brother's arrest and incarceration, visit him, or attempt in any manner to communicate with him, and I was more than ever satisfied of his guilt.

On the evening of the fifth day succeeding the robbery, Henry Barker suddenly took a train for Chicago. He did not leave Columbus like an honest man, but sneaked about the depot until the train was well under way, when he sprang aboard, giving my operative all he could do to accomplish the same thing and accompany him. At a way station the detective telegraphed me the condition of affairs, and I had two men at the depot in Chicago awaiting their arrival, one to relieve the man accompanying Barker, and another—my son William, to get a thorough look at Barker, so that he might be able to render any assistance necessary.

Barker at once proceeded to his "wealthy wife's" rooms in a disreputable quarter of the city. Here he remained well closeted from observation, but so thoroughly guarded that his escape was impossible, for one day. Then, with a small valise which his wife had been seen to purchase for him at a pawn-shop near their habitation, he set out leisurely in the morning, considerably changed in personal appearance but perfectly self-possessed and evidently with no fear of pursuit, for the Michigan Central depot.

Arriving here he purchased a paper and a cigar, and smoking the one and occasionally glancing at the other, he sauntered about the locality for a short time, when he walked to the ticket office and purchased a ticket for Canada, via the Michigan Central and Grand Trunk railroads. This much done and he went to the train, took a seat in the smoking-car, and resumed the reading of his paper as pleasantly and nonchalantly as though a reputable business man starting out on a summer trip to the Thousand Islands.

His presence at the depot had been reported to me immediately, and I authorized my son, William A. Pinkerton, to make the arrest. A carriage took him to the depot from my office in five minutes, and he arrived at the train at the same time as young Barker. Following him into the car, he waited until Barker had seated himself comfortably, when William approached him and said, pleasantly :

" Barker, sorry to annoy you, but you will have to delay your trip to Canada until later in the season. The express folks down at Columbus want you."

He made no resistance at all, but came along quietly,

seeming to feel grateful that he had been arrested in a gentlemanly manner.

He was then placed in the carriage which had conveyed William to the depot, and my son, taking a seat beside him, and an officer riding on the box with the driver, the whole party were in my private office in a few minutes.

He made no noise and seemed in no great degree alarmed. He submitted to being searched with the best of grace, not over fifty dollars being found upon his person. I was beginning to fear we had made a mistake, when I ordered one of the men to remove the lining of the valise. Barker grew deathly pale when I said this, but he said nothing.

This precaution rewarded me by discovering, neatly secreted within the lining, fourteen thousand dollars. Even then he had nothing to say, and I concluded to let him think the matter over for a little time while on the train to Columbus, which he, an officer, and myself were on board of the same night, Barker pretty well ironed, more for the effect I hoped it would have on him than from any fear that he would attempt to escape.

I gave strict orders that no word should be spoken to the man by any person, and engaging a stateroom of the sleeper for our party, shut him and the officer within it, compelling the officer to sit there like a sphinx, looking wise as an owl, but uttering never a word.

Late in the night, Barker could stand the silence and suspense no longer, and he begged piteously of his guard to permit him to speak to me. For a time he silently shook his head, but at last called me, when the poor fellow broke down altogether, begged piteously for mercy, and reveal d where twenty-five thousand dollars of the stolen money could be found buried in a vacant lot next that occupied by his mother's house, and gave me the whole particulars of the robbery, which I telegraphed in advance to Mr. Warner, who, with this aid, had secured a like full and free confession from the incarcerated express clerk, before our arrival at Columbus at noon of the next day.

The robbery had been planned by Henry Barker, and was the simplest thing in the world after his brother, the clerk, had consented to his share in it. The door was conveniently left open ; the assistant was given a heavy dose of chloroform ; then the clerk himself opened the safes and selected the packages of value for removal. Then the appearance of general confusion was arranged, and after the, bolt had been bent to give the impression that the door had been forced from the outside, Henry had given his brother a mild dose of chloroform, and departed with every dollar that the office contained, twenty-five thousand of which he had buried, and fifteen thousand of which he had taken with him from Columbus, it being the intention of the express clerk to join his brother in Canada when the storm had blown over a little.

But :

> " The best laid schemes o' mice and men
> Gang aft agley ! "

and the two robbers were subsequently given four years

each in the penitentiary, while the company was highly elated that I had been the means of recovering for them thirty-nine thousand dollars, out of what seemed an absolute loss of forty thousand dollars, and that, too, all within eight days.

CHAPTER XVI.

THE COST OF BUSINESS ARROGANCE.

SOME time in September, 1871, there was presented at the banking house of Henry Clews & Co., in New York City, a draft for the sum of $55 dollars. In the usual course of business, the draft was stamped thus:

> *ACCEPTED.*
>
> Payable at the Fourth National Bank.
>
> HENRY CLEWS & CO.

Two or three days afterwards, the draft was presented to the Fourth National Bank for payment. The figures had been altered to $5500, but not so as to attract attention.

The man who presented the check, however, was so nervous that the suspicions of the paying teller were aroused. He detained the man who presented the draft and sent a messenger to the house of Henry Clews & Co. to see if it was good. After some trouble the mes senger forced an interview with the junior member of the firm. That young gentleman seized the check, drew it through his jeweled fingers and said :

"Young man, there's our stamp on that draft right before your eyes. If that stamp was a bear, it would bite you. Tell your paying teller that time is valuable to us, and if we are to be interrupted in our business hours through his stupidity, the Fourth National Bank will have to make some other arrangements so far as Henry Clews & Co. are concerned ! "

So saying, he seized a pen, and before the messenger had recovered from his surprise and could tell him of the suspicions of the teller of the Fourth National, he wrote across the face of the check :—

Good for $5500.

HENRY CLEWS & CO.

This he handed to the young man, again rebuked him for bothering the great firm of Henry Clews & Co., and vanished.

The messenger returned to the bank, and the paying teller indignantly paid the money without more question. The gentleman who altered the figures went on his way rejoicing, and but two days afterwards the firm of Clews & Co. discovered the fraud.

They had lost exactly five thousand four hundred and forty-five dollars for the exhibition of a little arrogance.

CHAPTER XVII.

A CURIOUS CASE OF CIRCUMSTANTIAL EVIDENCE.

A CURIOUS case of circumstantial evidence was tried before Judge Paxon, in the New York Court of Quarter Sessions, some time since. A shoe manufacturer, named George Bruder, was tried for the alleged theft of three thousand dollars, which was in charge of a bank messenger, named Brooks. The latter left the Security Banking House with certain securities and money for the Clearing House, and on the way stopped at the shop of the shoemaker named, to pay a bill.

The messenger laid his pocket-book and the package on the counter, and placed his arm upon them while he wrote out a bill. When he got to the Clearing House, a count of the securities and money was had, and then, for the first time, it was discovered that there was a deficit of three thousand dollars. The messenger at once returned to Bruder's shop and made known his loss. The shoemaker denied having seen it, and a search was made of the place. Had the case rested here, there would have been very little upon which to base a belief that the shoemaker handled the money. The Commonwealth called a witness to prove that he was in the shop of George Bruder, *the day* after *the loss*, when his daughter came in bearing a package of money, saying that the shop-boy had found it in the cellar; whereupon the de fendant claimed that it was his, that he had put it there for safe-keeping, and that he supposed his dog had lug it out of its place of concealment. The shop-boy also testified to finding the money in the cellar, to which he had gone to chop wood. The package of money was upon the ground, and was done up in an almost precisely similar manner to that of the bank package.

There was proof that Bruder had a fire-proof safe in the store, which made it all the more strange that he should have his treasure lying around loose in the cellar. The only evidence offered by the defense to meet this case was that of good character, and the fact that he did not keep a bank account. The jury were together for some time, and then rendered a verdict of not guilty.

I think it would not be possible to make out a stronger case on circumstantial evidence than here presented. The remarkable fact of a package of money of the same amount, and in every other particular closely resembling the lost one, being found in the cellar by the shop-boy the day after the alleged loss, and the shoemaker's ex planation that he supposed his dog had found it and dragged it from its place of concealment, would be, it seems to me, strongly indicative of guilt. But the little instance is simply one of thousands which every year con trive to throw a strange fascination and interest of possi bility and doubt around all cases of circumstantial evi dence.

CHAPTER XVIII.

A PRIVATE ASSURANCE COMPANY AND A PUBLIC INSUR-
ANCE COMPANY.

THIS sketch relates to an insurance company and an
assurance company. The former got the worst o
it, and the latter *were* the worst.

The insurance company in question was the Royal
Fire and Life Insurance Company of Liverpool and London, whose American office was, at the time I write of,
located at No. 56 Wall Street, in New York ; and the
Assurance Company was composed of the eminent Dan
Noble, Jimmy Griffin, Frank Knapp, and Jack Tierney,
sneak-thieves ; and while New York was their general
headquarters, it may be truthfully said that their operations extended into all cities of the United States, while
their risks were high and their profits very large.

Dan Noble himself has always been noted as a brilliant and gentlemanly rascal of the confidence game,
sneak-thief order, and, at about the time he organized the
company of precious rascals referred to, was at the height
of his business prosperity as a professional sneak-thief.
Noble never did much of the actual " sneaking " himself,
but he was a most brilliant general of these matters, and
was, nearly always successful in, first, planning a huge robbery ; second, in bringing the right parties together to

11*

assist in doing the work ; and, third, in having immediate and direct charge of all the neat little work of the rob bery itself.

Even as far back as during the early period of the war Noble was a noted criminal, but had always, through hi splendid appearance, ready money, and fine generalship, managed to elude the several clutches of justice grasping for him from all directions ; and in those instances where he had been compelled to taste the legitimate fruits of his villainous life the bitter experience had been short, and was, through the lavish use of his money, rendered as little disagreeable as possible.

Accidentally I was the cause of a little practical joke on Noble, which, although it occurred many years since, still clings to him with unusual freshness, and which created great merriment among sporting and criminal classes of the more polished order ; and even to-day, among this class, whenever "Dan Noble's steerers running old Pinkerton into a faro-house" is mentioned, a laugh at Dan's expense is the result, and, referred to in his presence, is invariably as good as an order for a bottle of wine.

The incident referred to happened in this way :

During the war, while I was at the head of the Secret Service of the Government, although here, there, and everywhere, my real headquarters were with General McClellan in the field, although official business frequent- ly took me to Philadelphia, Baltimore, Boston, and New York.

On one occasion, when I was in the latter city for the

purpose of seeing Colonel Thomas Key, whose head quarters were then at the Fifth Avenue Hotel, having not as yet established my large New York agency, I took quarters at the St. Nicholas, on Broadway.

I had arrived late in the afternoon, with the intention of seeing the Colonel during the evening, which would permit of my return to Washington the same night, or, at least, the next morning ; and, having secured a hearty supper and purchased a cigar—for I was a great smoker then —I strolled aimlessly and leisurely about the rotunda and public rooms of the hotel.

I had been enjoying this solitary promenade but a few minutes, when one of two gentlemen came up to me with extended hand and smiling face, and, heartily grasping my hand, which I readily gave him, most enthusiastically ejaculated :

"Why, Colonel Green, this *is* a pleasure ! When did you get in ? Why, here, Edwards, you know the Colonel ? "

"Certainly, certainly," promptly responded that gentlemen. "We had no idea of meeting you here, Colonel. Are you stopping at the St. Nicholas ? "

Of course I understood the whole matter in an instant. The game was old, very old, and besides, I knew the men. My first thought was to have the couple arrested, but I saw a capital chance for a little fun at the expense of the two, who were regular " steerers " for the house where Dan Noble was " dealing " a faro game, and pretty fair confidence men. So I permitted the game to

go on, and, assuming an air of opulent rural simplicity
I responded :

"My friends, you have the advantage of me. Don'
believe I'm the man you're lookin' for."

"Why, you're Colonel Green, aren't you ? " persist(
the scamp, with a beaming face and a look which was
intended to convey the impression that he would forgive
any pleasant raillery like that from his dear old friend,
the Colonel from Hackensack.

" No, you're wrong," said I, pleasantly ; " my name's
Smith—Major Smith, of the Quartermaster's Department."

" And you positively say that you're not Colonel
Green ? " said the roper, with a very handsomely gotten-up
look of perplexity, wonder, and amazement stealing over
his features.

" Not much," said I, tersely.

" Well, I'm damned ! " he retorted, turning to his
friend. " Edwards, I never made a mistake like that
before in my life ! "

" Well, *I* have, once or twice," remarked Edwards,
thoughtfully ; " but, by Jupiter ! it is the most remarkable
likeness I ever saw—most remarkable ! "

" Remarkable ! Well, I rather think so. Why, Major
Smith—beg pardon, would you favor me with a light ?
Thank you. Do you know, I've sold this Colonel Green
goods right along for fifteen years, every season, until this.
But come, let's sit, and you must pardon me for being
so rude, Here's my card. I am the ' Preston ' of the

firm; and this is my friend, Mr. Edwards—same business, but another house; and, do you know, I'd have bet an even thousand dollars that you were Colonel Green?"

"Yes, and I'd have gone you 'halves' on that. What department did you say you were in, Major Smith?" asked Edwards, carelessly.

"Quartermaster's," I replied; "'Swindling the Government,' the newspapers call it."

"Indeed!" ejaculated the roper calling himself Mr. Preston, attentively noting every word I uttered.

"Yes, I am over here to New York now for a thousand cavalry horses."

Now, it would take a good deal of money to buy a thousand cavalry horses; and Mr. Preston's eyes fairly sparkled as he thought of the rich lead he had struck. I was dressed roughly, was very much tanned by exposure in the field, and undoubtedly *looked* the character of the rough Quartermaster's Department man I had assumed to perfection, and I led the two men to believe me easy prey.

"Let's have another cigar, Edwards, and then take a stroll up to the club house," said Preston; and then addressing his conversation more particularly to me, he asked: "Major Smith, won't you walk up with us? We merchants have got a cozy little place up here a few blocks, where, after the business and down-town banging of the day are over, we can go and have a quiet, sociable time, all by ourselves. Won't you take a walk up with us?"

"Well, I don't mind," I replied reflectively. "But I can't stay long, for I've got to attend to part of my buyin to night."

At this remark, indicating to Preston that I probably had a good supply of ready money on my person, as well as large resources, being an army contractor, his eyes snapped again, and I could just imagine the fellow devouring me in his mind and thinking : "Oh, won't we have a sociable time carving up this old stuffed turkey— oh, won't we though!"

A moment later we were on the street, and within five minutes were entering what appeared to be a most elegant private mansion, on the east side of Broadway, and but a few blocks from the hotel.

"Fine place you have here," I observed, as we stood in the vestibule, and the alleged Preston stepped to the bell-knob and gave it a pull.

"It's one of the most complete 'club-rooms' in the country. The boys have good times here occasionally."

While he was replying to me, I distinctly heard the soft tinkle of another bell besides the one that the "steerer" had rung, and I at once conjectured that it was a signal, given perhaps by Preston's companion, to those within, that another fool with a fat purse had been captured, and that everything should be ready within for a proper reception of him ; and, although I had not the slightest fear of personal harm, I dexterously whipped out my revolver from my hip-pocket and slipped it down into my front pantaloons pocket, where I conveniently held its handle with my right hand, quite ready for anything that might occur; and, with my hands in my pockets and my hat on the back of my head, quite countrified in appearance, I strolled in after the two precious scamps.

It is needless to give my readers any detailed descrip tion of the place into which we were now ushered. It was a magnificent gambling-house, and that was all there was of it.

When we had arrived within, quite a pleasant scene was presented. To one uninitiated it would have ap- peared to be just what the "roper" stated that it was— a business-man's resort, where he could enjoy himself among clever companions. Here sat a group of persons talking of stocks and bonds, and gravely discussing the effect of certain war movements upon securities; at another place were a couple chatting on social topics; and, again, a little party seemed to have some connection with newspaper matters. Everything was beautifully arranged to create a fine impression upon a rural stran- ger, and, as the bank-note reporters used to say, was "well calculated to deceive."

In the rear room of the suite stood a regular faro table, and several gentlemen were gathered about this, chatting and laughing, and occasionally making a play. After introducing me to several of the inmates and re- lating the incident bringing us together, vhich he termed "a most ludicrous though agreeable error," Preston led the way toward the gaming-table.

I did not follow him immediately, but, with my hands

still in my pockets, and my hat still upon my head, I lounged about the place in a very lawless and country fashion, curiously examining and handling different articles of *bijouterie* and ornamentation, and occasionally asking information about the cost or quality of any article which struck my fancy, as it appeared, of whoever might be standing near me.

Finally Preston carelessly remarked: " Come, Major, step over here and have something."

" Well, I believe I will," I replied, making a lunge toward the magnificent sideboard. A half-dozen other persons followed, and were introduced in a high-sounding manner, while the spruce negro attendants served to each of us such liquor as we might fancy ; and I recollect that the whisky I got was some of the finest I ever drank.

During this pleasant diversion I heard the voice of the elegant Dan Noble, who was dealing the game—and right here let me say that I could not have, for my life, told whether it was faro, keno, or any other game, for I never played a game of cards in my life, and never expect to— urging the " cappers " and " steerers " to lose no time, but bring me to the table and begin the operation of fleecing me ; while they, evidently somewhat impressed with my stubbornness, protested in low tones that there was plenty of time, and that they would " work me " shortly.

After this refreshment, I resumed my appearance of curiosity, and again began my strolling ; while several of the pretended gentlemen crowded around the gaming table, and made heavy winnings—all of which of course was for the purpose of arousing my curiosity and tempting me to join the game ; while, without appearing to do so, I noticed that the keen, sharp eyes of Dan Noble followed me wherever I went, and he appeared anxious to try his hand at fleecing me so thoroughly that I would remember it so long as I lived.

The appointments of the place were simply magnificent, and I took my own time to examine them, while the two "steerers" I had met at the St. Nicholas, by every manner in their power, persistently sought to induce me to join the parties playing; and I could not help enjoying a hearty laugh internally, so hearty, in fact, that I could at times scarcely repress a roaring-out burst to see the ingenuity of the men so handsomely yet so fruitlessly exercised, while I mentally noted the interest exhibited by their confederates and the chances they seemed to take in their own minds as to the probability of gaining my supposed wealth from me, although they each and all, true to their habits and profession, made a great effort to support the character of being elegant business or other gentlemen, at .eisure for the evening, and bent on having a good time all to themselves.

Finding that I resisted all these ingenious attacks, re course was again had to the sideboard ; but this time, to the dismay of the gamblers, I only took a cigar. The cigar was as fine as the liquor, and, enjoying its splendid aroma, I now straggled up to the table.

Everybody was now in high spirits.   Jokes and wit

flowed freely, and the betting began to run high, those risking their money very singularly winning largely; while the magnificent Mr. Noble, slick and trim as a bishop, and with a solitaire diamond as large as a big hazel-nut gleaming from his shirt-front, greeted my presence among the gentlemen around the green cloth with a nod and a smile of welcome.

"Gentlemen, won't you please make room for Major Smith?" said Noble, with a voice as sweet and pleasant as a blooming country schoolma'am's; while instantly at least three chairs were made ready for my occupancy.

But I stood there very provokingly disinclined to be made a victim of, and remarked, extremely innocently, after a little time :

"Well, I guess I won't play any to-night.   I don't understand the game."

Immediately I was appealed to from all sides with "*Do*, Major ; just one play, Major!"   "Major, try your luck with the rest of us !" and all that sort of thing ; while Noble himself remarked pleasantly : "You must remember, Major Smith, that we are all gentlemen here !"

At this I looked at Dan a few moments in a quizzical, comical way, and finally, as if suddenly being struck by a remarkable recollection, I blurted out :

"Come over here, dealer, and have a drink, and then I'll tell you something funny."

There was a noticeable confusion about the table. Everybody was surprised and some bewildered.   Noble at first hesitated ; but as I led the way to the sideboard he followed me mechanically, and his face began to express wonder, perplexity, chagrin, and even rage, in rapid succession. Several of the gamblers followed, and the liquor was swallowed by all in silence. Scarcely had I set my glass upon the sideboard, when Noble said, in a perplexed, curious, and half-alarmed tone:

"Who in hell *are* you, any how ? "

I seized him by the hand, and gave it a squeeze that made his fingers crack, from which he writhed as if hurt.

"Why, Dan Noble, don't you remember me ? You ought to, Dan ! How long since you came from Elmira ? Are you going to get out of that scrape, Dan ? You don't know how glad I am to see you, Dan !" and I gave his hand another powerful grip, that made him squirm again.

" But damn it, who are you ? " he said hotly.

" Come over here, Dan, and I'll tell you," and I jerked and dragged him aside, and then whispered in his ear :

" Allan Pinkerton."

"You know me now, Dan," I continued uproariously. " You see I know *you*, and *you*," I roared, grasping the hand of Jim Laflin, the gambler. " How long have you been away from Chicago, Jim ? I'm damned glad to see all you good fellows ! And you, Sears," said I, crossing to another gambler whom I knew ; " how's luck been with you lately ? And *you*, and *you*, and *you* !" said I rapturously, nodding to half the people in the place, and calling each one of them by name, and clinching the

knowledge of each by some little reference to their pre
vious criminal acts. "Why, boys, this *is* a surprise to
me ; so glad to see you all, you know. Perhaps you're
all a trifle surprised. But don't mind me. I'm just a
common sort of a fellow. Come, Dan, old boy," said I,
turning to Noble, who stood there as though a bomb-
shell had exploded in the room ; "let's all have a good,
sociable, friendly old drink together."

"But you don't want me, do you ? " gasped Noble trem-
blingly, after the liquor had been drank, with many toasts
to Mr. Pinkerton, instead of to "Major Smith, of the
Quartermaster's Department."

"Oh no, not just now; but remember, Dan, if ever I
do want you, it will not be a hard matter to get you."

"I know that, I know that," said Noble, in a concilia-
tory tone ; "but are you after anybody else here ? "

"Oh, no, I guess not; not just now, anyhow. It
would be a pity to disturb a party of so eminent gentlemen—bankers, newspaper men, society people, etc. ; and,
as I have had a very pleasant call, I think I'll go and attend to buying those thousand horses."

My identity had leaked out by this time to all, and several of the scamps took occasion to slip out ; but most
of the inmates gathered about me with great protestations
of friendship and admiration ; and, after lighting a fresh
cigar, I left the place, having caused the greatest sensation it had ever known, and left to Dan Noble the legacy
of a practical joke that his criminal companions will jest
him upon to the day of his death.

But his ingenuity and ability to plan and assist in the execution of "sneak" work were of the highest order, as the robbery of the Royal Fire and Life Insurance Company of Liverpool and London evidenced.

On December 10, 1866, all New York was thrown into a great state of excitement by the announcement that the office of the company in question had been robbed of a quarter of a million dollars ; and the public interest in the matter was none the less when the manner of the robbery became known.

A meeting of the American directors of the company had been announced to be held at their office, at noon of the day in question, and at about half-past ten o'clock of the same forenoon a tin box, usually deposited for safe keeping in the vaults of the Merchants' Bank, and containing about a quarter of a million dollars in Government bonds and negotiable securities, had been sent for, to be used or inspected by the directors in the event of any change in stock, as was the usual custom at such meetings.

The box with its contents was placed in the vault opening from the inner or back room of the office of Mr. Anthony B. McDonald, the agent, and the inner iron door of the safe closed, but not locked.

At about a quarter past eleven two well-dressed and apparently respectable men called, and, expressing a desire to be informed regarding the conditions of life insurance, were shown into Mr. McDonald's apartment.

One of them, a young man about thirty years of age

and having the appearance of an able commercial traveler on a fine salary, immediately entered into conversation with the agent; and, taking a seat on the opposite side of the table, inquired the terms on life policies, stating that he and several other individuals wished to effect an insurance on their lives, as they were about leaving to go down the Mississippi to New Orleans on a quite extended trip for their different houses.

He then made some remarks, to the effect that they were undecided as to whether they would take a traveler's risk or insure for a life period, and stated that, as he had just been married, he felt an additional anxiety to secure his wife against prospective poverty.

During the time this business-like conversation was going on, the other gentleman, from occasional timely remarks, indicated to Mr. McDonald that he was one of the commercial travelers desiring insurance, and that the person talking to him was the spokesman for the whole party. After a little time, while the agent and the inquirer after rates and terms were busily employed together, the friend remarked that he thought he would step out for a few moments, and would return shortly.

The vault was situated to one side and to the rear of where Mr. McDonald was at work upon his tables and statements, and the young man who remained entered into the business so arduously that Mr. McDonald made some calculations from a table of risks to satisfy his inquiries regarding the policies for his friends.

During this time the young man who had left the

office returned, and resumed his careless manner of walk-
ing about tne room and interestedly examining the pictures and other articles of ornamentation hanging upon
the walls.

After a little time he made some casial remark about
not being able to keep a certain appointment unless his
friend excused him then ; and, after agreeing to meet him
at a later designated hour at the house of a prominent
business firm, he bade the two gentlemen good-day and
left the office.

A few minutes later the gentleman who had been such
an interested inquirer in insurance matters, after thank-
ing Mr. McDonald for his kindness and attention, and
promising to consult his friends and call again after so
doing, also withdrew.

The meeting of the directors was held according to the
call. Those gentlemen gravely considered such matters
as required their attention, and finally desired an examination of the bonds and stocks. The tin box was sought ;
but lo ! it was gone. The greatest consternation pre-
vailed ; but it was soon seen that the company had been
robbed in a most brilliant manner, and that the two gentlemanly pretended travelers, who wished to provide for
their wives so tenderly, were the skillful sneak-thieves who
did the work.

Now, Dan Noble had planned the whole matter, knew
that the directors' meeting was to be held, knew that the
tin box which traveled so frequently between the insurance office and the Merchants' Bank contained bonds or

other valuables, and also had learned all about the habits and methods of conducting the inner office.

He therefore organized a " gang," as it is called, con- sisting of Frank Knapp, Jimmy Griffin, and Jack Tierney, to do the work.   Himself and Jack Tierney were to dc the " piping " on the outside, as also to hold a carriage in readiness, either to remove the plunder or enable the " sneaks" to escape, should their object be discovered before it should have been consummated.

Frank Knapp represented the inquiring commercial traveler, and Jimmy Griffin was the " sneak " who repre- sented the friend who was compelled to go out, and then, after his return, was unable to remain on account of keep- ing a certain appointment.

Knapp took a seat at agent McDonald's table, so that the latter's back was toward the vault, and then Knapp shrewdly kept him so thoroughly engaged that he paid no attention whatever to the supposed friend, who, with an overcoat thrown lightly over his arm, carelessly walked about the place, apparently whiling away the time in a cursory examination of the ornaments on the walls.

During this sort of thing Griffin slipped into the vault, noiselessly opened the safe, abstracted the tin box con- taining the bonds, arranged his coat over it neatly, and then came back, standing within two feet of the agent and Knapp when he stated to them that he would have to go out for a few minutes.

He went out, gave the box and the overcoat to Noble and Tierney in the carriage—the latter instantly leaving--

and then, after a short delay, returned to the insurance office to make his excuses and leave the second time.

The leaving of Knapp has already been described, and no one can question that the scheme, in its planning and cool, leisurely execution, was one of the most perfect and brilliant in the entire annals of crime.

Knapp and Griffin at once fled to Canada, being urged to that course by Noble, who only gave these men twenty-seven thousand dollars out of a booty of over a quarter of a million; and this unfair deal at last led to troubles between the thieves, resulting in Noble's arrest, conviction, and partial punishment for this particular crime. Fifty-five thousand dollars' worth of the bonds were recovered by the company, on payment of a premium or reward of fifteen per cent.

Noble eluded punishment for over four years, but was finally convicted at Oswego, New York, in February, 1871—his great wealth, entirely secured by crime, having been utterly exhausted in his long battle with justice.

He was sentenced to ten years' imprisonment at Sing Sing, but escaped from there in 1872, having served "prison time" but a little over one year, and then fled to Europe, where he began anew his career of crime. He attempted to perpetrate a daring "sneak" job on the Paris Bourse in 1873, on a broker's office, but was caught in the very act, convicted, and sentenced to five years' penal servitude, which full time he served, only being liberated in the summer of 1878, just in time to attend the Paris Exposition, and continue his brilliant conspira-

12

ries. But, as I have said, wherever Dan Noble goes, or whatever luck he may have in a criminal way, the story of his "steerers running old Pinkerton up to his brace game" will always remain a practical joke upon him, which can never be run away from and never shaken off.

———————◆———————

CHAPTER XIX.

A BIT OF DETECTIVE-OFFICE ROMANCE.

O F the tens of thousands of strange and interesting incidents connected with prolonged and far-reaching detective service, undoubtedly that portion containing the richest veins of romance, the brightest humor, and the deepest pathos, is comprised in the demands made on the detective agency for numberless kinds of assistance by men and women who are unfortunate enough to become complicated in family troubles involving the supposed unfaithfulness of the husband or the wife.

I wish to say, at the beginning of this bit of romance, that I am bitterly and irrevocably opposed to touching that kind of work. No honest and honorable detective will soil his hands with it. For thirty years, and through hundreds of thousands of applications for the services of myself and my men, I have shunned and avoided it for the unclean, poisonous thing that it is. In all modesty, and for the purity and honor of the detective service of America, as one who has spent the best half of his life in its elevation and bettering, I wish to, here and at all times, urge upon those younger and less experienced than my-self, who may be at the threshold of their life-work, the absolute necessity of turning a deaf ear to applications for this class of assistance.

There may be, there often are, exceptions in this re-gard, where men and women, from the highest and most honorable of motives, desire and have a right to certain information, which may more thoroughly establish a wife, a husband, or a near friend in their regard and esteem, or permit a decision which, though hard and heart-breaking to make, is the only dignified and honorable thing to be done, when the one under suspicion proves himself or herself utterly unworthy of confidence or respect ; but these are unusual exceptions, and nearly every instance where women apply to the detective to watch the hus-band, or the husband the wife, the mistress the man, or her "friend" the mistress, there will be found something disreputable and degrading behind it.

To put detectives on such low errands of espionage is to demoralize them and utterly unfit them for higher work. The detective must have a clean mind and clean hands, or he sinks to the level of the criminal, and is no better than he ; and there is no way in which he can become so completely corrupt and unbalanced as to place him where he becomes the spy and the football between animal passion and revenge.

The instance I am about to relate, where I took a case of this kind, is only an exception proving the general rule which I have laid down, and was one so pitiable, and yet so ridiculous, that I cannot restrain a hearty laugh whenever I recall it. It occurred but a few years since, and is still as fresh in my mind as though it happened but yesterday.

One summer afternoon, about three o'clock, a pretty *coupé* halted in front of my present offices on Fifth Avenue, Chicago. The sweet face of a young woman appeared at the window and looked up at the large building with evident trepidation and fear. Even the negro footman, that quickly descended to serve the lady, seemed possessed of a certain solemnity and awe, which indicated at least some well-defined unpleasantness in the household where he was employed, and momentous importance attaching to this visit. Alighting upon the sidewalk, the little lady looked nervously about her, peered into the open door of the fine station on the first floor, where my large night watch, the preventative police, are quartered, where she saw a few officers and patrolmen quietly sitting about on day duty ; and then, seemingly quickly satisfying herself that this was not the detective department, hastened rapidly up the broad stairs.

She had determination in her manner ; but in every feature of her fine face there was a quiver and tremor that told of acute suffering. It was not common that so remarkably fine-looking a lady, so distinguished in appearance, sought the mysteries of detective service ; and, as she swept into the main office, casting a flushed and startled look about her, the groups of sub-officers and bevies of clerks, by long custom grown quick and keen in judgment of such things, knew, without being told, something of what the case *might* be, and in their minds unanimously pronounced it : " Particularly pitiable."

My office-boy—also taking in the situation at a glance, and seeming to understand that the lady was much con fused by the, to her, unaccustomed surroundings—at once conducted her into my superintendent's consulting-room, and proffered her a seat opposite Mr. Warner himself.

Superintendent Warner, who has been in my employ for nearly twenty years, is a very staid, sober gentleman, one who has a reputation, among my other officers and men, of never looking at a woman save sidewise, and then only for the tenth part of a second—(a man who is so proverbially modest in this particular that it is even re- ported of him that he passes words, when reading, unless certain that they are of the masculine gender) ; but the very woe that spoke from his visitor's face affected him so strongly that he looked up over his gold-rimmed quizzers from his papers and dispatches, and regarded her curi- ously with his cold gray eyes for fully three seconds.

Then the handsome, elegantly-dressed, beautiful lady began sobbing and talking.

Superintendent Warner, looking straight out of the win- dow, adjusted his quizzers, and began listening.

The lady—whom I will call Mrs. Saunders—after several sobs, which she finally mastered with a great effort, said, in a voice of repressed emotion :

" Mr. Warner, I am in great trouble—great trouble."

He could see it ; and he hinted as much, resuming his attitude of attention.

"Is it necessary to tell my name ? "

" Most certainly."

" And tell you where I live ? "

" Yes."

" Oh, this *is* awful ! " she said, more as if speaking to herself than the superintendent.   " Well, I live at No. — Indiana Avenue "(a very aristocratic thoroughfare).   " My husband is the senior member of the firm of Saunders, Rice & Co., on State Street."

Yes, Mr. Warner knew them very well.

" And you know about our trouble ? " she asked, in a way showing that the poor woman felt certain, as people always do, that *her* grief was certain to occupy the attention of all the world.

" Well, I think it would be better for you to give me *your* version of it," he replied quietly, but already nervous at the probable prospect before him.

" Oh, dear !—well—" she began, with a flushing and paling face.   " My husband is rich.   We have a beautiful home ; it seemed as though the world was very bright before *this* ! " (Sobs.)   " He always came home to dinner, and never, never passed the evening away save with me ! "

" How long have you been married, madam ? " respectfully asked the superintendent.

" Only eighteen short months," she replied, crying bitterly.

" Have you a child ? "

" One darling babe." Another sob.

" Well ? "

The superintendent was getting anxious for particulars, and troubled for the result.

" Well, sir, about two weeks ago we had a slight misun derstanding."

Mr. Warner nodded his head, as though he knew what *that* meant.

" But it wasn't much, sir ; truly it was hardly a quarrel. But we began taking our meals separately, each too proud to make any concession, each full of spirit, and thinking the other was in the wrong, but both gradually growing away from each other until finally—— "

Here the good little lady paused and blushed deeply. It hurt her to say what was on her tongue, but it had to come.

" Well ? " queried Mr. Warner, wiping his quizzers and blusning to the very top of his bald head.

" Until we finally occupied sleeping apartments in quite opposite parts of the house ! "

Mr. Warner saw it was the old story, one that had floated ten thousand times into the office, ever since he had been in it, and he began to fidget about in his chair as the lady resumed her weeping.

" Well, sir, he acts *so* strangely. He slams the doors, and won't even look at the baby I hold up in my arms for him to see ; and, about a week ago, I noticed that he did not get into the house until two or three o'clock in the morning. I couldn't get but a glimpse of his face, but he

looked *guilty* . I hate to tell you this, sir, but I am *sure*
some bold, bad woman is at the bottom of it all. He has
been away from home for three whole nights, sir—for
three long, dreary nights.   I *know* he is with this woman.
Oh, sir ! I don't know what to do ! I don't know what
to do ! But if you can only some way get my husband to
realize what a terrible thing he is doing, and then capture
this bad woman, and do something awful—*just awful !*—
with her, you shall have any—yes, any sum you have a
mind to name ! "

Here the poor lady, seeing that there was but little
hope for her in my superintendent's face, pleaded piteously, between really heart-rending sobs, that her " dear
hubby" might be brought back, and this horrible woman
completely annihilated, and explained how, for several
days, *she* had been dodging about the city herself, to
ascertain where the supposed cause of her husband's
misdoing lived, and how she might wreak a deserted
wife's vengeance upon her, and, finding that she could
accomplish nothing, discouraged and disheartened, she
had come to my office hoping for help.

Superintendent Warner really pitied his fair visitor, and
hardly knew what to do.   He glanced for courage along
the wall, where one of the framed mottoes from my " General Principles" for detective work hung in its frame.
The motto read :

" *These Agencies will, under no circumstances, operate
in cases arising from marital difficulties !* "

He tried to get courage and bravery enough from this

but the misery of the little woman got the better of him ;
and, trying to look very sympathetic and at the same
time severe, he stammered out, as he rose to indicate the
termination of the interview :

"Sorry ; d—— very sorry, madam ! But much as I de
plore your trouble—pardon me for saying this—is—well-
ha, hum !—well, one of that *kind* of cases, you see, where
I will have to confer with Mr. Pinkerton before giving
you any answer of a definite character. I can hold out
no hope for you whatever to-day. Mr. Pinkerton will
be in shortly. I will lay the matter before him. You may
call at the same hour to-morrow. I can give you a decision then."

The little woman dried her eyes, thanked the superintendent as best she could, and was shown out the private
door of the outer consulting-room, Mr. Warner murmuring sympathetically :

"Good-day, madam ; good-day. Sorry ; d—— *very*
sorry !"

It is a custom of mine, which has been observed without exception for several years, to ride in my carriage,
rain or shine, snow or sleet, for from two to four hours
of every afternoon. I find not only genuine pleasure in
it, but health and vigor, and, above all, a relief from a
crush of business, which, with me, seems never to be done,
and to increase beyond measure as I advance in life.

These rides are taken in every direction from my
office ; sometimes through and through the heart of the
city ; sometimes to some outlying suburb ; and often ten

twenty, and frequently thirty miles straight out into the country. I have thus formed a regular acquaintance with little roadside inns, where I always find my bevy of beggars and vagabonds ready to hold or water my horses, for the change they as invariably expect ; and I have thus come to know every sign in the city, every alley or by-way, every nook and corner; and, in numberless instances, the almost perfect information so secured of every peculiarity of Chicago and its surroundings has proven of invaluable service in facilitating whatever work of a local nature I might have in hand.

On the day in question I had been out over the roads adjacent to Chicago's beautiful North Shore, and had determined to return through Lincoln Park along the wide, smooth boulevard which borders the white beach where the waves come tumbling in. It was one of those rough, raw days when the clouds go scurrying across the sky, and the water upon the broad expanse of Lake Michigan had a steely-blue color intervening between the scudding white-caps. The park was deserted, and not a carriage save my own was to be seen down the miles of drive, level as a floor. Turning from the highway into the drive, I saw, a mile beyond, like a dark *silhouette* against the water, the form of a solitary man, pacing rapidly back and forth upon the sands. Swiftly he sped up and down the shore, like one with no purpose, but impelled by some strong and overwhelming excitement.

As I neared him, he took no notice of either myself or carriage, and I saw that his face was pale, and that all of his actions betokened great mental trouble. My de tective instincts, or curiosity, or whatever it may be called, were at once aroused, and I directed my driver to pass the man slowly. Arriving opposite him, as we were now going in opposite directions, I noticed at once that he was a young business man of my acquaintance.

" Hallo, Saunders ! " said I.

"Well, what do you want ? " he returned, in a hard, hurt kind of a way.

" I want you to get right in here with me," I replied sternly, knowing that the man required a superior will to manage him.

He got in the carriage and sat down beside me without a word.

" What is the matter, Saunders ? " I abruptly asked.

" I'm all gone to pieces," he answered, with a moan.

" In a business way ? " I asked.

" No, at home," he replied bitterly.

" Now, tell me the truth—nothing else ! " said I, se-verely.

" Well, friend Pinkerton," he answered slowly, and as though his whole life and heart were in the reply, " my wife is going wrong ! "

" I don't believe it ! " I replied, warmly.

"Yes," he said, after a pause ; " yes, it's true. A few weeks ago we had one of those family quarrels that curse married people. It was a little thing at first—a *little* thing—just one of those family misunderstandings that bring hell between a couple. I wouldn't give up, not

would she. At first we were very proud, and would not
recognize each other. Soon we took separate meals.
Then my wife got high-toned, and took a bed in another
part of the house. I followed suit, and took *my* bed as far
away from her as I could get it in the house. For nearly
a week past she has been spending the days and nights
out. I have been trying to get at the secret of her estrange-
ment. For the last three days and nights I have been out
constantly. I have had several of our most trustworthy
employees watching the house and following her, but I
am entirely at a loss ; some human devil is taking advantage of our family trouble to ruin her. Pinkerton, I made
up my mind to come to you. But I recollected that you
never touch these matters, and I had about determined
to do something desperate ! "

My heart opened at once for the man, and I concluded
to break over my rule at any cost, get at the bottom of
the trouble, which, I could see, he had only made worse
by his attempting to play the detective, and then, if it
were possible, show the wife the wretchedness and misery she was causing, and in some way, not then quite
clear to me, but which I felt assured would in good time
transpire, bring about a reconciliation and peace to the
family of my young friend.

I told him this ; and it made a new man of him at once.

We were soon at the agency, and we proceeded together at once to my own private office. I immediately
summoned Mr. Warner, and began explaining matters
with a view of having him get a thorough understanding

of it with me, and then make a detail of men when neces
sary for thorough investigation.

This had hardly been entered into when I observed
that my superintendent was conducting himself very
strangely. He "hummed" and "hawed," cleared his
throat a half-dozen times as if to speak, but each time
seemed to change his mind and repress himself by the
greatest effort. On several occasions I came near asking
him the reason for his singular action, but refrained on
account of the presence of my friend.

No sooner had he departed, with the understanding
that I should pick him up at a designated spot on the
next afternoon, and before he had hardly reached the
street, than Mr. Warner burst into such an irrepressible fit
of laughter that I could not resist joining him, although I
confess the whole proceeding was quite beyond my power
of comprehension ; but when he had sufficiently recovered
to explain himself and relate the interview with the
beautiful lady an hour previous, the ludicrousness and
complete absurdity of the entire situation came over me
with such force that I am afraid I was quite as badly affected as my superintendent, and certainly myself indulged
in a roar of laughter which must have been heard to the
remotest part of the great building, and possibly, as I have
capital lungs, beyond into the street.

But my readers may be very sure that the cases were
taken.

The next afternoon the lady called, was informed that
Mr. Pinkerton had deviated from his fixed rule in her

behalf, and such necessary information was secured as would give color to the evident planning of a thorough investigation. Superintendent Warner also gave her such hope and courage as he could; and the little woman went away with the understanding that she should call at the same hour on the next day, and looking much brighter and happier for the hope that had risen within her. He also elicited the fact that her husband had returned to his home early on the previous night, had retired early, and had certainly remained in the house during the whole night.

On the same afternoon I had my young friend in my carriage for an hour, gave him some hint that the object of our search would be captured, possibly by the next day, and in all probability everything would terminate much better than I had at first feared—in fact, wholly as it should. I was also able to learn that his wife had certainly passed the preceding night at home. He was sure of it, but did not seem to wish to tell me how. Altogether, he had become sunnier and more hopeful.

On the third afternoon the little woman came as true as time to the minute of her appointment with my superintendent.

"Well, we have the truth of the matter at last. I hope it won't prove too bad!" he continued, reassuringly, as the little lady, womanlike, now that the suspense of it all was nearly over, burst into tears.

"Tell me, tell me all about it! Do tell me! If it kills me, I must know it all!" she sobbed violently.

"My dear madam !" replied Mr. Warner in a soothing tone, "you *must* compose yourself. I am not at liberty to give you the particulars. I can only say this much : We shall in a few minutes have this party who has caused the trouble in our office. You are to take a seat in one of the parlors. We will then have the party introduced to you, and you can then, having everything in your power, secure a confession as we have done, and extort a lasting pledge !"

With this the lady was conducted to one of the several small parlors, or reception-rooms, near my own private office, frequently found necessary in my business. The room was conveniently somewhat darkened, and, on leaving the superintendent at the door, she said, with some trepidity and evident fear :

"Oh, what shall I do alone with this fiend ? "

"Just use your very best judgment, madam," Mr. Warner replied ; "nothing shall harm you."

With this the door closed, and the little woman was alone. What were her feelings and thoughts I cannot attempt to picture. One thing, however, was certain. As she paced the floor with a quick stride for the few minutes which should intervene, her fingers worked nervously, as though her spirit and indignation could not be restrained, and that she must wreak vengeance upon the fiend who had come between her and all that she loved.

Half an hour before I had left my young friend at his store. I had informed him that I had "run in the

party he " most wanted to see ; " that the person was then
in my office ; that I had extorted a full confession, the
details of which, however, I declined to give, as I had
determined he should be given an opportunity to confront
the person himself and see with his own eyes and heal
with his own ears the object of *his* fruitless detective service and the whole story.   He was greatly moved, and
said he feared he would do the d——d villain bodily
harm.   I told him that if he did he would forever forfeit my friendship ; and he pledged himself solemnly to
confine his indignation and punishment to his unexpected
presence and words alone.

The last words of mine to him, as he alighted from my
carriage at his store, were :

" Now, Saunders, if you bring a revolver or anything
of that sort, or in any way break faith with me, I will
make you suffer for it.   *I won't have any scenes in my
office !* "

I had arranged that he should take a certain course to
get to the agency.   This brought him to the second floor
and near my room by a private entrance, so that there
might be no danger of any of his friends seeing him.

I shortly heard his footsteps upon the stairs.   He
halted occasionally, as if to gain strength for his terrible
meeting.   At last he entered my room, and said :

" Pinkerton !   My God !   this is too much !   Where—
where is he ? "

" There ! " I replied, pointing to a sliding-door, through
which a parlor was reached.

He stepped to the door, put his hand upon the knob, paused a moment nervously, then, drawing himself to his fullest height—and looking so much the man, every inch of him, that I was proud of the fellow—strode into the room.

There was silence for a moment—I confess that to me it was an awful silence. It was a thrilling moment, and had a thousand times more in it than I ever hoped.

Then there was a little shriek, a strong voice tremulously choked and stifled, a rush of a true husband and a devoted wife across what had seemed an impassable gulf, safe and sure into each other's arms.

I did not disturb them. For an hour they were there together. What love had been renewed, quickened, doubt dispelled, hopes brightened, everything that is tender and true in life resurrected and bettered, I cannot tell , but I *do* know that two more grateful people never existed on the face of this green earth.

And I also know that they both went home in the little *coupé* together, and have never occupied " separate apartments " since.

CHAPTER XX.

BOGUS DETECTIVES AND WOULD-BE DETECTIVES.

IN my upward of a quarter of a century's detective career many strange circumstances have continually arisen, and are constantly arising, to make the experience of my every-day life both remarkably painful and pleasantly romantic. The position which I occupy gives me an unusual opportunity to see life from the under side, and the worst as well as the best phases of human charac ter are forced upon my notice, until they become, by sec ond nature, a matter for study.

Among the peculiar experiences which are forced upon me are some from a class which have risen directly from the world-wide reputation which has been secured for my agencies and my methods of detection. Many unthink- ing people have come to believe that there is something mysterious, wonderful, and awful about the detective. All my life, and in every manner in my power, I have endeavored to break down this popular superstition, but it would seem that it could not be done.

Many persons seem to desire to believe that a detective holds some supernatural power, or yet is possessed of some finer instinct or keener perception than other mor- tals; and hence the bogus detective has the elements of success as a swindler when he even makes the shabbiest pretense of being a detective.

This foolish fancy as to the power of the detective comes, I am aware, from that element, nearly akin to fear in all of us, for anything mysterious or unexplainable. But I have always contended that the criminal could not best be brought to justice *by* the criminal, but by the clean, healthy, honest mind, using clean, healthy, honest methods, and those persistently and unceasingly

It is undoubtedly true that the successful detective must be possessed of faculties fitting him for his peculiar character of work, and ten thousand men may possess those who live and die without the slightest hint of such capabilities. Into nearly every prominent profession or vocation men drift because they are by nature best suited to fit them. The successful merchant becomes so not, as a rule, through good fortune, but by keeping his work well in hand, being capable of managing a large number of employees, making his investments safe and certain, and being content with *gradually* acquired credit and wealth. But he *must* have the disposition and the ability to do all this, or he is quite likely to fail. And so with every other profession or business ; and the detective must possess certain qualifications of prudence, secrecy, inventiveness, persistency, personal courage, and, above all other things, honesty ; while he must add to these the same quality of reaching out and becoming possessed of that almost boundless information which will permit of the immediate and effective application of his detective talent in whatever degree that may be possessed.

And this is all there is to the very best of detectives.

If there is mystery attached to his movements, it is simply because secrecy is imperative, and that will never consist in vague hints and meaningless intimations. These are the surest signs that he is an impostor. If he *is* a detective, and an able one, he will not go about publishing the fact. Any thinking person can readily see how utterly useless would be the efforts of such a person to accomplish anything worthy.

I have been led to say this much, not only to dispel the

popular idea concerning detectives, but to also call the attention of my readers, and the public generally, to the almost countless instances where business men and private citizens are imposed upon and subjected to every manner of indignity and annoyance by the veriest swindlers extant, who pursue petty thievery or petty blackmailing schemes through the pretense of being detectives, and particularly of being " Pinkerton's detectives."

One of these scamps will call at some little provincial town, where communication with large cities is poor, and, after getting "the lay of the land," will call upon some business man of the place—the more ignorant the better—and vaguely intimate that he is there in his interest. If the person should fail to understand, the bogus detective will buttonhole him, take him into a quiet corner, when the following conversation is likely to ensue :

" Pinkerton, you know ? "

" Pinkerton ?—Pinkerton ?   Well, what about him ? "

" I'm one of his men ! " the alleged will reply, with an air of great importance.

"Well, I've heard of Mr. Pinkerton often ; but what may your business be ? "

" That's just what concerns *you !* "

Here the assumed detective will probably show some forged letters or some cheap star, or something of the kind, with a pretense that it is his "authority" for acting in the business.

By this time the country merchant is half-frightened,

wholly curious, and altogether mystified, and, very naturally, wishes to know what the nature of the man's business is, and what is about to happen.

Upon this the bogus detective branches forth into a talk
about Mr. Pinkerton having discovered that on such and
such a night his store is to be broken into and robbed,
and that he has been sent there to inform the merchant
of the proposed burglary, and to act with him in prevent
ing the same.

Now, nothing will more work upon a man's fears than
the conviction of impending danger—some evil which
still lies in the dark, but which seems certain to transpire ;
and so soon as the bogus detective has laid this foun-
dation, nothing is easier than for him to get upon the most
confidential terms with his unsuspicious victim.

In the meantime the impostor has taken board at the
best hotel in the place—if he has had assurance enough for
that—and soon lets his pretended business be known in
certain quarters, though always exhorting the strictest
secrecy, and he soon has the reputation about town of
being "one of Pinkerton's men ! "

He will now probably begin operations by making a
pretense of communicating with me, and, in the presence
of some party whom he is desirous to impress with his
importance, will seal and direct a massive "report" or
letter to me, which, however, he is very careful not to
mail.   He will then hint at mysterious comrades--all my
men—who are close at hand, but under cover, and who
will be ready to assist him at the necessary moment, and

that he proposes to make a clean job of the thing, **and** forever rid *that* place of robbers and criminals.

In this manner, and in various other ways, he gradually worms himself into public confidence. And this class of a fraud has sometimes even the audacity to telegraph me, in meaningless jargon, unintelligible combinations of words or sets of figures, until everything is ripe; and then, on the strength of my reputation as a business **man** and a detective, strikes right and left for money or **any** other thing he can get, and leaves the place between **two** days, having beaten everybody possible.

Others of this class will accidentally ascertain some foible, or possibly criminal act, of the private citizen, and will at once make known his object to be the arrest of the party on a certain charge—also quietly hinting that he is sorry for the publicity which must ensue, but that he feels compelled to do his whole duty. Perhaps he will inform the victim that he may be allowed his liberty for a day or two, in order to arrange his business affairs, and, in the interim, pretend to keep a close watch upon him. By this time the party is in a proper condition to be bled, and shortly is so worked upon that a snug sum is got, when the villain immediately decamps.

This pretending to be in my employ is a favorite dodge of impecunious wanderers and " dead-beats " who find themselves stranded at hotels. I have a large personal acquaintance among hotel-keepers and other public business men, so that, in my kind of business, circumstances might occur, as they have frequently occurred,

where courtesies and favors from them have been of great
benefit. The dead-beat has found this of use, and, with
his keen insight into possible chances of extending his
stay, or of getting away without the detention of his bag-
gage, should he have any, he has frequently made such
liberal use of my name as to permit his peaceful departure.

Even in communities where citizens are usually well
informed, and perhaps I had recently brought some important case to a successful termination, some unprinci
pled lawyer or official, possessing a petty spite or grudge
against a neighbor, has dimly hinted that he and myself
understood each other ; that when the proper time came
he would cause an explosion, and that Pinkerton's men
were then in town, and keeping their eyes open too !

Slouching individuals of all manner of kind, traveling
to or stopping at all manner of places, when the last re
sort has failed for raising the wind, or carrying out some
miserable scheme, immediately transform themselves into
pseudo-detectives, and nearly as often make a pretense of
some near or remote connection with my business for as
many various purposes as there are different swindlers.

But a short time since a mysterious individual appeared
at the residence of a wealthy family of Iowa farmers, who
are immediate relatives of a gentleman prominently connected with the Philadelphia *Inquirer*. He exhibited a
letter purporting to be from my office, authorizing him to
follow and hunt down certain Missouri outlaws, and also
called their attention to an item from a Chicago paper

relating an affray between one of my operatives and a criminal whom he was arresting, where the operative lost his finger from a pistol-shot. The name of the detective was given, and it corresponded with that of the bogus letter ; while, sure enough, the impostor had lost just that finger spoken of.

The vagabond intimated that he wished to remain with them for a short time for his " detective " purposes, and also stated—which secured his admission to the family— that while he was there he would quietly keep his eye upon the members of a neighboring family with whom the former had been at feud for nearly fifteen years.

The actions of the man were incomprehensible. He was of course mysterious, and made a pretense of being out much of nights, and keeping very closely within the house during the day. He told great tales of miraculous doings with criminals, exhibited many wounds he had re- ceived in the assumed pursuit of his duty, and in various other ways played the rôle of a detective according to the stage rendering and the popular conception of that character, remaining with the family several weeks. But at last the real character of the man became known.

A brother of the farmer was a wealthy stock-man, and, after his trips to Chicago, always returned to the farm for a few days' visit, generally with a considerable amount of money in his possession. On his first arrival there after the appearance of the bogus detective, the latter conceived a cock-and-bull story about having discovered a counterfeiter's cave in the woods near the farm, which

was occupied during the day, but always deserted at
night, and he endeavored to induce the stock-dealer to
accompany him on a tour of inspection.   At first he consented to go ; but his suspicions finally became aroused,
and he refused unless also accompanied by his brother.
This the scamp opposed, offering some excuse, which
further inclined the people to believe he was an impostor.
The same night the rogue suddenly left, and the parties
found that every pistol or revolver in the house had been
so tampered with that its effective use would be simply
impossible.

It had been this particular bogus detective's plan to get
into the good graces of the family until such a time as the
drover appeared, and then decoy him into the woods at
night, where he might rob him or murder and rob him at
leisure.

Not succeeding in this. and finding that the locality was
becoming too warm for him, he decamped.   The same
night he robbed the post-office in the village near at
hand, and was captured.   He got one year in the penitentiary for this.   But, strange as it may seem, I was never
informed of his pretensions concerning being in my employ until after he had served *his* term and been discharged, when, evidently out of mere curiosity, the gentle
man referred to as prominently connected with the Philadelphia *Inquirer* gave me a history of the matter and
desired information as to the man's genuineness.

I could give the reader hundreds of similar instances
where people are daily permitting themselves to be im

13

posed upon by these shrewd tramps and petty swindlers who, under the guise of " Pinkerton's detectives," carry on their villainous schemes of blackmail, and exasperating, although paltry swindles.   I am continually receiving telegrams and letters asking if such and such persons are in my employ ; whether they have been authorized to take certain proceedings, or whether I will be responsible for any indebtedness they may incur.   And I am certain that a modest estimate of the sum I have expended in running down these pests and assisting in bringing them to justice would not fall short of ten thousand dollars.

But if " bogus detectives " have proven of constant annoyance and occasional absorbing interest, there is an other class of persons that have been still more persist ent in endeavoring to attract my attention, and at all times a source of infinite amusement.

My mails are daily burdened with their communications.   I am run down and cornered most ingeniously. I never have peace from their obstinate endeavors.

These are the would-be detectives.

They are legion.

They exist in all parts of the world, are in all sorts of positions or conditions of impecuniosity, and have every manner of ability imaginable.   They *will* be detectives whether or no ; and, if I do not give them a chance, they threaten to distinguish themselves on their own account. Every time word comes to the public of my agencies hav ing succeeded in an operation of any magnitude these applications come in shoals, although the daily receipt is so large in number that the Government at least must be greatly benefited. I try to have them all suitably answered; but many of them defy a sober consideration and even a translation. These are turned over to Chief Clerk Robertson, and consigned to what I have appropriately named the "Lunatic File;" and I am sorry to confess that this is a wonderfully large monument to detective aspiration.

There seem to be three things which are the ambition of a very great class of men and women who have arrived at a point where they are desperately in need of employment. They wish to go upon the stage, become an author, or turn detective; and it is about an equal chance which way they go.

One of these people writes me :

"I am traveling around a great deal, and want you to send me a roving commission as one of your detectives. I see many instances where the power of such authority would be of great benefit to me."

Now, here was an individual who really and honestly believed that I in some way had the power to grant him a "roving commission" to make an ass of himself on any occasion which might offer; and if there was one thing in the world that the precious scamp was sincere about, it was that I would go into ecstasies over being able to secure just such talent as his.

A benighted female writes from Detroit that she is "alone in the world;" that she is certain of being "born a detective;" that she is at present boarding at a certain respectable boarding-house, where there is a thin partition separating her room from another, in which she is sure a noted gang of burglars have their rendezvous ; that in the silent and witching hours of the night these men talk over the situation in deep and solemn voices, and arrange future plans for depredation and robbery ; and that her ear is constantly applied to this partition, until she has become a sort of an Edison phonograph—in fact, a repository of wonderful secrets, which she will divulge—like the machine, give forth when she is unwound ; and that all that is necessary for me to become possessed of such information as will enable me to distinguish myself and win fame, is to send her forty dollars. Think of it ! only forty dollars ! This will enable her to liquidate a slight outstanding indebtedness at the aforesaid boarding-house with a thin partition, when she will proceed to the ends of the earth, if necessary, and dog the footsteps of this band of robbers, and, by getting into rooms at hotels, and otherwise, will continue the phonographic business indefinitely.

Now, here was a genius that ought to have received encouragement ; but unfortunately she did not set a sufficiently high value upon her services.

A gentleman, addressing me from the Grand Hotel, San Francisco, relates that he is writing a book from observation on the Pacific coast, and that he thinks a commission from me, authorizing him as a detective in that section, would prove of great benefit to him. In return for this he solemnly promises to give me and my business a "splendid puff" in his book, which he is sure (what author was ever not) will "sell like hot cakes."

I felt a sympathy for the man, but was compelled to decline becoming responsible for his hotel and other bills, even at the risk of losing so excellent an opportunity for a place in his swiftly-selling book.

A party from a large town in Kentucky, who is in the piano and organ trade, writes that his income is becoming small, through the cutting on prices of base interlopers, and that, as his business is fast going to the devil, he has made up his mind to fling himself, as it were, body and soul, into the detective business ; and, while certain that his services are worth to any employer or corporation from four to five thousand dollars a year, he will sacrifice himself to the cause of justice at a mere pittance. He concludes his interesting application with this *naïve* and spicy remark :

"As I am a married man, with six cherubs, my mother-in-law being a permanent fixture with me now, I can leave home indefinitely."

It might have been that here was the secret of a man, worth four or five thousand dollars to any employer, being willing to leave home indefinitely for a mere pittance.

Mothers-in-law have been the cause of even greater instances of desperation than this.

Away up from the cotton-fields of Texas I receive an application from a party who says he is with me every day and hour in my fight against criminals and law-break ing. He says he is "nothing but a common cotton picker," but confesses that he has a great mind, and that to a massive intellect " cotton-picking has its drawbacks." He bids me God-speed in my good work, and remarks that he knows a thing or two that I am not "up to," even if I did come from Scotland, closing his letter with the proposition that, whenever I want a man who can get right at the bottom of things, he will leave the fair fields of Texas at a moment's notice.

Poor fellow ! I could almost see a man who had had better fortune in the years before, and who had written me more as an outburst of his own desperation at his cotton-picking fate in the burning sun of Texas, than because he had the remotest idea that he could be of any service to me or that I could more than kindly reply to him.

Another person, writing from a southern Illinois town, puts the matter in this concise manner :

"There is a band of burglars here.   I'm going to hunt them out, if *you* can't.   I'll come to Chicago for fifteen dollars a week, twenty dollars advanced."

In the man's efforts to appear wise and terse, he neg.' lected to sign his name, and so I could not forward him the amount required.

Another would-be detective, with an inventive turn, writes me :

"I have a sure method of detecting crime or persons.   I will disclose the same to you for two thousand dollars in money , or I will accept a position under you in your force, at a salary commensurate with the importance of my discovery, and use the system in connection with my operations."

Out of mere curiosity I looked into this matter, and found the applicant to be an impecunious half-crazy "mind reader" and spiritualist.

A party from Pittsburg explained some of his abilities as follows :

" In the character of a common laborer or Irishman I can handle a pick and shovel admirably. As a negro I can transform my appearance and dialect, so that I could pass undetected among negroes themselves. I can pass in the best society as a titled foreigner, or play ' coachy ' in a gentleman's household. I can take any character to perfection, and, if you will indicate anything you wish assumed, I will put up a forfeit of any reasonable amount that I can assume it, or enact it so as to even deceive yourself. Salary is no object.

"I know I would love the detective's life ; and if you don't want me, I shall go it alone."

Never having made a bet in my life, I could not conscientiously take this wager, and therefore was compelled to inform the Pittsburg aspirant for detective honors that he would have to " go it alone."

The district attorney of one of the wealthiest counties in Wisconsin recently wrote me, asking to become a detective. He stated that he had a lucrative practice ; had been very successful in his office ; could give the highest commendations from lawyers, members of the Wisconsin Legislature, senators, and from the press ; but that he had become fascinated with his idea of the life of a detective, and that he felt that he must enter my service. He agreed to leave his business entirely, devote himself honestly and earnestly to the work, and prove himself in every way worthy of my best respect and esteem.

Now, here was an application worthy of all consideration; but I saw that the man was simply momentarily flushed with the supposed romance of the work, had never considered the numberless instances of ill-success and hard, grinding labor; in fact, that he had had—as a person will witness a grand theatric performance and become momentarily "stage-struck"—his mind fixed upon some brilliant achievement of the detective order, and was for the time being actually "detective-struck," if that term is admissible. And I frankly told him so, showing him that his course did not lie in that direction. The result was: second, sober thought; and the man to-day thanks me for an honorable standing among the legal fraternity of Wisconsin.

Now, these are but a few samples, at random, out of thousands of applications from would-be detectives the country over. They are before me, as I write, in huge piles; from women who have a mission; from men who want a commission; from traveling preachers, who confess that there is much roguery even among church people which they wish to bring to light—always providing they can make a few dollars out of the business; from country bumpkins, who are dissatisfied with the plain ways of the village or the farm, and who imagine there is great glory and perennial romance in the detective's career; from all

Sorts of men, who imagine they have a scent of all sorts of crime, and who only want my indorsement and a little, just a little, money to make the thing a grand success; from authors, who wish to become familiar with crime, in order to depict it, and who absolutely need, so they say, a connection with my agencies to accomplish it; from sailors, who promise to climb to the cross yards, stand on their heads, and do other daring nautical feats while scattering circulars to advertise my business; from wandering pedlars; from strolling tinkers; from traveling clock-repairers; from gypsies, and even from thieves in countless numbers!

Each one and all have abilities—on paper—that are simply marvelous. Each and all show me what a sacrifice they are making to take upon themselves such a life, and how brilliantly successful they will be in my service. And each and all want money, immediately and continuously.

Now, I have just this advice to offer to all with detective aspirations: Let well enough alone. If you are in any employment, remain in it; attend to it faithfully and honestly. You *might* become a detective; but where one becomes a successful detective, a thousand fail utterly and completely—or, worse, become blackmailers and vagabonds, if not actual thieves and criminals.

CHAPTER XXI.

EXTRAORDINARY SELF-ROBBERY.

ONE day in December, 1870, the president of one of the Chicago national banks called at my office and desired a private interview with me.

His statement was, that the deputy county treasurer of a county in Iowa, while alone in his office, had been assaulted by some unknown ruffians, nearly murdered, and sixteen thousand dollars taken out of his safe.

It was desired by some correspondent of the bank's, at the county seat where the assault and robbery had occurred, that the bank president should confer with me and secure my assistance.

Having but these bare outlines of the matter, I could do no more than at once dispatch one of my most able men to the point, with such general instructions as at that time could be given. This man—a keen, shrewd Irish-American named Hanlon, upon whom had previously devolved the successful working up, under my direction, of several heavy bank and safe robberies—proceeded immediately to the place, and there met a gentleman named Wooster, who had authorized the operation, and who, being on the deputy treasurer's bonds, was naturally very anxious that the burglars and would-be murderers should be apprehended, and the large amount of money taken—or at least a portion of it—recovered.

The result of a careful preliminary examination into the matter was telegraphed me as follows :

On the night of the ninth of December, in the year mentioned, a gentleman named Newcomb, desiring to purchase a county bond for some customer, went to the court-house, where the deputy treasurer, a gentleman named Benton Emery, was accustomed to remain until about nine o'clock—his office being a sort of general rendezvous for a few of the county officials and several business men of the town.

On entering the treasurer's office, Mr. Newcomb was startled to find a prostrate form upon the floor. He immediately procured a light, and found a man covered with blood, and apparently dying. Blood was upon the floor and flowed from several wounds of the presumably murdered man. The room betrayed evidences of a severe struggle ; the lamp had been thrown upon the floor, and the odor of the oil showed that it had been broken in the fall. The chairs were thrown about and broken, and, what was more conclusive, and seemed to give some little clue to the mystery, was the circumstance that the door to the safe stood wide open, and papers and parcels were scattered in every direction around it.

Mr. Newcomb took all this in at a single glance, and, half suspecting what was to follow, found the wounded man to be no other than Benton Emery, the deputy treasurer himself. He was immediately taken home, and in a few days, though he barely lived through the terrible wounds he had received, was able to give an account of the robbery, as it undoubtedly was.

He stated that just after dark two men in oil-cloth coats called at his office, and stated that they desired to purchase some revenue stamps. They asked for five dollars' worth, and tendered a one hundred dollar bill in payment. He took up a glass to examine it, and, after scrutinizing it and becoming satisfied of its genuineness, turned to open the safe. No sooner had he done so than one of the men sprang upon him, drawing a dagger, and grasped him violently by the throat. He was unable to utter a sound, but struggled with his assailants, clutching the dagger by the blade. The ruffian drew the dagger through his hand, and inflicted an awful gash, nearly severing the thumb at the ball. Weakened from his struggles with his burly foe and the pressure on his throat, he was compelled to gradually relax his efforts, when he received several stabs in his side. He then fell to the floor insensible.

An examination of the wounds proved that, though they were dangerous, they were not necessarily fatal. There was a gash on the hand, as stated, and four wounds around the heart, which, though deep, were not dangerous. The throat was wounded, and a frightful cut in the head disclosed the skull underneath.

The safe was overhauled, and sixteen thousand dollars, chiefly county funds, with a few small sums placed in the safe by merchants for safe-keeping, had been taken.

Now, these were the outlines of the matter, and it would

reasonably be supposed that a bold and outrageous robbery had occurred and a brutal murder almost committed.

In fact. hardly any other theory could account for the
terrible wounds which Mr. Emery sustained.

Some delay had ensued before I had been called upon,
so that by the time my operative had arrived in the village
Mr. Emery had so far recovered from his wounds as to
be able to take an active part in the endeavor to detect
the perpetrators of the crime. He was a man of wealth,
was engaged in no speculations which might have embar-
rassed him, so that while no possible clue to the robbers
could be secured at that time, and with the information I
then possessed, the last thought to enter my mind was
any possible suspicion that the deputy treasurer himself
had the remotest connection with the robbery.

But every other possible theory and clue were finally
exhausted.

I reasoned that professional criminals of the sort capable of so daring a crime, in nearly every instance leave
some clue by which their character as criminals can be
established, and subsequently their identity pretty clearly
arrived at. In my thirty years of detective work these
things became so marked and fixed that, on reading a tele-
graphic newspaper report of a large or small robbery,
with the aid of my vast records and great personal experience and familiarity with these matters, I can at once tell
the *character* of the work, and then, knowing the names,
history, habits, and quite frequently the rendezvous of the
men doing that class of work, am able to determine, with

almost unerring certainty, not only the very parties who committed the robberies, but also what disposition they are likely to make of their plunder, and at what points they may be in hiding.

I hardly believed this robbery to have been committed by professional bank robbers. This conviction was verified by the fact that the closest inquiries failed to show that any strangers who could not be accounted for had been seen in the village for weeks before. The town, though the county seat, did not contain at that time a population of over five hundred, and in a place of that size the face of a stranger is always closely scanned, and he cannot remain in the place without being quizzed and questioned.

I could not believe the robbery had been done by any of the class of outlaws who generally commit depredations upon express companies, isolated banks, and the like, in the more sparsely settled portions of the West; for a scouring of the country, in every direction, failed to discover the slightest clue to any persons having ridden to or from the place, or reached or departed from it on foot or by any manner of conveyance.

This consequently narrowed the investigation to the townspeople of the place itself. So here I directed my operative to dig away persistently, and leave no stone unturned toward the solving of the mystery. But it was of no use. The history, antecedents, occupation, habits, and financial condition of every male person in the village was secured, and where any person was found who might have, by the remotest possibility, been connected with the affair, he was made to give a thorough account of himself. But at last this course utterly failed to develop anything material to the case, and I found myself balked in every direction.

One day, while sitting in my private office, puzzling my brain over the matter, and going through and through my operative's reports from beginning to end, with the vain hope of picking out of it all some slight thread upon which to hang even a theory of the robbery, I came to this sentence in one of the reports :

" Mr. Emery is ceaseless in his efforts to assist me, but seems to be very much opposed to my going so hard upon some of the people of the village, as he constantly insists that it was done by professional robbers from a distance."

In the mood I then was, my mind continually reverted to this. Why was Mr. Emery so solicitous about his fellow-townsmen while there remained the barest chance of the robbers being found among them ? And why did Mr. Emery desire to constantly impress my operative with the idea that the robbery was done by professional robbers from a distance ?

Pass this paragraph as often as I might, I always came around to it, stopped at it, and began asking myself these questions about it. I could not rid myself of the feeling, the longer I studied over it, that the impression was gradually but surely becoming fixed in my mind that there was behind all this a motive.

Now what was that motive ?

I felt that the suspicion which was gradually creeping into my mind was unjust to Mr. Emery ; but the line of investigation it suggested, and which I now determined upon, was the *dernier ressort.*

I therefore immediately instructed my operative to continue his investigations as zealously as ever, but to at once devote more attention to noting every act and expression, as well as the manner and bearing of Mr. Emery, without in the slightest degree betraying to the deputy treasurer his double duty.

The result of this was, that in a few days I had before me reports which fully justified the course taken.

Emery seemed to be worried and anxious, and to relax his interest in endeavoring to track the robbers. There was a great load of some kind upon his mind. He appeared to have relapsed into a listless condition, from which any newly-proposed plan by my operative would awaken him into a state of genuine nervousness and excitement, and it soon came to be his half-expressed desire that the operation should be abandoned.

At this point I decided to further test my new theory of the robbery.

I arranged that an anonymous communication should be forwarded to the place from Dubuque, intimating that two suspicious characters could be found at a certain designated place in that city, whom the writer had reason to believe were the two persons that had committed the robbery. The descriptions sent tallied exactly with those given of the robbers by the deputy treasurer himself ; and accordingly my operative and Mr. Emery set out for Dubuque to endeavor to secure an identification of the suspected parties.

But my operative found it hard work to even get him away from home. He protested that he had no faith in anonymous letters, and would wager any amount that it would all prove a fool's errand ; and although he finally consented to make the trip, nearly every remark made by him concerning the matter tended to show that Mr. Emery knew as well as I did that no robbers of his treas-ury were to be found in Dubuque.

I had instructed operative Hanlon to *insist* both that the parties were to be found, and that, if there was any-thing like an excuse for doing so, he should arrest the men and take them back with him. When this was said pretty forcibly and decidedly, Emery seemed to be utterly at a loss for an opinion ; but finally, as if overwhelmed by the possible complications which such a course might involve, very hotly urged the injustice of such a step ; and finally, just before reaching the city, came out flatly, and said that he had been thinking the matter over, and had come to the conclusion that, if the real robbers were brought before him, it was very doubtful whether he would be able to identify them at all!

All of this and much other, tending to show a *guilty knowledge* of the robbery on Emery's part, and a great anxiety to be rid of the whole matter, was telegraphed me from Dubuque ; and I instantly decided to arrange a ruse by which Emery could be brought right into my office, where I could watch him, converse with him, per haps play upon him a little, but, at all events, where I might be able to form a better judgment of the man, and conclude whether he was in any way connected with this affair, which, in looking at it from any standpoint, I could not but regard as very mysterious.

I could scarcely imagine *what* connection Emery had with the matter. I confess that I *suspected* he had robbed himself. But how were the horrible wounds that had nearly caused his death to be accounted for?

Surely no sane man in Emery's position in life would cut his hand nearly off, stab himself a half dozen times most desperately over and about the heart, and lay open his skull as a fearful sabre stroke would do!

I could hardly imagine any solution to the mystery. Possibly he had not been guilty of the actual robbery, but perhaps it had been done by persons who had since approached him, and represented to him that they were too shrewd to be punished, and, having convinced him of this, for a liberal share of the stolen funds, secured from him a pledge that he would prevent, as far as possible, the efforts which were being made for their capture.

In any event, I had decided that Mr. Emery *was guilty of something!*

I therefore at once telegraphed operative Hanlon, at Dubuque, that the parties he had expected there had got an inkling that their whereabouts had been discovered, had fled to this city; that I had had them arrested, and was now detaining them; and directing him to leave there at once for Chicago with Mr. Emery, whose presence would be absolutely required.

This done, I set about preparing matters at my office so as to give color to the genuineness of the arrest when Mr. Emery arrived.

I selected two stalwart men from among my force, and, by change in dress and sundry other little manœuvres, made them answer the description of the supposed burglars who had robbed and nearly murdered Mr. Emery. They were heavily ironed and strongly guarded, and certainly, under the circumstances, presented a very hard and desperate appearance.

The next morning operative Hanlon and Mr. Emery arrived in Chicago.

The very moment I set my eyes upon the man I knew him to be guilty.

He was a gentleman of fine appearance naturally, but in every movement of his person, in every feature of his face, in every changing tone of his voice, in every startled look from his downcast eyes as they met my own, there was as strong an evidence of guilt as I ever had looked upon, and as true a proof that Emery was the criminal as though he had been a robber, had robbed and half-murdered another man, and come into my office under arrest rather than as a guest.

I saw all this at once, and endeavored to reassure him with the belief that we had at last captured the right parties.

He hoped so, he said; and this was all that could be got out of him.

Soon we proceeded to the apartment where the pretended desperate criminals were guarded.

They played their parts well, and made every possible apparent effort, without overdoing the matter, to prevent recognition. Emery was white as a ghost when he was brought before them. He seemed at an utter loss of knowledge how to act, but finally ventured to say that, while he might have seen them, he could not swear to their being the parties.

Returning to my private office, I invited Mr. Emery to a seat, directed the door to be closed, and, seating myself before him, remarked pleasantly :

" Mr. Emery, we are having pretty hard luck in this matter ? "

" Very ! " he replied, with a dry throat and a good deal of huskiness in it.

" What would you say, Mr. Emery," I remarked, with a meaning smile, " if I should tell you that, although you fail to identify the parties under arrest here, I now have the perpetrator of this crime within my office."

His face grew livid and white by turns, and his eyes seemed starting from their sockets.

"Yes," I continued, with great severity; "and what would you say if I would show you the man in this very room ? "

" Where ? where ? " he gasped, giving a startled look in every direction,

"There! there! See him! Look at him!" I almost shouted, turning him at one motion in the revolving chair where he sat, and bringing the poor fellow squarely in front of a huge pier-glass, and then forced him squarely upon his feet against it by main strength.

I never saw a more ghastly face than that of this self-robber's.

He sank into his seat and gasped:

"For God's sake, Mr. Pinkerton, you don't mean——"

"You *know* what I mean, Emery. You *know* it! Now out with the truth, like a man!"

There is but little more to tell. Emery now *knew* that I *knew* he committed the robbery, and the poor man went right at it, confessing the whole matter in a few minutes.

It was to the effect that he had no need for the money, was wealthy and beyond any possible want for life, but, being there in the office, shut up with so large a sum of money so long, he had first thought of the ease with which *he* might be robbed; then, revolving this in his mind so frequently, he finally conceived the idea of robbing himself. At last this became a sort of all-absorbing idea with him, which he could not by any possibility shake off, until actually, to give himself relief from it, he stole the money, hid it under the side-walk in front of the office, broke up the office furniture, and scattered papers and things, so as to give an evidence of a struggle, and at last inflicted upon himself the terrible wounds from which he had nearly died in order to give color to the story he was obliged to tell of being assaulted.

But the saddest part remains to be told. Emery was put in charge of the same operative, and returned to Iowa a prisoner, where he had left three days before a respectable citizen and a trusted officer. The money was all found just where Emery had said it was hidden. But the shame and disgrace of it all was more than the deluded man could sustain, and the second day after his arrival home he ended all his troubles by committing suicide ; this tragedy terminating one of the strangest incidents of my detective career.

----◆----

CHAPTER XXII.

A BRILLIANT CONFIDENCE SWINDLE IN HIGH LIFE.

IN looking over the events of my most eventful life, as the frequency of criminal occurrences of similar character often compels me to do, I cannot but reflect over the strange gullibility of the general public, and wonder at the great fertility of schemes and successful conspiracies on the part of criminals. Every day of the year some apparently new development in the way of criminal ingenuity is apparent, and the best detective minds of the time are constantly kept at their keenest friction to devise some means and expedients to cope with the advanced and apparently cultivated brains that are forever busy with fresh devices for living a life of elegance and ease without honest labor.

And yet to one who has spent the greater part of his life as I have done, in conscientiously studying the philosophy of crime and the peculiar traits and characteristics of criminals, there appears to be nothing startlingly new in all these matters. There is change in manner of operation, there may be fresh method in execution, but the main principle of crime, as well as of its detection, always remains the same ; and with the thousands upon thousands of warnings and public lessons coming to light every year, it would almost seem that respectable citizens refuse to profit by the bitter experience of others, and by their apparent simplicity and unguardedness really invite upon themselves the manipulations of keen rogues and educated rascals; and so true is this of people of all grades of society, that frequently, while doing everything in my power to assist those who have been almost ruined by their own foolishness, I could not resist the reflection that they had been served as they deserved.

An instance of carefully-prepared planning, neat work, and successful swindling of this kind came under my notice in Baltimore, a few years since ; and whenever it is recalled to my mind I am in doubt whether I shall more admire the handsome manner in which the scheme was done, or condemn the foolishness of the educated victim, who, after I had unearthed the scoundrels that had cruelly deceived and swindled the party, refused to prosecute them, out of some mawkish sentiment or fear of public ridicule.

In 1868 an old gentleman—whom I will call Willet—

died in Baltimore, leaving behind him a young and charm ing widow and a big fortune. After a year's becoming retirement and mourning, Mrs. Willet reappeared in society, and was warmly received within her circle, as her accomplishments were apparent and her wealth well known. Her grief was very easily drowned in a moderately gay society life, and consequently many real admirers and more genuine adventurers came in contact with her.

Among those with whom she became acquainted was one Henry Halliot, a son of a retired officer of the Union army during the rebellion. He was at one time, and was supposed then to be, a young gentleman of promise, wealth, and good connections, and, being a handsome, pleasant sort of fellow, he possessed just those traits and habits to easily captivate impressible women.

Halliot had been introduced to Mrs. Willet by a French lady, named Mlle. Villiers—a recent arrival in the society in which Mrs. Willet moved, but reputed wealthy and as being very select in her society. This Jeannette Villiers was unmarried, vivacious, witty—in fact, fascinating as only spirited and handsome French women can be. She was a charming brunette, full of blood, vitality, and positiveness, and soon began to exercise a certain magnetic influence over Mrs. Willet, with whom she soon became very intimate, and who was a dreamy-faced blonde, with but little strength of character.

Perfectly charmed with the young and volatile French woman, Mrs. Willet, after an acquaintance of three months, took her to her home as a guest, to remain there

Just as long as she pleased, and share the luxuries of the splendid house, the servants, the plate, and the rich wine of the cellars, which Mrs. Willet had previously had all to herself.

Of course young Mr. Halliot called occasionally to visit the widow and her charming *protégée*. But his attentions were for a purpose, as will be shown, most marked toward the wealthy widow. It was not long before the handsome fellow made an impression upon the heart of Mrs Willet; and it was not much longer before it became evident that two years would not pass and leave Mrs. Willet a widow. Strange as it may seem, Mlle. Villiers appeared to look favorably upon the suit of the young soldier. Indeed she had been instrumental in forwarding the courtship, but had done so rather under cover, so that no complicity could appear between herself and young Halliot.

In the meanwhile the splendid French woman had gained a complete mastery over the rich widow. She was her inseparable companion. She guided her in all things, even down to the last minute of going and coming. She selected her books. She managed her servants, and what was more to her purpose, advised her regarding the disposition of certain large and valuable pieces of city real estate in the hands of a joint executor. In fact, the wily girl—for she could hardly be called a woman—so wound herself about the widow's affection that, if it is possible for one woman to be in love with another, Mrs. Willet was in love with Mlle. Villiers.

14

Mrs. Willet imagined that all her troubles were removed whenever her friend was at hand; and Halliot, the handsome young ex-officer, who still paid his devoted attentions to the widow, often jokingly remarked that ne had but one rival in all the world to fear, and that one was the dear little French woman who had brought them together.

Mlle. Villiers also seemed pleasantly jealous of Halliot; but, without seeming to do it, she always put in a good word for Halliot, and brought the couple together on every possible occasion. In a few months they had become three inseparables, and the executor, who had been a life-long friend of the deceased husband, looked on with a smiling approval as long as money was not needed and his young charge seemed to be so happily situated.

In September, 1869, Mrs. Willet disposed of a valuable piece of real estate, and received a cash payment of forty thousand dollars. Her husband had left her everything, and she was perfectly free to sell or lease any or all or none of the property, and duly appropriate the proceeds to her use as she saw fit. It was not supposed that the officer-lover knew of the widow's vast wealth, or cared to know the same; but Mlle. Villiers *did* know it, and took good care that Mrs. Willet, who knew nothing of law or business, should not be troubled with details or dry figures, and she generously performed all the labor of looking after the property for her friend. Kind soul! *she* expected no reward. Not she! Had she not plenty of her own? Did she not own an entire castle full of retainers, all in the south of *la belle France?* So she had told the widow, along with other delightful and bewitching romances of her sunny land beyond the sea; and, besides, her industry and good management of the Willet mansion were proverbial.

"How shall I ever repay you?" Mrs. Willet would ask, with an impulsive, affectionate enthusiasm.

"Oh, *mon amie*, speak never more of so little things!" the handsome French swindler would respond, throwing her arms around her friend's neck and adding the grace of impetuous ingenuousness to the pretty charm of her bewitching, broken English.

And so the fine French drama went on, with its gushing affection, its pretty wit, and its splendid intrigue.

Mlle. Villiers was always provided with funds from some mysterious bank account, and very frequently dropped, as if by accident, casual remarks concerning Parisian bills of exchange, the rents of her tenantry, and the like, which quite bewildered any of her chance acquaintances, and wholly deceived the poor dupe, upon whose bounty she was almost entirely living.

For all that could be seen by Mrs. Willet, Halliot and Mlle. Villiers were merely friends—*her* friends, and her true and steadfast friends; but if her eyes could have witnessed their secret meetings, and what occurred at them, and if her ears could have overheard the cold-blooded planning and scheming and comparing of notes, concerning the plucking they were soon to give her, there would have been an awakening, and that soon enough to prevent her from suffering great loss.

Soon after the sale of the property in September, when the forty thousand dollars had been invested in Government bonds, Halliot, who had now become the recognized lover of Mrs. Willet, was taken suddenly ill. He occupied fine apartments at an up-town hotel, and thither Mlle. Villiers and the sorrowing widow proceeded to find the handsome ex-officer terribly emaciated in appearance. No words could express the sorrow of Mrs. Willet and her friend. Ascertaining that a considerable bill was standing against Halliot at the hotel, Villiers only had to hint that his illness had probably caused it, when every penny's indebtedness was liquidated as well as a month's advance payment made, while orders were left that every attention possible should be shown the invalid.

Word kept coming to the Willet mansion that the sick man was growing worse and worse ; and the little French rascal, Villiers, so artfully worked upon the widow's fears, sympathies, and love, that she became nearly beside herself with grief as well as utterly helpless and pliable in the hands of her pretended friend.

Soon Mrs. Willet received a message, signed " your dying lover," summoning her to Halliot's bedside. She begged and entreated Mlle. Villiers to accompany her. No, no ; she could not, she would not ; she knew something terrible was about to happen. Finally Mrs. Willet went alone, half frantic at the sudden overwhelming cloud that had fallen upon all she held dear, and nearly fainted at the door of Halliot's room.

Rushing to his bedside, she took him impulsively in her

arms, and, sobbing like a child, begged that he might be spared to her.

Some touch of pity for the woman's fidelity must have come over the shamming scamp as he lay there upon the white pillows, propped up in a picturesque position, for it was a long time before he seemed to dare to speak of the subject uppermost in his mind; but finally it came, and after the following manner :

While holding the betrayed woman to his heart, he confessed, in a seeming agony of remorse, that he had cruelly deceived her; that he had long loved Jeannette Villiers, the beautiful French woman, and, worse than all, that the woman was his wife !

He was on his death-bed. He could not die without Mrs. Willet's forgiveness, nor would he give up the ghost unless Mrs. Willet would swear, upon her bended knees, that his wife and soon-to-be-born child should be her care, her wards through life. The broken-hearted woman took the oath, and departed. She meant, in all honesty, to keep it too. She vowed that she should never let this woman suffer, and, in her simplicity and loyalty to an honest friendship, was not altogether dis-pleased that events had so culminated that she could now show, in a practical manner, her kind feeling to the beautiful French girl, who was now, the simple Mrs. Willet thought, in a pitiable condition of dependency, and would soon be in a more pitiable plight with a father-less babe in her arms.

On her return to the now miserable mansion, there was

a sad scene of reproach, forgiveness, and sobbing; but it all resulted in Mrs. Willet's taking Villiers into her heart and affection again, and, although both women were undergoing great anguish and grief, yet both women were happy. Mrs. Willet was happy because she had done a magnanimous act. The French woman was happy because the French drama, of which she was "leading lady," was getting on so successfully.

The next day the young ex-officer died—so Mrs. Willet was informed; and the Baltimore newspapers contained notices of his death, while the obituary editor of the Philadelphia *Ledger* wailed out (at a dollar a line) a fitting stanza of grief. This information and the previous excitement completely prostrated Mrs. Willet, and she did not attend the funeral. But Jeannette Villiers *did*. At least she went where Mrs. Willet supposed the funeral of Halliot occurred, and the charming rascal wore the deepest of mourning and looked more charming than ever. She also evidently mourned deeply and felt keenly the loss of her husband, while Mrs. Willet was simply inconsolable — the whole matter, if it had been real on the part of Villiers, presenting the almost inconceivable instance of two handsome and intelligent women, one the wife and the other the denied lover, both mourning the loss of the same man, and both continuing an ardent affection for each other.

About a month after the supposed death of Halliot Mrs. Willet consulted an attorney, and thence went to the executor of her husband's estate, where she received ten thousand dollars. With this she proceeded to a prominent hotel with Villiers, where, in the presence of witnesses—which had of course all accidentally been provided by the latter—she placed this large sum of money in the hands of the French woman as a free gift. This was, as she said, partially fulfilling the solemn vow she had taken before Halliot on his death-bed.

In three months more there was a birth at the Willet mansion. The sprightly, vivacious, charming Villiers, or Mrs. Halliot, as she was now called, had become the mother of a healthy boy. The heart of Mrs. Willet was further touched, and the strange fascination upon the woman still pursued her and prompted her to still greater generosity. As soon as the mother dare leave the house, she was once more taken to the hotel, and there again, before witnesses, presented with forty thousand dollars in Government bonds.

Jeannette Villiers wept, and protested that her dear friend was too kind; but Mrs. Willet insisted that she had it to spare, and felt that she was only keeping the binding oath she had taken.

Strange to relate, however, one week from the day when the last presentation was made Mrs. Halliot and the child went out in a carriage for an airing.

Mrs. Willet pressed the use of her own *coupé* upon her; but no, she could not think of such a thing, and secured one on hire. Night came, and the mother and child did not return.

" They will surely come to-morrow!' said the deserted widow. And she fairly wept herself to sleep that night for lonesomeness at being separated from her "dear Jeannette." But "to-morrow" came, and another to-morrow, and a week sped, but no charming little French woman came.

Mrs. Willet was now nearly insane, at least so the story went. Weak and tractable in the hands of a design-ing French woman before, now she was apparently wild with dread that something terrible had happened to her *protégées ;* and it was not until she had consulted her exe-cutor that her eyes were opened. He had not been made aware of the last gift of forty thousand dollars in Gov-ernment bonds. When Mrs. Willet gave the ten thou-sand-dollar check, he made no objection ; but now he was utterly dismayed at the turn things had taken, and at once applied to me for assistance to unravel the mystery, although the widow bitterly protested against such a course.

I felt that little could be done, simply because the vic-tim of the conspiracy was unwilling to take any steps toward exposing the villainy of the rascals who had duped her ; and I imagined I could see behind all more than the mere desire to shield persons whom she had once held in high regard, and consequently pursued my investigations with no possible hope of bringing two precious rascals to justice, but with a personal interest in fathoming the *ause* of Mrs. Willet's peculiar tenderness.

For some time my researches were balked in every par-ticular. To begin with, Mrs. Willet was very chary of

How the "French Drama" was played.—Page—

giving information. Not only this, but Jeannette Villiers, on leaving the Willet mansion, had taken the precaution to not only remove her handsome photograph from Mrs. Willet's album, but had also destroyed or removed every little keepsake or article of *virtu* by which some possible clue of her whereabouts might be secured.

I let this feature of the matter drop for a time, and finally turned my attention to Halliot's rather mysterious death. Quite accidentally (through my extensive acquaintance among army officers) I learned that he had been seen in the West, but my informant could not recollect where or under what circumstances. Being confirmed in my opinion, however, that the dashing ex-army officer was alive and in the enjoyment of as good health as myself, I next turned my attention to the circumstances attending his alleged death.

Pursuing this line of investigation, a certain hotel clerk was found, who had been discharged for irregularities, and who, for an enticing remuneration, freely confessed to assisting Halliot in pretending to die He stated that Halliot had represented to him that the sham was necessary to prevent a marriage which he loathed. He had helped him simply as one good fellow would help another out of such a scrape, and had been given a handsome present for his trouble. I further ascertained from this man that Halliot was living in elegance in St. Louis, and had recently married a French widow, who had a very young child ; but that Halliot was now living under the assumed name of Hilliers, which, the reader will recollect,

14*

bore a striking similarity to Villiers, the name of the charming French woman who had so mysteriously disappeared from Mrs. Willet's home in Baltimore.

I could not but put these names together in my mind, and was now certain that I had found a clue to the shrewd pair, who were probably living in elegance in St. Louis on the proceeds of the generous woman they had both wronged; but still I was unable to wholly account for the singular determination of the wronged widow to let them live in peace wherever they might be; for by this time she was as fully convinced as myself and the executor that she had been coolly and deliberately swindled by the couple.

The executor was determined to probe the matter to the bottom, whether or not any of the fifty thousand dollars could be recovered; and I confess that my professional interest and curiosity made me quite as anxious for the same result.

It was a matter now of no difficulty to ascertain definitely that Halliot, or Hilliers, as he now called himself, was living with the beautiful and fascinating French lady as his wife in St Louis; that the man was in a lucrative business; that the woman was supposed to be a handsome and wealthy Parisian widow, who had smitten the husband while traveling in Europe; and that both were very happy in the enjoyment of their ill-gotten gains; and it was a matter of scarcely greater difficulty to place an operative, a dashing man-of-the-world, in Halliot's society in such a way that he soon won his confidence and compelled the revelation of what is the most interesting,

romantic, and dramatic feature of the whole affair, show
ing that the shrewdness of the two, their boldness, their
cunning, and, above all, their supreme assurance, were all
supremely incredible.

Piece by piece the revelation was made that Halliot had
exhausted the means left by his family, had in the meantime married the beautiful Jeannette Villiers, but had kept
such marriage secret, and that both, for purposes of plunder, had pretended in society to being single ; that, as
soon as the acquaintance of Mrs. Willet was formed by
Mlle. Villiers, the conspiracy to relieve the widow of her
surplus wealth was arranged ; that Villiers then won her
confidence and esteem, then introduced Halliot, who won
her affection to an overwhelming degree ; that then Halliot
pretended to die, having made the dying confession and
secured the oath that Villiers should remain Mrs. Willet's
care, knowing that the latter's generosity would be touched,
and that she would do the handsome thing, which she had
done to the extent of a ten thousand dollar check ; and
that then, after this much had been secured, Halliot suddenly came to life, before Mrs. Willet, at a place where
Villiers had shrewdly arranged to have the widow so that
a scene should be prevented ; and that, though Mrs.
Willet nearly died of fright and astonishment, she was so
overjoyed at his being alive, that the scoundrel moulded
her to his purposes like putty, and then and there again
made a confession that he had *pretended to die so that he
might relieve himself of Jeannette Villiers*, who had never
been his wife, but only his mistress, and that he loved the

widow to distraction, and could never be happy without her.

Then, in the joy and happiness of this reunion, the double-dyed scoundrel so worked up the woman's feelings and real love for him, that, before they had left the room where Jeannette Villiers had brought them together, Mrs. Willet had agreed to a scheme to get rid of her little French friend by giving her the forty thousand dollars, which had been given, as already related ; and, when the entire fifty thousand dollars had been secured, the scheming and brilliant couple quietly left Baltimore and the doubly-wronged and deceived widow, to begin life in the West under the circumstances previously recited.

But it was all of no use. Mrs. Willet positively refused to prosecute the parties; and the operation, while a success in reaching the parties sought and securing the information desired, failed to bring to justice two of the keenest unprofessional swindlers I have known.

Halliot, *alias* Hilliers, is now a hale, hearty man of forty, well-to-do in the world, while Jeannette Villiers, his wife, is a magnificent-appearing woman of a few years younger ; and, stranger than all of the strange things connected with this romantic affair, the Halliot family and the family of Mrs. Willet—who was, a few years since, happily remarried —are on the best of terms and as good friends as though this villainous though brilliant confidence swindle had never been performed.

THE END.